Race and the Avant-Garde

ASIAN AMERICA

A series edited by Gordon H. Chang

The increasing size and diversity of the Asian American population, its growing significance in American society and culture, and the expanded appreciation, both popular and scholarly, of the importance of Asian Americans in the country's present and past—all these developments have converged to stimulate wide interest in scholarly work on topics related to the Asian American experience. The general recognition of the pivotal role that race and ethnicity have played in American life, and in relations between the United States and other countries, has also fostered the heightened attention.

Although Asian Americans were a subject of serious inquiry in the late nineteenth and early twentieth centuries, they were subsequently ignored by the mainstream scholarly community for several decades. In recent years, however, this neglect has ended, with an increasing number of writers examining a good many aspects of Asian American life and culture. Moreover, many students of American society are recognizing that the study of issues related to Asian America speak to, and may be essential for, many current discussions on the part of the informed public and various scholarly communities.

The Stanford series on Asian America seeks to address these interests. The series will include works from the humanities and social sciences, including history, anthropology, political science, American studies, law, literary criticism, sociology, and interdisciplinary and policy studies.

A full list of titles in the Asian America series can be found online at www.sup.org/asianamerica.

Race and the Avant-Garde

EXPERIMENTAL AND
ASIAN AMERICAN POETRY
SINCE 1965

Timothy Yu

STANFORD UNIVERSITY PRESS
STANFORD, CALIFORNIA

Stanford University Press
Stanford, California

Printed in the United States of America on acid-free, archival-quality
paper

Library of Congress Cataloging-in-Publication Data

Yu, Timothy, Ph.D.
   Race and the avant-garde : experimental and Asian American poetry
since 1965 / Timothy Yu.
      p. cm. — (Asian America)
   Includes bibliographical references and index.
   ISBN 978-0-8047-5997-7 (cloth : alk. paper)
   1. American poetry—Asian American authors—History and criticism.   2. Experimental poetry, American—20th century—History and
criticism.   3. Race in literature.   I. Title.   II. Series.
   PS153.A84Y8 2009
   811'.5409895—dc22

                         2008029274

Typeset by Bruce Lundquist in 11/14 Adobe Garamond

Contents

Acknowledgments

My greatest intellectual debt is to Marjorie Perloff, whose book *Radical Artifice* first sparked my interest in Language writing. She has been a mentor and friend whose support has never wavered. Her responses to my work—engaged, enthusiastic, challenging, and always delivered with remarkable speed, whether from home or halfway around the world—have pushed my thinking to its best. Albert Gelpi, a fount of knowledge on modern poetry, has been a thoughtful and thorough reader and a supportive friend whose enthusiasm for poetry, and life, inspires me. David Palumbo-Liu helped me to become a more rigorous and critical thinker; his interdisciplinary, boundary-crossing work has been an example to me in its sense of the importance of historical and political contexts, and his insights and wisdom have provided a crucial grounding for my project. Sianne Ngai's intelligence and patience helped focus this project in its earliest phases, and her energy has continued to animate it; our conversations and debates have often led to breakthroughs I could not have achieved on my own. I also owe a debt of gratitude to Nicholas Jenkins, whose encouragement gave me the confidence to pursue this work, and whose insights have always sharpened my thinking.

Much of this book was researched and written during an invaluable fellowship year at the Stanford Humanities Center. I am grateful to John Bender, the Center's director, and to the fellows and staff for creating an intellectual atmosphere that was so productive for me and many others.

Funding from the Stanford English Department and the Phi Beta Kappa Northern California Association also helped support my work.

Steven Mandeville-Gamble of the Stanford University Library's Department of Special Collections helped me gain access to the then-uncataloged Emory Lee Papers, a wonderful cache of Asian American materials that included complete runs of *Aion* and *Bridge* magazines; he and Michael G. Olson also made it possible for me to use Allen Ginsberg's "auto poesy" recordings, tracking down obscure catalog codes and transferring the reel-to-reel tapes to usable cassettes. Lynda Claassen and the staff of the Mandeville Special Collections Library at the University of California, San Diego, were a great help both during my month of research in the Archive for New Poetry there and in granting permission to quote from the Ron Silliman and Charles Bernstein Papers. My research at UCSD was supported by a grant from Stanford's School of Humanities and Sciences.

The intelligence, support, and friendship of my wonderful colleagues in the Stanford English Department made my time there a pleasure, and the department's remarkable staff provided life-saving assistance on more than one occasion. My colleagues in the Department of English at the University of Toronto have offered warm support and encouragement in helping me to finish this project. I have also been assisted by two generous research grants from the University of Toronto's Connaught Fund.

Part of the excitement of working on this project has been the opportunity to correspond with the poets themselves. I am grateful to John Yau, Ron Silliman, Janice Mirikitani, Alan Chong Lau, Lawson Fusao Inada, Charles Bernstein, and Bruce Andrews, who graciously answered my queries and granted permission to quote from their work.

Some of my material on Cha and Ginsberg was presented at the 2002 and 2003 MLA conventions, and my work on Yau was part of a conference at the University of Salamanca in 2000; I am grateful for the helpful responses generated by those presentations. The Asian Americas Workshop and the Workshop on Contemporary Poetry, hosted by the Stanford Humanities Center, also provided crucial forums for much of this work. An earlier version of my final chapter appeared as "Form and Identity in Language Poetry and Asian American Poetry" in *Contemporary Literature* 41.3 (Fall 2000), © 2000, reprinted by permission of the University of Wisconsin Press; the anonymous readers' reports helped me improve the project.

I also thank Colleen Lye for suggesting the term "ethnicization," which I happily adopted.

I am indebted to Gordon Chang for helping bring this work to the attention of Muriel Bell, who ushered it through the review process as one of her final projects at Stanford University Press. Stephen Fredman and another anonymous reviewer provided generous and detailed feedback on the manuscript, responding comprehensively to the book's arguments and offering invaluable suggestions for improvement. Stacy Wagner, Jessica Walsh, and Joa Suorez shepherded the book through every step of production, cheerfully demystifying the process.

None of this would have been possible without my family. My parents, Linda and Philip Yu, my grandmother, Sophia Pan, and Pat Valenza have supported me in every possible way. Robin Valenza and I have taken every step of this journey together; her brilliance and strength have been an example to me, and her love has gotten me through the hardest times. This work is as much hers as it is mine.

Race and the Avant-Garde

Introduction

Toward a Sociology of the Contemporary Avant-Garde

Race and the avant-garde have been linked since the dawn of the twentieth century, when avant-garde artists such as Picasso, Ezra Pound, and Gertrude Stein found inspiration in African masks, African American culture, and Asian literature. At midcentury, Jack Kerouac and other Beat writers drew energy from their identifications with blacks, Asians, and Latinos. And Charles Olson, founding figure of the Black Mountain school of poetry, famously likened his poetics to the jazz of Charlie Parker. For these white European and American avant-gardists, racial others offered an escape from Western aesthetics, serving as a source for the revolutionary breakthroughs that have characterized the twentieth-century avant-garde. But such non-Western sources remained largely in the realm of folk culture or ancient tradition. For much of the century, white avant-gardists rarely felt the need to acknowledge the presence of nonwhite artists as peers and contemporaries.

In the latter part of the twentieth century, however, the racial dynamics of the avant-garde shifted. Rather than being able to appropriate the cultural productions of nonwhites in the service of avant-gardism, contemporary white avant-gardists, particularly in the United States after 1970, found their positions in the forefront of revolutionary culture actively challenged by writers of color, as these latter writers were awarded increasing degrees of moral, political, and aesthetic authority by readers and critics. Although movements such as the Harlem Renaissance offered earlier examples of racialized avant-gardes, I argue that after 1970 the question of race became central to the constitution of *any* American avant-garde, as writers and artists became increasingly aware of how their social locations inflected their aesthetics. My second claim is perhaps even more surprising: that the communities formed by contemporary American writers of color can themselves best be understood in the terms we have developed for the analysis of the avant-garde.

It might be objected that these claims confuse two different kinds of artistic groupings. Categories such as "Asian American poets" or "African American writers" are, after all, defined socially, by the race of their members, whereas avant-gardes are defined in aesthetic terms. But the analytic power of the concept of the avant-garde is that it reminds us that the aesthetic and the social are inseparable. An avant-garde is an aesthetic *and* a social grouping, defined as much by its formation of a distinctive kind of community as by its revolutionary aesthetics. As such, it can serve as a corrective to essentializing views of any kind of artistic community.

In examining two groups of contemporary poets—Asian American poets and the group known as the "Language" writers—I suggest that these groups share key traits that enable us to see them both as avant-gardes; at the same time, they display a distinctively contemporary concern with social identities that is most often centered around the discourse of race. Both groups identify themselves with the political left, seeing poetry as a revolutionary practice and issuing manifestos to justify their work; both emerge from and respond to the political and social upheavals of the late 1960s. Both dissent from the conventions of mainstream American poetry of the 1970s and 1980s, and both develop their own institutions of publication and distribution, from magazines to small presses to anthologies. But central to both is a surprisingly acute sense of how race can inflect aesthetics, and of the relations of power that racial difference creates among contemporaneous avant-gardes. Those relations of power are described in a provocative paragraph in Paul Mann's *The Theory-Death of the Avant-Garde*, where Mann acknowledges—albeit with great skepticism—that the contemporary avant-garde may have ceded the mantle of radical art in the late 1960s to women and artists of color, using language that places various avant-gardes in a competitive relationship:

> [T]he death of the avant-garde as a politics of aesthetic revolt is a means by which the same rhetoric of aesthetic opposition can be repeated just as vehemently in discourses that consider themselves radically different. The avant-garde is dismissed as white, male, etc.; now projects for the represen-

tation of gender, class, and race take its place, but perhaps without effectively restructuring their relations to the economy. (119)

Such arguments in the aesthetic sphere can be seen as corollaries of similar dynamics in the realm of politics and of ostensible divisions within the American left since the 1960s. The new left of that period has often been characterized as an alliance between the civil rights and antiwar movements—and thus, implicitly, between black activists and white student radicals. What is less often discussed, however, is the sense among many white radicals that the language of resistance and revolution truly belonged to oppressed minorities and that white activists could only hope to borrow it. In *The Sixties*, Todd Gitlin quotes white student leader Tom Hayden expressing his admiration for black civil rights activists: "Those Negroes are down there, digging in, and in more danger than nearly any student in this American generation has faced. . . . We should speak their revolutionary language without mocking it" (128). Such accommodations were possible within the idea of a racially integrated new left but would become an increasing source of tension in the late 1960s with the rise of black nationalism and of what would come to be called "identity politics." In his autobiographical work "Under *Albany*," Language writer Ron Silliman recalls watching Black Panther drills with a friend in 1966 and feeling that "the Left was splintering" with "no room for us in that world, how then did our Left fit together with it?" (325). In such a political context, any avant-garde art that claimed to have revolutionary power would have to cope with the fact that the rhetoric of revolution seemed to have moved outside the province of white men.

As writers of color, from the members of the Black Arts movement to the radical Asian American poets published in journals like *Aion*, began to employ techniques and rhetoric inherited from earlier avant-gardes, white writers in the 1970s could no longer simply claim the mantle of "*the* avant-garde" that had previously been awarded to white male experimentalists. Instead, writers such as the Language poets had to acknowledge themselves as a socially as well as aesthetically delimited group, characterized by their own racial, gender, and class positions in a manner comparable to that of writers grouped together as Asian Americans, African Americans, or Latinos. In this context, what is needed is not an account that simply delineates the aesthetic traits of the avant-garde and then judges which works fall under that rubric, but what we might call a sociology of the avant-garde, which acknowledges the existence of multiple and even competing groups whose practices we might recognize as avant-garde and whose aesthetic programs are inflected by their differing social identifications.

My characterization of such a project as sociological draws on Renato Poggioli's assertion in his classic *The Theory of the Avant-Garde* that the avant-garde must be understood "not so much as an aesthetic fact as a socio-logical one" (3). In Poggioli's account, what is distinctive about the avant-garde is not any particular style or method but its emergence as a "social fact," a "society in the strict sense" that positions itself against "society in the larger sense" (4). It is thus to be distinguished from the idea of an artistic "school," with its focus on "techniques, training, and apprenticeship"; the avant-garde, instead, follows the modern model of the "movement," whose primary characteristic is its interest in "passing beyond the limits of art" toward a wider worldview that "extends to all spheres of cultural and civil life" (18). Perhaps most relevant here is Poggioli's vision of the avant-garde as complete community, one whose principles are not only aesthetic but social, psychological, and ideological:

> On the one hand, the anarchistic state of mind presupposes the individu-alistic revolt of the "unique" *against* society in the largest sense. On the other, it presupposes solidarity *within* a society in the restricted sense of that word—that is to say, solidarity within the community of rebels and libertarians. . . . The modern artist replaces that particular environment, determined by his family and social origins, with what the French call *milieu artiste*. There, sect and movement become a caste; hence a social fact in a primarily psychological way, motivated by vocation and election, not by blood or racial inheritance or by economic and class distinctions. (31)

Such an image of the "declassed" artist might seem radically at odds with the goal of accounting for the relative social positions of different avant-gardists. Writing in the early 1960s, Poggioli could hardly have anticipated the explosion of work by U.S. women and writers of color that would char-acterize the following decade. But other moments in Poggioli do suggest how his characterization of the avant-garde as social fact might help us link contemporary aesthetic and social identifications.

Poggioli argues that the avant-garde came to define itself against popu-lar culture, though not against the same forms of popular culture idealized by the Romantics. What Poggioli calls "purely ethnic cultures," with their "more deeply rooted traditional values" and "less self-conscious and more spontaneous traditions," are, he says, "almost completely disappearing from Western soil" (121), to be supplanted by a culture that is "fabricated (indeed 'prefabricated') on the lowest intellectual level by the bourgeoisie itself" (123). It is the latter, bourgeois form of popular culture against which the avant-garde defines itself.

Although Poggioli's critique of the culture industry is a familiar one, what is novel is his sense of a potential analogy between the position of "ethnic" cultures and that of the avant-garde. The unity of traditional culture is supplanted by the stylistic pluralism and eclecticism that characterize bourgeois culture, a culture that has "broken all the links between artisan and artist" in favor of a production of culture as a commodity for consumption (121). The avant-garde presents itself as a critique of this eclectic and presumptively universal culture by means of "stylistic dissent" (120), insisting on and agitating for the particularity and distinctiveness of its own style in order to achieve "the radical negation of a general culture by a specific one" (107). Although a restoration of "ethnic" culture is no longer possible, the avant-garde becomes an analogue of that culture through its artificial construction of a community whose social being and ideology can be directly expressed in aesthetics. The declassed avant-gardist can thus be seen not as a monad but as a participant in a kind of community no longer imaginable within bourgeois culture. Poggioli's reference to such a community as a "minority culture" (108) or, more cryptically, as "an almost unforeseeable diaspora of isolated intelligences" (92), suggests that the avant-garde, so understood, might be organized in a fashion not so distant from that of the kinds of communities we now describe with the terms "minority" and "diaspora."

In fact, our contemporary "ethnic" categories are every bit as constructed as the avant-garde formations Poggioli describes. The term "Asian American," for instance, is an invention of the late 1960s, designed to tie together disparate ethnic groups (Chinese, Japanese, Korean, Filipino, and so on) under a single political and cultural umbrella. A category such as "Asian American culture" can thus claim no organic continuity with any particular ethnic culture; it must be understood not as a traditional racial category but as a modern rubric that yokes together different groups and individuals, regardless of ethnic or socioeconomic origin, for the purposes of political organization and dissent. Indeed, the process of forming an "Asian American" consciousness strongly resembles Poggioli's description of the formation of an audience for avant-garde art: "almost by spontaneous generation, by means of single and independent joinings of isolated individuals, a group emerges that is not easily determined geographically or socially, individuals who end up finding, in the object of their own enthusiasm, reasons for community as well as separation" (91). The Asian American artist, like the avant-gardist, puts forward a tendentious argument for cultural particularity—invents a culture—both as a means of organizing a specific artistic community and as a means of critiquing the larger culture.

Poggioli's concept of the avant-garde, with its sense of a profound connection between the social and the aesthetic, can thus be applied to a wide range of contemporary literary communities. This insight may also give us a new perspective on perhaps the most influential theory of the avant-garde, that of Peter Bürger. Bürger's *Theory of the Avant-Garde* argues that the avant-garde's goal is to "reintegrate art into the praxis of life" (22), in contrast to bourgeois art, which insists on its autonomy from life. Bürger's characterization of this avant-garde gesture as a *re*integration acknowledges that in prebourgeois times—namely, in the periods of "sacral" and "courtly" art—art was still integrated into social life; even though Bürger's typology does not precisely correspond to Poggioli's notion of "ethnic" culture, both imagine a premodern culture in which the aesthetic and the social are inseparable. But if Bürger, like Poggioli, sees the avant-garde as in part a return to this unity, he also makes clear that the avant-garde's strategy is not a reactionary or nostalgic one. In an era in which the links between art and society have been decisively severed, the avant-garde imagines not an art that grows organically out of society but rather the reverse: a social life that is itself grounded in art. This is not a mere attempt to integrate art into the "means-ends rationality of the bourgeois everyday" but an "attempt to organize a new life praxis from a basis in art" (49). The avant-garde is thus a kind of echo of socially grounded, collectively produced and received art in an era when such groundings are no longer possible—an attempt to create a community by aesthetic means.

The category of "avant-garde" should thus make us more aware both of the social elements of a grouping like Language poetry, whose coherence may seem largely aesthetic, and of the aesthetic elements at work in the constitution of an apparently social grouping like Asian American poetry. Although Language poetry is now identified primarily with a set of aesthetic principles, such as a critique of lyric subjectivity, a challenge to linguistic reference, or the use of nonnarrative techniques to structure a text, an examination of Language writing's formation in the 1970s suggests that Language writers also understood themselves as sharing a social identification, a community. Reading series, publications, and anthologies were only the most visible manifestations of this community.

At the same time, Asian American poets of the 1970s, far from taking race as the unifying ground from which their work emerges, actually approached questions of Asian American identity through debates about poetic form. Conventional accounts of Asian American and other ethnic writings tend to proceed from the social to the aesthetic, positing an Asian American culture or experience that then finds expression in Asian American art. As noted previously, however, Asian American culture is itself a composite that attempts to include vastly different historical experiences. The prominent role literature has taken in Asian American discourse since the 1970s—from the poetry sections regularly featured in Asian American publications to groundbreaking anthologies such as *Aiiieeeee!*—suggests that it is, in fact, through literature that Asian Americans have sought to define Asian American experience. The work of writers such as Lawson Fusao Inada, Francis Oka, and Janice Mirikitani shows a willingness to experiment with different poetic forms—from haiku to protest poetry to jazz poetry to first-person lyrics—in an attempt to create a distinctively Asian American sensibility. In the work of these writers, the question of what it means to be Asian American is as much a formal as a social or political one. Asian American poetry of the 1970s represents a concerted attempt to perform precisely that task Bürger finds characteristic of the avant-garde: to organize a distinctively Asian American life praxis from a basis in Asian American art.

To describe Language poetry and Asian American poetry as avant-garde in their origins and impulses is not necessarily to claim that they have remained unstintingly avant-garde throughout their histories. For both groups, the 1970s represent their most strongly avant-garde moment—the period in which Language and Asian American writing dissent most radically from the dominant institutions of art. During this decade, both bodies of writing existed almost exclusively in small, fugitive publications, accompanied by aggressive rhetoric against what both groups of writers saw as a conventional art that served the needs of capitalism and imperialism. The poetry that appeared in Asian American publications like *Aion* and *Gidra* and in language-oriented journals like *This* bore little resemblance to the writing appearing in mainstream publications like the *New Yorker* or the *Paris Review*. Writers and readers tended to be part of geographically delimited communities, often centered around reading series or activist organizations in San Francisco, New York, and Los Angeles, and displayed little interest in mainstream literary success.

Not until the later 1970s and 1980s did Asian American and Language writing gain some visibility outside their initial channels, changing not only the public profile of the work but each group's internal dynamics and avant-garde orientation. Among Asian American writers, this shift was evident early on in the professionalizing tendencies of a writer like Frank Chin, who, as I discuss in Chapter 3, touted mainstream success as a key goal for Asian American authors. Whereas Asian American publications of the early 1970s disdained and even ridiculed conventional lyricism or poetic subject matter, by the end of the decade Asian American journals began to make themselves over in the image of conventional literary organs, sponsoring contests and prizes and attracting a somewhat younger generation of poets who emphasized personal experience over politics. At the end of the 1970s, Language writing—whose membership and audience had seemed so constrained as to draw charges of insularity and exclusion from fellow poets— was also reaching a larger audience through the publication of the journal *L=A=N=G=U=A=G=E* (a title that also helped, of course, to cement the movement's name), whose emphasis on critical writings provided an abstract, theoretical foundation for what had previously been a largely local phenomenon.

In short, the categories of Asian American and Language writing were gradually unmoored from their original social contexts, allowing them to take their places within mainstream poetic discourse. The conjunction of the social and the aesthetic—which marked the avant-garde moment within each group's development—was replaced by the now-familiar divide between the two, with "Asian American poetry" becoming a primarily social category and "Language writing" becoming a largely aesthetic one. Such definitional shifts were necessary for these modes of writing to be comprehensible within the universalizing framework of mainstream literary discourse—for Asian American and Language writing to become categories that signified beyond a purely local community. Asian American writing, rather than being marked by a particular political orientation or a specific context of small-scale production, came simply to signify any work whose author "happened to be" of Asian descent, a shift that tended to exclude work that did not conform to mainstream aesthetics. It is no accident that the understated, apolitical, first-person lyrics of Cathy Song, which stand in sharp contrast to Asian American writing of the 1970s, were the first poems by an Asian American to gain widespread critical attention.

In the case of Language writing, it was not until mainstream critics and readers came to be aware of something called "Language poetry" in the mid-1980s that it became imaginable for writers outside a small group to be read as doing "language writing." As the term became a broadly stylistic rather than a more narrowly avant-garde one, writers such as Michael Palmer and Susan Howe, who did not identify themselves with the more specific project undertaken by Silliman and his colleagues in the 1970s, would come to be called "Language poets" as well, with the term coming to stand for a whole spectrum of formally innovative poetics. That this represented a radical shift from the work of the 1970s is evident in some writers' subsequent allergy to the term "Language poetry"; Silliman, who had frequently employed the term "language-oriented" in the 1970s to describe his project, was enraged by Douglas Messerli's decision to name a mid-1980s anthology *"Language" Poetries* and declared in a letter, "I am not a language poet." Language writing was not, in this vision, an aesthetic project in which just anyone could participate; rather, it was attached to a specific community at a specific moment in time and, for participants like Silliman, was emptied as soon as it was removed from that particular social context.

The current status of Asian American and Language writing as literary categories, then, cannot be read backward into those categories' origins. In fact, perhaps the most crucial reason to examine the history of these categories—separating the avant-garde moment of the 1970s from the mainstreaming of the 1980s—is that our sense of the value of these categories, and of their political implications, still derives largely from the logic of the work of the 1970s, even though subsequent writers seem to have repudiated the cruder versions of that decade's aesthetics and politics. It would be nearly impossible to make an argument for the political value of the poems of Li-Young Lee or David Mura without relying to some degree on the more pointed political engagement of the writers of the 1970s who established the need for a category of Asian American writing. Nor would it be easy to establish the political credentials of "experimental" styles in current poetry without returning to the arguments advanced by Silliman, Bernstein, and other Language writers. If the product of these categories now seems to be a group of distinguished individual writers—Silliman, Hejinian, Howe, Lee, Cha, Yau—we must also remember that the profound shift in literary values that allows us to appreciate their work was an achievement of the avant-garde impulses of Language and Asian American writing in the 1970s.

Although I argue that Asian American and Language writing grew from a similar avant-garde impulse, it must also be said that there have been few organic points of connection between the two. Indeed, both Language and Asian American writing were emerging in the same politically charged Bay Area atmosphere in the 1970s, but there is little evidence that either group of writers was actively aware of the other.[1] The poets and institutions of Asian American poetry in the 1970s, which I discuss in Chapter 3, are all closely connected with the Asian American political movement that coalesced around the student strike at San Francisco State in 1968–9: poet Janice Mirikitani was a student there, and her magazine *Aion*, the first Asian American literary magazine, emerged from that context.[2] The major figures of Language writing, including Charles Bernstein, Bruce Andrews, Ron Silliman, Barrett Watten, and Lyn Hejinian, were educated at Harvard or at the University of California, Berkeley; their poetic affiliations did not, in general, emerge directly from university-based political commitments or social interactions.

Although they are not direct lines of influence, the connections that can be drawn between the two groups may nonetheless give us a clearer sense of their relative social and cultural positioning. The first link is the powerful role Asian cultural influences play not only in twentieth-century American poetry but in American culture of the 1960s more broadly. As Josephine Nock-Hee Park shows in her recent study *Apparitions of Asia*, the deep legacy of Ezra Pound's turn to Chinese models and materials in his poetry is extended into the mid-twentieth century by Beat writers' engagement with Buddhism. But the appeal of Asian cultural models is evident at all levels of American culture in the 1960s and 1970s—an appeal that gains a political edge from growing opposition to the war in Vietnam. In this rise of what I call "postmodern orientalism," Asian culture becomes a site for identification and appropriation by American artists and activists, even as it remains other and foreign to American culture.

As I discuss in Chapter 2, composer Steve Reich, whose work *Drumming* was a major influence on poet Ron Silliman, has frequently cited the impact of Asian music on him, noting his desire to "think Balinese" in his work. Silliman, in turn, named his long poem *Ketjak* after a Balinese chant. In his essay "The Turn to Language and the 1960s," Barrett Watten cites Allen Ginsberg's use of Buddhist chants and the Black Panthers' use of Mao's *Little Red Book* as politically charged moments of Asian identification. At the same time, Watten characterizes these Asian texts as empty signifiers, "incomprehensible" symbols whose primary function is to mark a position utterly outside any possible system.[3]

Even though such appropriations of Asia were undoubtedly productive for white writers and artists, postmodernist orientalism placed Asian American poets in a peculiar situation. In theory, the counterculture's embrace of Asia could have offered writers of Asian descent a significant opportunity to find a wide audience for their work. There can be little doubt that Asian American writers and activists were themselves inspired by such importations from Asia, from Asian American activists' own embrace of Mao's philosophy to Mirikitani's engagement with Japanese poetic forms. In practice, however, white Americans' interest remained fixed on Asia itself, not Asians in America; the search for otherness led overseas (Ginsberg to India, Snyder to Japan) but not to the domestic productions of Asian Americans. Indeed, as Park argues in *Apparitions of Asia*, Asian American poets defined themselves by writing against what they saw as the appropriation and exoticism practiced by poets like Snyder. So while white experimental writers and artists like Ginsberg, Snyder, Reich, and Silliman gained critical and even popular recognition for their citations of Asian culture, Asian American poets struggled until well into the 1980s to gain a mainstream readership.

On those rare occasions when Asian Americans did gain recognition from white avant-gardists, the results were mixed. The reception of Theresa Hak Kyung Cha's *Dictée*, which I discuss in Chapter 4, suggests that the category of Asian American writing was still unacknowledged by many white experimentalists as late as the mid-1980s. Through the lens of postmodern orientalism, Cha's avant-gardism was understood as a sign of her essential foreignness. Not until the 1990s did Asian American critics begin to link her work to that of other Asian American writers.

We may also get a sense of the relative locations of Language and Asian American writing through their vexed relationship to a third body of work: African American writing. In the late 1960s and early 1970s, African American culture provided a powerful but ambiguous example for both

Asian American and white experimental writers. Nathaniel Mackey's and Aldon Lynn Nielsen's authoritative studies of experimental African American poetry suggest that black experimentalists formed an avant-garde in which social dissent and aesthetic dissidence were profoundly consonant; as Mackey puts it, such poetry displays an organic link "between ethnicity and formal innovation, social marginality and aesthetic marginality" (7–8). Most influential for Asian American writers in particular was the Black Arts movement, at its apex in the early 1970s; anchored by the politically charged work of Amiri Baraka, it advocated "a poetic diction rooted in black speech and black music" (Nielsen 9). But as Nielsen demonstrates, African American influences can be found throughout the history of the American poetic avant-garde, particularly in the influence of jazz, a model for the work of African American, Asian American, and white poets alike.

As Asian American activist and musician Fred Ho notes in his "Tribute to the Black Arts Movement," many Asian Americans "have admired the black American struggle and especially what we perceive to be the strength, rootedness, and communality of the black American cultural experience" (142). Ho's own jazz group, the Afro Asian Music Ensemble, is a tribute to such connections. Indeed, as Ho suggests, it was jazz that offered the best example of a politically resonant avant-garde: "Malcolm X represented the vanguard of revolutionary black nationalism. John Coltrane represented the musical and cultural vanguard. . . . A dynamically dialectical interplay existed between both political and artistic energies" (145). Jazz, more than any direct influence of African American poetry, had a major impact on Asian American poets, most notably, as I discuss in Chapter 3, on the work of Lawson Fusao Inada.

But Ho acknowledges that Asian Americans never developed a true counterpart to the Black Arts movement. The closest equivalent, Ho writes, was "a very small bicoastal activist circle" of the 1970s that included Inada and a few others (150). Thus, black cultural nationalism could also serve as a reminder of what Asian Americans lacked; as Ho puts it, "Where is our Asian Malcolm X? Or Langston Hughes? Or John Coltrane?" (142). Although I argue that Asian American poets did function as an avant-garde in the 1970s, they never achieved the coherence and prominence of the Black Arts movement. Poets like Inada and Mirikitani did not exert a strong influence on non–Asian American writers. As a result, Asian American poetry would not gain wide recognition until the 1980s, when it would be defined not as avant-garde but by the more mainstream aesthetic of Cathy Song, David Mura, and Li-Young Lee.

The relationship between African American and Language writing is also a complex one. Even though no Asian American poet was acknowledged as a peer by white experimental writers until quite recently, the avant-garde scene of the 1950s and 1960s did include Amiri Baraka, who (as LeRoi Jones) was the only black writer in Donald Allen's anthology *The New American Poetry*. As Mackey notes, Baraka was a "bridge figure" among the avant-gardes of the period, variously affiliated with Beat, Black Mountain, New York school, and African American writing (7). More important than the direct influence of Baraka, however, is the wide-ranging impact African American culture—especially music—has had on the American avant-garde in the twentieth century. Reminding us that Charles Olson and Robert Creeley, like many other white writers, where compelled by the rhythms of bebop, Mackey cites Olson's widely quoted remark on projectivist poetics: "[T]here was no poetic. It was Charlie Parker" (8). Nielsen even suggests a powerful jazz genealogy for Language writing, noting the strong influence of the music and poetry of Cecil Taylor on the work of Clark Coolidge, who in turn was a major model for Ron Silliman and other Language poets (258).

Identifying such connections, however, should not obscure the fact that Language writers counted no writers of color among their ranks, and very few among their allies. In the debates around the founding of the journal *L=A=N=G=U=A=G=E* that I discuss in Chapter 2, the only black writer named as a potential contributor is Lorenzo Thomas. In this respect, the canonization of Language writing simply follows a literary-critical tradition in which groups of white writers are seen as constituting "the avant-garde," with nonwhite artists and cultures relegated to the status of mere "context" or "inspiration." But the situation of Language writing, I argue, differed from that of earlier avant-gardes in a significant way. Like Asian American writers of the 1970s, Language writers emerged at a moment of heightened awareness of race; it was no longer possible, as it might have been in an earlier era, to simply remain ignorant of the rise of African American, Chicano/Chicana, or Native American political and artistic groupings.[4]

I suggest that Language writers responded to this shifting landscape in a two-pronged fashion. First, they developed an occasionally uncomfortable awareness of their own social particularity—becoming, in Silliman's work, an almost "ethnic" sense of his position as a progressive white male writer.

But they also reacted against what they saw as more doctrinaire forms of identity politics, hoping to create in their work an aesthetic that could integrate diverse materials within elaborate formal structures. It might be said, in effect, that Language writers sought to continue the politics of the 1960s by other means, steering away from the perceived perils of separatism and violence toward an analysis of language.

This last argument is one suggested by Barrett Watten in his 2002 article "The Turn to Language and the 1960s." Watten provocatively proposes analogies between the social movements of the 1960s, from the civil rights movement to the Berkeley Free Speech movement, and the "radically formalist poetics" of Language writing (139). What social movements shared with "language-centered" poetics, Watten argues, was the establishing of a position "outside" a given order, whether that of the liberal university, of institutionalized racism, or of language itself. Charles Bernstein's 2000 essay "Poetics of the Americas," although on a very different topic, makes an analogous argument: the techniques of Language writing can be allied with the dialect poetry of ethnic minority writers because both represent "nonstandard language practices" (113).

But both Bernstein and Watten acknowledge that they are writing revisionist histories, testifying to the gaps between Language poetry and other modes of writing in the very act of seeking to bridge them. While Bernstein argues that it is now possible to see the "intimate formal and sociohistorical connection" between black and white modernisms, he also notes that "the fact of the color line" meant that "these developments often took place without reference to each other" (113). And although Watten asserts that it is possible to retrospectively construct a common political genealogy for Language poetry and the writing of poets of color, such connections were less than obvious at the time. "The textual politics of the Language school," Watten observes, "are commonly opposed to the expressivist poetics (Black Arts, Chicano, feminist, gay/lesbian) that emerged in the same decade, for good reason" (139). Watten categorizes his own account as a "thought experiment" rather than a history precisely because there were few organic links between Language writers and poets of color in the 1970s.

Indeed, there is some reason to think that forceful articulations of African American identity were a negative example for Language writers. Watten's extended critique of the "irrational" and "distorted" politics of the Black Panther Party suggests that black separatism forms a kind of limit case for his argument, threatening to disrupt the emancipatory coalition of the left (172)—much as Ron Silliman, as described previously, wonders what the rise of the Black Panthers means for the future of the left. As I will suggest of Silliman, Watten offers language-centered writing as a response to the political fragmentation of the 1960s, a potential force for the reintegration of the left: "The language-centered poetics of the 1970s permitted the recovery of a totalized *outside* that was a casualty of the conflict between expression and representation in the 1960s" (183).

Language writing, like Asian American poetry, is therefore less a parallel development to the rise of the Black Arts movement than a response to it. But unlike Asian American poetry, which sought (with limited success) to model itself on Black Arts, Language writing's focus on "language itself" can be read as an effort to move beyond more obviously identity-based categories. This has allowed critics to grant Language writing a kind of monopoly over the aesthetic—regarding its politics as purely formal—while relegating Asian American and African American poetry to the realm of identity politics. Whereas Language writing has reached a significant academic audience (although not without generating significant controversy), with several of its practitioners now university professors of poetics, Asian American poetry is still sufficiently overlooked that a panel was convened at the 2007 Modern Language Association convention to inquire into the neglect of poetry in Asian American studies.[5]

In studying Asian American and Language writing, my goal is not to produce a revisionist account that would erase the historical gaps between the two bodies of work. My argument that both groups can be understood as manifestations of the avant-garde should not occlude the very different goals of Language and Asian American writing or the very different paths they have taken. Indeed, I hope that understanding both as avant-garde formations may help us explain their complex and frequently misunderstood positioning in the contemporary American poetic landscape.

Understanding Language and Asian American poetries as divergent manifestations of the contemporary avant-garde distinguishes this project from the approaches adopted by Nathaniel Mackey and Aldon Lynn Nielsen, whose groundbreaking studies have conclusively established the existence of a vibrant tradition of experimental African American writing. My interest is less in outlining a history of experimental Asian American writing than in showing how Asian American and Language writing emerged as parallel avant-garde formations. I also distinguish my framework from the one adopted by Ann Vickery's *Leaving Lines of Gender*, which persuasively argues for what Vickery calls a "feminist genealogy" of Language writing; my interest lies in the vexed history of division between the two bodies of work I study, rather than in any argument for their unification.

Several recent critics have sought more actively to bring Asian American poets into discussions of experimental writing. Juliana Spahr's *Everybody's Autonomy* holds up experimental texts such as Theresa Hak Kyung Cha's *Dictée* as examples of works that "decolonize" reading through both their form and their content, and Brian Kim Stefans's essay "Remote Parsee: An Alternative Grammar to Asian North American Poetry" offers an alternative canon of innovative Asian American poets that includes John Yau and Mei-mei Berssenbrugge. Such projects, however, with their focus on formal categories, do not offer an argument for the distinctiveness of Asian American writing; they also do not offer an explanation as to why the work of most Asian American poets has not previously been recognized as experimental. Viewing the categories of the Asian American and experimental comparatively, through the lens of the avant-garde, can help us answer some of these questions, revealing the linked history of both bodies of work, the reasons for their divergence since the 1970s, and the conditions that seem now to be allowing a renewed sense of their connections.

My point of origin for these concerns is the work of Allen Ginsberg, not because Ginsberg should somehow be seen as the progenitor of either Asian American or Language poetry—though his influence is quite evident in both—but because one can see, coexisting in his work, those political and aesthetic issues that will ultimately give rise to Language poetry and Asian American poetry. Chapter 1 focuses on Ginsberg's poetry of the later 1960s, composed by dictation into a tape recorder and called "auto poesy." In these poems, Ginsberg hoped to combine the media's generalizing power with the humanity of the individual consciousness. But his original recordings reveal a subjectivity that is uncertain and self-revising, relying not on spontaneous thought but on will and assertion to create its desired effect. These aspects of Ginsberg's work are emblematic of the fragmentation of the new left in the late 1960s into the identity politics of the 1970s—a situation to which both Language poetry and Asian American poetry arise as responses.

The work of Language writer Ron Silliman, the subject of Chapter 2, extends Ginsberg's vision of a poetry that realistically portrays society; but

Silliman employs formal techniques, such as the parataxis of the "new sentence," that attempt to guard against Ginsberg's excesses of subjectivity. With the breakup of the left in the 1970s, Silliman's project is threatened by the limits of both individual and group subjectivity—by boundaries of race, gender, and sexuality. In studying correspondence among Language writers, I show how Silliman and other Language writers adapt by redefining the avant-garde, positing Language writing not simply as an aesthetic movement but as a social identity, in a process that might be dubbed the "ethnicization" of the avant-garde.[6] Silliman's first major work, *Ketjak*, is both a convincing map of the contemporary social landscape and an often uncomfortable exploration of white male consciousness—a sensibility awkwardly aware of its own "pervasive presence."

Although one might assume that Asian American writing of the 1970s would be less prone to such anxieties, Chapter 3 shows Asian American poetry engaged in comparable struggles over identity and poetic form— a response, in part, to self-conscious comparisons to the strength of black nationalism. Poetry fulfills an avant-garde function in early Asian American publications, not by reporting on but by actively creating an Asian American culture. The work of such poets as Janice Mirikitani, Francis Oka, and Lawson Fusao Inada, in which the Asian American subject is visibly under construction, reflects a dynamic fusion of Beat, jazz, and populist influences.

During the 1980s, as Language writing and Asian American writing became visible to mainstream readers, their common avant-garde orientations were obscured, making their practices seem radically separate. I explore this process in Chapter 4 by documenting the reception of Theresa Hak Kyung Cha's book *Dictée*. Although Cha was known in white avant-garde circles in the 1970s and 1980s, she was neglected by Asian American readers until the early 1990s. *Dictée*'s difficult career illustrates the avant-garde continuity of Language and Asian American writing but also cautions against any simple attempt to integrate the two. The multiple and often conflicting structures that organize *Dictée*—linguistic, poetic, mythical, historical, personal— make it a text in which the impulses of experimental and Asian American writing meet in mutually critical fashion.

By the 1990s, the term "experimental Asian American poetry" had emerged to describe work like Cha's. Chapter 5 offers a critique of this concept through a survey of the work of John Yau. Yau's use of ethnic signifiers allows his work to be positioned within the discourse of Asian American writing; at the same time, he adopts the Language poets' conception of a self constructed in language. But in hanging on to the emptied-out structures of ethnic identity, Yau gains a foothold from which to critique Language poetry's attempt to incorporate the "marginal." Far from providing a synthesis, Yau's work stages the history of and conflict between these contemporary avant-garde modes.

A sociology of the contemporary poetic avant-garde is crucial if we are to understand the roles that categories such as Asian American and Language writing have played, and continue to play, on the contemporary American scene. At stake are the very terms of contemporary literary value, in which aesthetics are strongly linked with the social. Perhaps most important, this project seeks to provide the historical context necessary to understand the distinctive contributions of a wide range of poets, from Allen Ginsberg to John Yau, and to grasp the inescapably political ramifications of these poets' negotiations with poetic form.

ONE

Auto Poesy

Allen Ginsberg and the Politics of Poetry

To begin a discussion of race and the avant-garde with the work of Allen Ginsberg may seem a curious choice. Race plays little explicit role in Ginsberg's work, and Ginsberg and his fellow Beat writers are rarely discussed in terms of the avant-garde.[1] But for the politicized era of the 1960s, Ginsberg's poetry, for better or worse, offered the most powerful example of the political claims of American avant-garde writing—an example both imitated and critiqued by white experimental and Asian American poets of the succeeding generation. Ginsberg's early work gives us a crucial glimpse of the avant-garde vision in America at midcentury; his later work suggests that vision can never be a truly universal one—an insight that helps account for the proliferation of contemporary avant-gardes differentiated by race.

To revisit Ginsberg, then, is to return to the concept of the political, seeking to grasp how the idea of a contemporary American political poetry emerges in Ginsberg's work. Taking a public role in the anti–Vietnam War movement, Ginsberg became an example to numerous other poets who became politicized in the 1960s.[2] In a 1989 interview, Ginsberg would, perhaps arrogantly, give Beat writing credit for providing a "spiritual lib" that paved the way for "many different kinds of liberation . . . Women's Lib, Gay Lib, even to some extent, Black Lib" (*Mind* 506).[3] Both Audre Lorde and June Jordan, Ginsberg said, "appreciated what we [the Beats] had done as a kind of liberation of language and a feeling, so that they could manifest their private world and not . . . imitate the academic white" (509).[4] Nor was Ginsberg's influence limited to these groups; white experimentalists such as the Language writers would admit, albeit grudgingly, the relevance of the work of Ginsberg and other Beat writers.[5]

If we look for the politics of an early Ginsberg poem like "Howl," we will not find it in any endorsement of party, position on the issues of the day, or polemic against government policy. Instead, "Howl" responds to discourses of power in large part through its form: the wild juxtapositions that cross cultural and moral boundaries, the anaphoric structure that rejects hierarchy, the collage created with a faith in an organic, rather than artificial, order. In drawing on these techniques, Ginsberg extends a sense of the politics of literary form established by poets such as Ezra Pound and T. S. Eliot, whose long poems are structured as models of entirely reordered civilizations. But we can further see Ginsberg as participating in a distinctively avant-garde political project, one perhaps best described as utopian. The political visions of historical avant-gardes such as Italian and Russian futurism can be seen less in their explicit allegiances to political movements of the left or right—rarely apparent in their works themselves—but in the utopian allegories they offer, the models of revolution and of future social organization they create in their shattering of traditional forms and their embrace of new poetic languages.

What Ginsberg adds to this formal politics is a conscious awareness of the avant-garde as social fact. His desire to depict the "minds of my generation" has led critics like M. L. Rosenthal to see him as an originator of the "confessional" strain in contemporary American poetry, but we might more accurately understand this impulse as sociological, grounded less in personal expression than in the attempt to represent the situation of the group of which the poet finds himself a member. Ginsberg's "Howl" combines a political critique grounded in the poem's form with an awareness of the social location—that of the Beat coterie—from which that critique emerges. Although the Beat community itself may have been an exceedingly small one, Ginsberg's insight that a contemporary avant-garde political critique would have to register the social site of its emergence would prove formative for later American avant-gardists.

Indeed, that need for a social grounding for the avant-garde may help explain why the power of Ginsberg's poetry declined even as his direct political involvement deepened. For while "Howl" marked its origin in a particular community, it also implied the potential universality of that community, creating a paradoxically inclusive coterie. Such universality was, of course, an illusion, one that collapsed under the increasing political pressures of the 1960s. Later works like Ginsberg's "Wichita Vortex Sutra," although far more explicit in their political content than earlier poems, ground their universalist claims too heavily within the individual subjectivity of the poet, weakening their persuasiveness. For writers of the 1970s, it became clear that the avant-garde's continuing power would be in its particularity, in its marking of the racial, class, and gender locations of its formal innovations.

Explicit political commitments played little role in the early Beat movement. Ginsberg admits as much in a 1972 interview, collected in *Spontaneous Mind*: "[W]e were definitely thinking in non-political terms, apolitical terms. The first necessity was to get back to Person, from public to person" (286–7). Nor did Beat writers toe a party line: while Ginsberg increasingly identified with the left in the 1960s, Jack Kerouac became an outspoken conservative.[6] More recently, numerous critics have called attention to the sexism, racism, and homophobia underlying the Beats' ostensible program of liberation.[7] Yet there can also be no doubt that Ginsberg's "Howl" was seen by many readers of the 1950s, and by the critics who followed, as a radical statement whose impact was felt in political as well as in aesthetic terms.[8]

A reading of "Howl" is unlikely to uncover any particular political platform. The poem's primary villain, Moloch, cannot be identified with any political figure, system, or government. Indeed, such an attempt to locate the signified of "Moloch" would be beside the point. Although Ginsberg's poetry of the 1960s takes on specific targets (drug laws, the Vietnam War, the U.S. government's foreign policy), no one—least of all Ginsberg himself—would argue that the primary impact of "Howl" is as a rallying cry for the left. In fact, if we are to understand the significance of "Howl" for the politics of poetry, we should look neither to the denunciations of Moloch in Part II of the poem nor to the countercry of the Footnote, "Everything's holy!"[9]—both examples of what many readers have criticized as simplifying rhetoric. Instead we should look to the longest, most powerful, and most memorable section of the poem, Part I, whose impact, and political resonance, can be attributed to Ginsberg's distinctively avant-garde techniques.

Ginsberg's shocking juxtapositions of unlike words and images, a version of collage through which Ginsberg hopes to create an alternative to rational discourse in "incarnate gaps in Time & Space," gives the poem its avant-garde form. But that form is also joined by avant-garde content: the evocation of an alternative community of "beats," rendered with novelistic and even sociological detail. It is this link of the aesthetic and the social realms that gives the poem its distinctive political vision. "Howl" both imagines an alternative society and, through its distinctive structure, offers a model for organizing that society—seeking, as Peter Bürger would say of the avant-garde more broadly, a grounding for a new life praxis in the materials of art.

Ginsberg describes his version of avant-garde juxtaposition in two lines toward the end of Part I of "Howl":

> and who therefore ran through the icy streets obsessed with a sudden flash
>   of the alchemy of the use of the ellipsis catalog a variable measure
>   and the vibrating plane,
> who dreamt and made incarnate gaps in Time & Space through images
>   juxtaposed, and trapped the archangel of the soul between 2 visual
>   images and joined the elemental verbs and set the noun and dash of
>   consciousness together jumping with sensation of Pater Omnipotens
>   Aeterne Deus
>
> (*Howl* 6)

Ginsberg's litany references a wide range of influences on his own practice: the "catalog" poems of Christopher Smart and Walt Whitman; the "vibrating planes" of Paul Cézanne's paintings; the "variable measure" of William Carlos Williams; the "sudden flash" of vision produced by Ezra Pound's imagism. All of these methods rely on the notion of things "juxtaposed," working across "gaps in Time & Space" rather than through logical connections and generating a transcendent, quasi-religious "sensation." And by making these artists and writers part of the cast of "Howl," Ginsberg presents formal choices as acts of social rebellion, paralleling modernist innovators with those other characters in his poem "who howled on their knees in the subway" or "who walked all night with their shoes full of blood" (4).

This sense of modernism as dissent can be attributed in part to Ginsberg's dissatisfaction with his literary education at Columbia, where the writers Ginsberg felt to be most valuable were neglected. In a 1972 interview, Ginsberg recalled that one instructor told him "Whitman was not a serious writer because he had no discipline and William Carlos Williams was an awkward provincial, no craft, and Shelley was a sort of silly fool!" (*Mind* 279–80). And in the aftermath of the publication of "Howl," Ginsberg would write to his former professor Lionel Trilling, "Eliot & Pound are like Dryden & Pope. . . . Whitman will be seen to have set the example and been bypassed for half a century" (*Howl* 156). Ginsberg's expulsion from Columbia, memorialized in "Howl," thus becomes an exemplary rebellion, equal parts aesthetic and social: "who were expelled from the academies for crazy & publishing obscene odes on the windows of the skull" (3).

Juxtaposition in "Howl" operates on several levels. First, and perhaps most strikingly, it works at the level of the individual image—"hotrod-Golgotha," "nowhere Zen New Jersey," and Ginsberg's own favorite, "hydrogen jukebox." Ginsberg writes of the last phrase that "tho quite senseless [it] makes in context clear sense" (*Howl* 153); elsewhere he cites it as an example of "the juxtaposition of disparate images to create a gap of understanding which the mind fills in with a flash of recognition" (*Howl* 130). Ginsberg's "flash" echoes Ezra Pound's classic account of the working of the "image" as "that which presents an intellectual and emotional complex in an instant of time" (Pound 86). But whereas Pound's "In a Station of the Metro" is grounded in a haikulike juxtaposition of two simple images, Ginsberg's images use a vocabulary already loaded with associations; his words often evoke an entire cultural milieu: *Zen, hotrod, jukebox*. In Ginsberg it is frequently not two objects but two contexts—religious, historical, political—that are juxtaposed, and the effect of the images is in the forcing of one set of associations up against another.

Ginsberg pushes this modernist technique into an avant-garde realm in part through images that are willfully perverse, chosen for maximum dissonance and grotesque effect. The result is a kind of surrealist burlesque, producing one-liners like "Zen New Jersey" that juxtapose the mystical and the notoriously mundane. But the images' subversive power comes ultimately from the connections they insist on making between ostensibly separate realms. "Hydrogen jukebox" suggests an alliance between the technologies of atomic apocalypse and mass entertainment; "nowhere Zen New Jersey" not only (comically) brings together East and West but refigures anomic suburban exile as a state of spiritual potential. Although Ginsberg's stated aim may be to unify disparate parts of the mind, his juxtaposition of context rather than objects draws connections across a divided social landscape, a key to the poem's political power.

Juxtaposition also operates at a broader level in "Howl" through the technique of the catalog. Ginsberg's model is, of course, Whitman, whose catalogs, like Cézanne's canvases, create "grand spaciousness in 'list poems' moving thru varying geographies, trades, sounds, stages, multiple precise but discrete observations" (*Howl* 130). The "gap" that Ginsberg posits between the individual words of an image is also meant to be present between each of the long lines of "Howl"; just as Cézanne's paintings "create the appearance of gaps in space without recourse to conventional perspective lines" (*Howl* 130), the catalog holds together the long poem without the conventional means of syntax or narrative. It is the catalog form that allows Ginsberg to construct his enormous cast of unlikely characters without regard for social or narrative proprieties, juxtaposing middle-class students "who passed through universities with radiant cool eyes," junkies "suffering Eastern sweats and Tangerian bone-grindings," advertising agents "burned alive in their innocent flannel suits," and criminals "who sang sweet blues to Alcatraz."

Ultimately, though, the logic of the catalog is centripetal, drawing these disparate characters together, in contrast to the centrifugal force of the individual images. Ginsberg's individual images take two words with rich but opposed connotations and force them together, creating a compound whose associational energies push outward. His catalogs, in contrast, have the task of taking a series of dramatic but isolated gestures and building them into a collective portrait of "the best minds of my generation." Ginsberg welds diverse experiences together to form a distinct society, a delineated avant-garde.

The catalog's juxtapositions are held together through the use of anaphora, the insistent "who" that opens nearly every line; borrowed from Christopher Smart's "Jubilate Agno," this technique turns the roster of characters into a litany, a directed address on a single subject. Faced with a chaotic mass of experience, Ginsberg imposes an order that is not narrative but grammatical, as the entire first section of "Howl" takes the form of a single sentence: "I saw the best minds of my generation destroyed by madness . . . angelheaded hipsters . . . who . . . who . . . who . . ." While such a method is leveling, refusing hierarchy in its parallel development, it is also centralizing, marshaling aesthetic, intellectual, political, and sexual experience into a demonstration of a group of people "destroyed by madness." Moreover, this group is defined in terms that are neither representative nor egalitarian; they are not simply "minds" but "the *best* minds," not persons of any age or even representative youths but "*my* generation." Much of a reader's response to the poem may depend upon her or his positioning with regard to these "best minds." Ginsberg certainly intends an irony here, as his "best minds" are precisely those whom a perverse society labels "mad." But how inclusive is the community that Ginsberg imagines? Does his celebration of these "angelheaded hipsters" merely set up another coterie, a new elite?

It is at this point that Ginsberg's formal allegory of a new community meets, and may even come into conflict with, Ginsberg's desire to portray the reality of an already extant group of comrades and friends. Although some readers bemoan critics' overemphasis on Ginsberg's life and on his Beat exploits,[10] Ginsberg made no bones about the biographical content of his work, arguing against "the hypocrisy of literature . . . which is supposed to be different from . . . our quotidian inspired lives" and calling for a poetry in which one would "talk as frankly as you would talk with yourself or with your friends" (*Mind* 23–4). There was no shame, Ginsberg insisted, in Kerouac's *On the Road* being about "a gang of friends running around in an automobile" (24).

Ginsberg's formal techniques may be modernist, but his emphasis on biographical material clearly marks his work as part of the post–World War II response to modernism, leading many critics to call Ginsberg a "confessional" poet in the vein of Lowell, Plath, or Berryman. In this reading, Ginsberg's response to academic, formalist modernism could be understood, like Lowell's, as an infusion of modernist forms with content that defies modernist ideals of impersonality. But what sets "Howl," at least, apart from other confessional works is its aspiration to the status of *collective* confession. It is certainly the case, as Steven K. Hoffman suggests of the confessionals, that "even the most personal dilemmas shed light on broader cultural conditions" (329); but a poet such as Lowell does this precisely by foregrounding his own status as a representative individual, not by claiming to speak for "my generation."

For whom, then, is Ginsberg speaking? What is the nature of the community he wishes to portray in "Howl"—who are its members, and can it really be said to represent a whole generation? "Howl" may gain much of its dramatic power from its perceived biographical roots, but its avant-garde politics ultimately rests upon its ability to abstract away from those roots in offering a broadly utopian and inclusive vision. Ginsberg's drafts suggest that his positions on such issues shifted throughout the writing of "Howl," as Ginsberg tacked between a highly personal, even insular approach and a broader but more abstract vision.

The annotated *Howl* that Ginsberg published in 1986 is itself testimony to the poem's biographical grounding. Ginsberg's notes reveal the identity of each "who" in the original draft, often fleshing out or providing context for an anecdote only hinted at in the poem. For example, the person "who fell out of windows in despair" is "ref. William Cannastra, legendary late 1940s New York bohemian figure, life cut short by alcoholic accident, body balanced out of subway window, knocked against a pillar, fell at Astor Place, Manhattan" (*Howl* 128). Indeed, the first draft is much more explicit than the final version in its evocation of specific personal experiences among a specific group of friends: "Ginsberg Kerouac Burroughs & Neal Cassady, I name them all" (*Howl* 23). Even the "Footnote to Howl," with its radically egalitarian assertion that "everybody's holy," begins in its first draft as a celebration of Ginsberg and three of his friends: "Holy Peter Holy Allen Holy Kerouac Holy Huncke" (99).

But Ginsberg chose to move away from this narrow focus on his friends as he revised the poem. The list of names is eliminated from subsequent drafts of Part I; Carl Solomon, the dedicatee, is the only one to remain, and even he is reduced from "Carl Solomon" to "Carl." Ginsberg's revisions show him condensing and compressing his lines, eliminating articles, prepositions, and other syntactical connectors in order to heighten the effect of imagistic juxtaposition; "who vanished into the New Jersies of amnesia" (13) becomes "who vanished into nowhere Zen New Jersey." These compressions often have the side effect of blurring biographical reference. Ginsberg's original, rather straightforward allusion to his dismissal from Columbia—"who were expelled from colleges for printing obscene odes in the dust of the sexless windows of men's dormatories [*sic*]" (19)—becomes a much more general and mystical proposition: "who were expelled from the academies for crazy & publishing obscene odes on the windows of the skull" (3). Even Ginsberg's first draft makes a generalizing gesture, turning his individual experience into the plural "expelled from colleges"; his revision goes further, making this event not a mere prank but an act of rebellion against "the academies," evoking a whole context of academic formalism and constraint. Similarly, the mundane, Williamsesque image of "men's dormitories" is spiritualized into the "windows of the skull," elevating Ginsberg's stunt to a mythical level that suggests a broader spiritual liberation.[11] As revision progressed, the poem became less directly biographical and more a riff on biographical details, which became raw material for the poem's larger vision.

One of the secrets of the appeal of "Howl," and that of Beat writing in general, has always been this careful management of biography. Ginsberg's

toning down of explicit biography is combined with generalizing gestures
to create a sense of inclusiveness that allows him to speak for a generation
and that allows a reader to feel part of the world he creates. At the same
time, Ginsberg's use of cryptic details evokes character and milieu without
pinning them down to a specific referent. "Howl" is full of mysterious and
only partially glimpsed characters, often marked by ethnic or geographical particularity but otherwise undeveloped. One striking example is the
character who appears in the final draft as "the Chinaman of Oklahoma."
In contrast to the generalizing impulse of some of Ginsberg's characterizations, this character begins in the first draft as a general category ("who
jumped in cars with chinamen" [23]), but becomes by the second draft a
specific figure, "the Chinaman," and is identified in subsequent drafts with
particular places—first as "the Chinaman of Illinois," then "the Chinaman
of Oklahoma." As the change in place suggests, there does not seem to be
any biographical source here; instead, Ginsberg creates an almost mythical
character who resonates with the Beats' fascination with racial others.[12] Perhaps the most significant effect of Ginsberg's formulation is that it creates
"insiders" and "outsiders"—"the Chinaman of Oklahoma" seems known to
Ginsberg and his intimates but can only remain a mysterious figure to other
readers. Yet Ginsberg's use of generic racial and geographical markers to
define the character—in contrast to Kerouac's extensive use of pseudonyms
in his novels—also makes the figure seem tantalizingly knowable, part of a
familiar landscape of "winter midnight streetlight smalltown rain" (4).

Ginsberg's delicate balance between biography and myth, between writer
and reader, insider and outsider, may be most evident in the figure of "N.C.,
secret hero of these poems" (4). "N.C." is, of course, Neal Cassady, legendary Beat personality and central character (as "Dean Moriarty") of Jack Kerouac's *On the Road*. As noted above, Ginsberg dropped his friends' names after the first draft of Part I of "Howl" in order to generalize and mythologize
his anecdotes. These names remain absent in the second and third drafts,
but in the fourth draft, Cassady reappears as the subject of a long paean:

> who went out whoring through the Midwest in myriad stolen night cars,
>   N.C., secret hero of these poems, cocksman and Adonis of Denver,
>   our long old love, heart of ten thousand bodies on another coast, joy
>   to the memory of his innumerable lays of girls . . .

>   (38)

Ginsberg, however, was still ambivalent about this inclusion. The next and penultimate draft of the poem retains the line but eliminates the identification and epithet, cutting everything from "N.C." to "coast." In the final version of the line, the initials are restored: "who went out whoring through Colorado in myriad stolen night-cars, N.C., secret hero of these poems, cocksman and Adonis of Denver—joy to the memory of his innumerable lays of girls . . ." (4).

Ginsberg's editorial vacillation may be attributed in part to the complexities of his own relationship with Cassady.[13] But it also betrays some uncertainty as to the audience for the poem, and the relationship of that audience to the community Ginsberg seeks to portray. The first draft of the poem reads like a highly personal document that celebrates a small circle of friends. Ginsberg's naming of Kerouac, Cassady, Burroughs, and Lucien Carr reflects little thought about the circulation of the poem outside that group—an issue raised almost immediately by Carr, who, as Ginsberg notes, "preferred his name be dropped lest it cause his life to cast a shadow beyond its actuality" (136). Carl Solomon, whose name was not dropped, bore the brunt of Ginsberg's underestimation of his poem's audience, growing deeply uncomfortable with the fame that resulted from what Ginsberg termed his own "naïve use" of Solomon's name (111).[14] Whereas Kerouac responded to the personal and legal difficulties of writing about his friends by employing pseudonyms and presenting his work as fiction,[15] Ginsberg dropped proper names entirely in an attempt to make a broader generational statement. The catalog of "who" seems infinitely inclusive, large enough to capture the experience of a whole society; what Ginsberg's removal of names conceals is that the vast majority of "Howl" surveys the experiences of only about a dozen people.

The designation of "N.C." as "secret hero" of "Howl," though, suggests Ginsberg's desire to hang on to his more intimate community, even as he works to open that community to a wider world. The very formulation— "N.C., secret hero of these poems"—is a study in contradictions. Ginsberg does not give Cassady's name, ostensibly protecting his privacy, but the initials suggest a kind of code, utterly transparent to some readers, opaque and tantalizing to others—again, creating insiders and outsiders. And what can a "secret hero" be? This is a curiously public secrecy, in which the sexual exploits of "N.C." are rehearsed in explicit detail; yet Ginsberg continues to insist that there is a "secret" at the heart of a poem based on utter frankness and exposure. It would seem that, after we read "Howl," there is nothing secret about "N.C." except his full name.

Ginsberg's "secret hero," then, has an odd effect on his audience. It clearly partitions his readers into the initiated and the uninitiated. At the same time, Ginsberg keeps the barrier of entry low by revealing enough information that we feel that we can not only know "N.C." and his comrades but that we could also participate, and be included ourselves in the litany of "who." This sense of the Beats as inclusive coterie, as a club to which anyone could belong, has always been part of the Beat appeal, however much it obscures the group's actual exclusions. It is this kind of community that "Howl" seeks to present: an avant-garde community that is marked by its isolation from everyday life but that is also exemplary, serving as a model for a much wider reorganization of social life.

Clearly, though, there remains a tension between the sociological content of "Howl" and its formal aspirations toward utopian allegory, between the particular portrayal of the experiences of a few and the desire to make a universal generational statement. Perhaps surprisingly, Ginsberg's gambit for resolving this tension is to insist on the essential accuracy and objectivity of what may seem like the purely subjective material of his poem. Ginsberg's poem aspires as much to be a historical and anthropological record of a neglected and repressed subculture as it does to be a denunciation of society or a call to arms. This sense of the poem as document has, for Ginsberg, an essentially modernist foundation, grounded in what he calls in a letter to Richard Eberhart "1920s W.C.W. imagistically observed detail" (*Howl* 154). But Ginsberg goes on to note that these observations are then "collapsed together by interior associative logic" (154). This is Ginsberg's version of the technique of "spontaneous personal narrative" pioneered by Kerouac, which Ginsberg describes in his annotations as "continuous scanning of writer's consciousness during time of original composition for simultaneous multilevel references sufficiently swiftly to include them in extended prose sentences" (126). Ginsberg imagines his poem, then, not as a direct image of reality but rather as a document of the mind's movements in perceiving reality, as it fills in sense data with association and emotion.

Ginsberg's interest in the stream of consciousness, however, does not mean that he regards the poem as a purely subjective artifact. Instead, he characterizes the "matter" of "Howl" as "*objective* acknowledgment of emotion" (xii, emphasis added). If Ginsberg is truly, in writing the poem, "leaping *out* of a preconceived notion of social 'values,' following my own heart's instincts" (152), subjectivity must be presented as accurately as possible in order to avoid self-censorship and self-consciousness, the imposition of artificial restraints and judgments. Ginsberg's desire for an accurate presentation of consciousness has often (mistakenly, I believe) been equated with such utterances as "First thought, best thought," understood as simply writing down the first thing that comes to mind, and abetted by such Ginsberg statements as "I don't have any craft and don't know what I'm doing" (*Mind* 249). The annotated *Howl* demonstrates definitively that "First thought, best thought" does not mean "First draft, best draft," and that, paradoxically, the most accurate possible representation of consciousness may require the most concerted poetic artifice.

Although the world of the poem may not be accurate in a journalistic sense—Ginsberg provides a quotation from a disgruntled Carl Solomon describing "Howl" as "apocryphal history" in which Ginsberg "enshrined falsehood as truth" (*Howl* 131)—Ginsberg does present the poem as a true representation of his own consciousness and its response to a historical moment. There is thus a continuing political tension in the poem, often conscious: What is the connection between the individual consciousness and the larger society of which it is a part? What is the link between the imagined world of the poem and the "secret" biographical and historical reality it adapts? Consider the following line from "Howl":

> who jumped off the Brooklyn Bridge *this actually happened* and walked
> away unknown and forgotten into the ghostly daze of Chinatown
> soup alleyways & firetrucks, not even one free beer

> (5, emphasis added)

What do we make of the qualifier "this actually happened"? This is hardly the most outrageous or implausible event in the poem. Does this cast doubt on whether the other actions in the poem "actually happened"?

"This actually happened" is a moment of self-consciousness in the poem, similar to Ginsberg's self-mocking exclamation in Part II: "the whole boatload of sensitive bullshit!" (7). It is a moment where Ginsberg calls attention to the precariousness of his own project, a humorous acknowledgment of the poem's excesses and exaggerations: sure, these other events may simply be the fantasies of a madman, but this jump off the Brooklyn Bridge—"this actually happened." Ginsberg likens such gestures to "the comic realism of Chaplin's *City Lights*" (*Howl* 124); they are gestures of good faith to a potentially skeptical reader, suggesting that the author is as capable as any critic of laughing at his own poem. But they also threaten the poem's goals of accuracy and objectivity, acknowledging error and subjective bias. The insistence that "this actually happened" opens a gap between the poem and the reality it seeks to document.

"Howl" is thus a poem of delicate balances. In its use of juxtaposition, it balances the centrifugal force of individual images with the centripetal logic of the catalog. In its portrayal of a community, it balances its sense of a small, actually extant and possibly exclusive coterie against its inclusive attempt to depict an entire generation. Finally, it claims to present an accurate picture of reality and consciousness but self-consciously and humorously calls attention to the gap between its own vision and the reality it seeks to portray. It is this balance of forces that makes "Howl" such a powerful and appealing poem. Ginsberg's techniques allow him to make broad claims, extending his reach into realms of politics, society, and religion; but the poem's countervailing pressures, and Ginsberg's own self-consciousness, also create a kind of modesty that pulls the poem back toward the personal, biographical, and "secret."

As Ginsberg's involvement in politics deepened through the 1960s, the pressure to close the gaps that "Howl" allows increased. Ginsberg came to take his bardic role more and more seriously; with the escalation of the war in Vietnam, the construction of an accurate picture of reality came to seem less a personal impulse and more a political imperative. The poem's language of truth could serve to oppose the language of falsehood spoken by politicians, corporations, and, above all, the mass media, which Ginsberg would come to view as the primary source of the language corrupting American life. But in its desire to make increasingly broad and explicit political statements, Ginsberg's work of the later 1960s departed from the avant-garde formula that gave "Howl" its power, abandoning the particularity of the Beat community in favor of universal statements that sought to reply to American political discourse in its own terms.

We can see this shift in Ginsberg's poetics in perhaps his best-known political poem of the 1960s, "Wichita Vortex Sutra," a polemic against the war in Vietnam. By the time of the poem's composition in 1966, Ginsberg had parlayed his earlier leftist inclinations, documented in such poems as "America" and "Kaddish," into a public, activist role.[16] Ginsberg spoke out against censorship, marijuana laws, and the war in Vietnam, becoming a featured presence at antiwar protests and participating in a whimsical attempt to "levitate" the Pentagon in 1967. Like many of Ginsberg's poems of the period, "Wichita" was composed using a method Ginsberg called "auto poesy," dictated into a portable tape recorder as Ginsberg crisscrossed the country by car.

Ginsberg's argument in "Wichita Vortex Sutra" can be stated quite simply: "The war is language"—more specifically, the "language / proliferating in airwaves," the language of media. Just as media language has come to constitute the American landscape through which Ginsberg moves, it is media language, spoken by politicians, generals, and pundits, that justifies and propagates the war, while simultaneously "bringing the war home" through reportage and television images. It is this claim that allows Ginsberg to position poetry as a means of responding to the war and of intervening in politics. In his 1968 "Improvised Poetics" interview, Ginsberg describes at length his goals in making, as he writes in "Wichita," a "Mantra of American language":

> So I wanted to—in the English language—make a series of syllables that would be identical with a historical event. I wanted the historical event to be the end of the war, and so I prepared the declaration of the end of the war by saying "I hereby make my language identical with the historical event. *I here declare the end of the war!*"—and set up a force field of language which is so solid and absolute as a statement and a realization of an assertion by my will, conscious will power, that it will contradict—counteract and simultaneously overwhelm the force field of language pronounced out of the State Department and out of Johnson's mouth. When they say "We declare war," their mantras are black mantras, so to speak. They pronounce these words, and then they sign a piece of paper, of other words, and a hundred thousand soldiers go across the ocean. So I pronounce *my* word, and so the point is, how strong is my word? . . . It was an interesting experiment, to see if that one assertion of language will precipitate other consciousnesses to make the same assertion, until it spreads and finally until there's a majority of the consciousnesses making the same assertion . . . the War is a Poetry . . . invented and imagined by Johnson and Rusk and Dulles . . . so the *end* of the War is . . . the Poem invented by Spock, or myself, or Phil Ochs, or Dylan. (*Mind* 152–3)

If the war is ultimately made by language, then it can be counteracted by other, more powerful language—that of the poet. The hope is that the poet's own "human consciousness newspapers," with its "personal communication of actual data" (*Mind* 198), can overcome the power of the actual newspapers, radio, and television and convince a majority of the public to end the war.

But Ginsberg's emphasis on his own "conscious will power" as the key factor shows the strain in this project; for it is precisely this will to order that Ginsberg has given up in turning to auto poesy. "Wichita Vortex Sutra" becomes a drama of the poet struggling to assert his own words and presence in a landscape of media language. It is perhaps most striking not as an effective statement against the war but as a demonstration of the crisis of avant-garde universality. Ginsberg has left behind the Beat community of "Howl" in order to address a wider, national audience. But since the avant-garde community is no longer available as a model of an alternative political order, Ginsberg must extrapolate a politics purely from his own subjectivity; and that politics ultimately looks very much like a mirror image of the politics it seeks to replace.

The second part of "Wichita" opens with Ginsberg listening to the radio program *Face the Nation*. The opening line is simply the program's title, "Face the Nation," immediately highlighting Ginsberg's project: he is trying to seize a piece of media language and restore its meaning, hoping to make his poem into a real conversation with America. Much of this section consists of ironic recitations of news reports, often accompanied by angry choruses of "language, language." One of the most powerful examples of this comes late in the poem, where Ginsberg's use of this chorus causes the entire news report to take on a chantlike, insistent, and diabolical tone:

> U.S. Military Spokesmen
>   Language language
>   Cong death toll
> has soared to 100 in First Air Cavalry
> Division's Sector of
>   Language language
>   Operation White Wing near Bong Son
> Some of the
>   Language language
>   Communist
>   Language language soldiers
> charged so desperately

they were struck with six or seven bullets before they fell
Language Language M 60 Machine Guns
Language language in La Drang Valley

(*Poems* 408–9;
Ginsberg Tape 70a1/025d)[17]

Ginsberg begins in medias res, as if we are coming into the middle of an ongoing news story, as if the whole war is blending into a single broadcast. His use of the refrain "language, language" emphasizes the monotonous and mechanical quality of the news, even as it reports the most appalling events (as when the Viet Cong soldiers "charged so desperately / they were struck with six or seven bullets before they fell"). As he moves through the passage, Ginsberg increases the frequency of the refrain, so that it begins to disrupt sentences and even phrases. The effect is to literalize Ginsberg's assertion that "the war is language"; in this passage, the war is fought with "Language M 60 Machine Guns." Ultimately, any sense of the events of the war is drowned out by Ginsberg's drawing of our attention to the language in which those events are conveyed to us.

But the simplicity of that formulation—"language, language"—has to make us wonder: Is the problem the specific language being used, or is the problem language itself? Are the events of Vietnam being expressed in the wrong words, or is the problem that they are being expressed in words at all?[18] Ginsberg, it seems, is hovering between these two positions, committed to confronting the language of war with his own, yet aware that the language of his own poem is contaminated by the language of war, as the recorder picks up everything coming over the airwaves. The result is a kind of wavering at the moments where he is most insistent on reclaiming the language as his own, and the poem's apparent failure to overcome the language of war. Indeed, the preceding passage comes *after* Ginsberg's bold declaration of an end to the war—a declaration that apparently does not keep the radio from broadcasting its dispatches from the front.

Part of the problem of auto poesy is that in its drive toward objectivity, it places the poet at the mercy of external stimuli, reducing the role of the ego and thus robbing Ginsberg's poetry of the biographical detail, associational brilliance, and self-conscious humor that helped to balance "Howl." But to overcome the language of the media landscape, Ginsberg acknowledges, requires an act of will, and "Wichita Vortex Sutra" is perhaps the most willed poem in the *Fall of America* sequence. Whereas many of the poems in this sequence are almost entirely landscape poems, "Wichita" has long stretches of introspection and intertextuality, as Ginsberg calls on Whitman and Melville and muses on the corruption of the heartland. The climactic section of the poem begins with such an inward turn, as Ginsberg declares, "I'm an old man now, and a lonesome man in Kansas / but not afraid / to speak my lonesomeness in a car, / because not only my lonesomeness / it's Ours, all over America" (405). This sense of the poet as representative self echoes the evocation of community in "Howl"; but the coziness of the Beat coterie is gone, and Ginsberg must make the much larger leap to a national community. It's a move that's possible, and necessary, because Ginsberg has shifted the field of action to that which he imagines all Americans to have in common—the American language: "I search for the language / that is also yours— / almost all our language has been taxed by war" (406).

To extrapolate from his own experience—the banal one of an old man lonesome in a car—to that of a nation requires an act of bardic hubris, and this is precisely what Ginsberg does. He announces, "I claim my birthright!" and calls a vast litany of Hindu, Buddhist, Muslim, Jewish, and Christian deities to "Come to my lone presence":

> Jaweh Righteous One
> all Knowledge-Princes of Earth-man, all
> ancient Seraphim of heavenly Desire, Devas, yogis
> & holymen I chant to . . .
> I lift my voice aloud,
> make Mantra of American language now,
> I here declare the end of the War! . . .
>
> . . .
>
> Let the States tremble,
> let the Nation weep,
> let Congress legislate its own delight
> let the President execute his own desire—
>
> (407)

The power Ginsberg wishes to claim is paradoxical: this "Mantra of American language" allows him to command, to have control over the imperative, "Let the . . . ," but what he wishes to command is that all should "follow [their] own delight"—essentially, that anarchy be legislated.

So what sort of political vision is "Wichita Vortex Sutra" offering? Far from offering an alternative method of organizing social life, Ginsberg leaves existing political structures in place in order to transfer those structures, in the following lines, to the level of his own individual mind; the declaration of the war's end really is a piece of legislation,

> published to my own senses,
> > blissfully received by my own form
> approved with pleasure by my sensations
> > manifestation of my very thought
> > accomplished in my own imagination
> > > all realms within my consciousness fulfilled

> > > > (407)

Ginsberg is, finally, unwilling to give up the authority offered by the existing language of power. These lines suggest that the individual self, in order to have real political authority, must make itself the mirror image of political institutions and must retain its allegiance to the language spoken by those institutions if it wishes to speak back to them. Where this leaves the poet, though, is still stranded within a media landscape he cannot hope to control: "60 miles from Wichita / near El Dorado," but not in it.

The limits of political vision in "Wichita" demonstrate the difficulty of translating avant-garde allegories into concrete political agendas. But perhaps more important, they demonstrate the delicate balance of the particular and the universal that accounts for the power of "Howl" and suggest that such a synthesis may no longer be possible in the social landscape of the 1960s and after. "Howl" depends for its effect on its portrayal of an inclusive coterie, rendered in a form that allegorizes—but does not delineate—the alternative social order that coterie might embody. "Wichita" largely abandons Beat particularity for a national vision, but this loss of the social fact of the avant-garde leaves Ginsberg with only the existing structures of power as a model.

In the following chapters, I suggest that Ginsberg's greatest influence on later poets of the American avant-gardes has been the particularity of his early avant-garde vision. Dissatisfied with the universalist political efforts of Ginsberg's later work, younger poets came to recognize that the power of contemporary avant-garde work could come from the manner in which it registered its social location. And unlike Ginsberg, who could imagine that his group of a few friends represented an entire generation, poets of the 1970s faced a political landscape characterized by a new awareness of race, class, and gender. These were the social facts that Language writers and Asian American poets, in their various ways, portrayed in their work, while continuing to seek forms that might suggest new ways of imagining their own political positions.

TWO

Ron Silliman

The Ethnicization of the Avant-Garde

In a 1975 letter, poet Ron Silliman, having "finally" gotten around to reading Allen Ginsberg's *The Fall of America*, gives the book somewhat reluctant praise: "[A]t its best [it] moves to *pure* description (I'm always attracted to people who carry some idea of language to that extreme, hence find James Merrill, Adrienne Rich interesting tho not the genres they've chosen)" (Silliman Letter to Bernstein, 8/10/75).[1] What Silliman seems to admire is the objectivity of Ginsberg's "auto poesy," its ability to turn the poem into pure recording device. But his remark also reflects doubts about the more subjective elements of Ginsberg's writing, which seem to provide an inadequate grounding for political critique. Although both Ginsberg's and Silliman's poetry aims at an accurate portrayal of contemporary landscapes, Silliman adopts formal methods designed to open the poem to collective experiences. The difference is perhaps best captured in the places each poet chooses to write. Ginsberg writes in a car; Silliman writes on a bus, opening his poem to the forces of politics, class, race, and gender on display in this mode of "public" transportation.

But this openness to social contexts also means that Silliman finds himself forced into a much greater awareness of the location, and the limits, of his own perspective. Even as he creates elaborate formal structures that can be seen, as Charles Bernstein has argued in *Content's Dream*, as an "allegory for a society that is nonauthoritarian . . . and multicultural" (314), the content of Silliman's writing, as well as his correspondence with his colleagues in the "Language" movement, suggests the particularity of Silliman's avant-garde work.[2] In a political landscape increasingly aware of divisions of race, class, and gender, Silliman puts forth the tendentious argument that Language writing is the form of avant-garde practice particular to politically progressive white men—a claim that allows him to see "Language poet" as analogous to "woman poet" or "Asian American poet," even as it has invited charges of racist and sexist exclusion. This "ethnicization" of the avant-garde—linking a particular poetic practice to a socially delimited group—has deeply troubled many of Silliman's readers; but it also reflects a contemporary context in which the discourses of race and of the avant-garde increasingly intersect.

Silliman's curious sense of Language poetry as social identity—a sense shared, to varying degrees, by his peers in the movement[3]—can be understood not just as an effect of the political realities of the 1970s but as a response to the crisis of avant-garde universality evident in Ginsberg's work of the 1960s. Silliman's long poem of the 1970s, *Ketjak*, is a study of urban landscape and social structure that is marked as emanating from the perspective of a white male avant-gardist; but its use of the disruptive and paratactic techniques of the "new sentence" seeks to act as a check against the limits of that perspective, aiming to create a broad-based account of contemporary experience that achieves a modicum of objectivity.

As a political gesture, Silliman's writing can thus be understood as a response to the disintegration of the coalitions—particularly interracial coalitions—that characterized the new left of the 1960s. Even though *Ketjak* does offer, through its form, an allegory of a new social order, it is rooted in social particularity. The coalitions imagined by post-1970 American avant-gardes, from Language writers to Asian American poets, are based not on broad appeals to national values but on the means by which each avant-garde delineates its own status as social fact.

In 1974, Silliman began writing a new work in the pages of a square blue notebook. Made in China, the notebook's pages were stamped with vertical red lines; to write in it, Silliman turned the book ninety degrees and wrote along these columns. This unusual format corresponded to an unusual style: Silliman's work, later named "The Chinese Notebook" and published in *The Age of Huts*, consisted of 223 numbered propositions—some questions, some assertions—written loosely in the manner of Wittgenstein's *Philosophical Investigations*. Yet Silliman insists throughout that his prose sentences be read not as philosophy but as poetry, laying the groundwork for his exploration of what he will call the "new sentence" in his long works *Ketjak* and *Tjanting*.

What may be most interesting about "The Chinese Notebook," however, is the glimpse it gives into Silliman's developing sense of the link between his poetry and politics, and into the historical moment from which that link emerges. In one late section from the notebook, Silliman stages a confrontation between himself and a skeptical interlocutor who doubts the value of Silliman's practice:

> 192. A friend, a member of the Old Left, challenges my aesthetic. How, he asks, can one write so as not to "communicate"? I, in turn, challenge his definitions. It is a more crucial lesson, I argue, to learn how to experience language directly, to tune one's senses to it, than to use it as a mere means to an end . . . [which] is, in bourgeois life, common to all things, even the way we "use" our friends. . . . But language, so that it is experienced directly, moves beyond any such exercise in despair, an unalienated language. He wants an example. I give him [Robert] Grenier's
>
>
>
> thumpa
>
> thumpa
>
> thumpa
>
> thump
>
>
>
> pointing out how . . . it is a speech that only borders on language, how it illumines that space. He says, "I don't understand." (*Huts* 63)

Silliman's incorporation into the text of a critique of his work—reminiscent of William Carlos Williams's inclusion of critical letters in *Paterson*—seems a risky gesture. Yet it serves quite neatly to position the work as political from the start. What seems like a straightforward aesthetic objection—Silliman's friend simply does not understand Grenier's or Silliman's poetry—is attributed to a political cause: this friend is marked not as a fellow writer or critic but only as "a member of the Old Left," and it is this position, Silliman implies, that determines his response to Silliman's work. By taking up a stance opposed to his friend's, Silliman is able to take for granted the political valence of his aesthetic practice.

Silliman's labeling of his critic as "Old Left" makes this aesthetic disagreement not only political but generational, implicitly allying Silliman with the "new left" that arose with the civil rights and student movements of the 1960s. Indeed, the debate Silliman stages can be read as a classic old/new left confrontation. The demand that a poem "communicate" something is linked by Silliman to the old left's outdated model of political change, one that focuses on large-scale political and economic institutions and that sees culture as nothing more than a conduit for a political position. Instead of simply opposing this view, Silliman makes a "new left" move by questioning the very terms of discussion, attempting to move outside established understandings and institutions. But what may be most characteristically new left here is Silliman's longing to "experience language directly," for "an unalienated language." Doug Rossinow's *The Politics of Authenticity* is only the most recent history of the 1960s to argue that this condition of alienation, and the desire to overcome it, was the primary intellectual force of the era. "[T]he new left," Rossinow writes, "came to argue that social and political arrangements caused inner alienation and that only radical social change would open the path to authenticity" (4). What Silliman wants is not simply a correct use of language but an *experience* of language that is unmediated and unencumbered by instrumental demands—finding a meaning, to paraphrase the new left's 1962 Port Huron manifesto, that is "personally authentic."

This identification of the work of Silliman and his colleagues, which would come to be known as "Language poetry," with the new left has enjoyed a resurgence of late, most notably, as discussed earlier, in Barrett Watten's "The Turn to Language and the 1960s." But such identifications elide the apparently wide gap between writing such as Grenier's or Silliman's and the vast majority of new left cultural production. Silliman's writing bears little resemblance to the work collected in Todd Gitlin's anthology of "poetry from the movement," *Campfires of the Resistance*,[4] and most Language poets would draw the sharpest contrast between their own work and that of such prominent antiwar poets as Denise Levertov and Robert Bly. Indeed, Silliman has pointedly criticized Levertov, whom he encountered as a teacher at Berkeley in 1969, characterizing her in a 2000 interview as someone who had "sabotaged her writing and her political credibility simultaneously."[5]

We can get a more precise sense of Silliman's political and historical position if we realize that, although Silliman implicitly identifies himself with the new left, his key work emerges, like that of other Language writers, not from a new left but rather from a post–new left moment. Born in 1946, Silliman was already politically active in high school and began attending college in 1965. He switched schools several times, however, and did not find himself in the political ferment of Berkeley until the 1969–70 school year.[6]

In fact, the first experience of higher education he mentions is his stint at San Francisco State, from which, according to an interview with Thomas C. Marshall and Thomas A. Vogler in *Quarry West*, he transferred after the "unsuccessful student strike in late 1968," which left him "totally demoralized about the possibility of a meaningful education there" ("Marshall" 10).

Silliman refers to the strike led by the Black Students Union and the Third World Liberation Front at San Francisco State from November 1968 to March 1969, which led to the establishment of black and ethnic studies programs at the college and helped spark similar movements elsewhere. That Silliman labels this strike a failure may simply acknowledge that all the strikers' demands were not immediately met. But it may also suggest a view of the strike as a sign of the new left's disintegration into what has been called "identity politics"—the splintering of a once-unified and interracial movement into competing factions and interest groups often defined by race and gender.

This narrative of the new left's decline and fragmentation is a feature of nearly every history of the 1960s—or at least those written from a white activist point of view. Rossinow provides a neat summary of this narrative:

> In the early and middle 1960s, a grand alliance for progress made great strides, especially concerning civil rights. Depending on who tells the story, either African Americans, under the influence of black power doctrine, first abandoned the coalition, or else they were pushed out by white liberals. . . . Then women, infected with the separatist virus, departed as well. "On the model of black demands came those of feminists, Chicanos, American Indians, gays, lesbians. " Soon the right began its easy domination of a divided opposition. (343)[7]

White student activists themselves split into increasingly polarized factions; the turn to violence by the Weathermen and other splinter groups marks, for Todd Gitlin and other commentators, the end of the new left vision.

In "The Chinese Notebook," Silliman considers the fate of two groups who seem to represent the perversion of new left ideals:

> 32. The Manson family, the SLA. What if a group began to define the perceived world according to a complex, internally consistent, and precise (tho inaccurate) language? Might not the syntax itself propel their reality to such a point that to our own they could not return? Isn't that what happened to Hitler? (*Huts* 46)

Silliman refers here to Charles Manson and his followers, who murdered eight people in 1969 in an ostensible attempt to ignite a race war, and to the Symbionese Liberation Army, which mounted a series of robberies and killings (along with the kidnapping of Patty Hearst) in 1973 and 1974 in the name of "revolutionary war."[8] The SLA would likely have had particular resonance for Silliman, since the SLA's core members met through the California prison reform movement, of which Silliman was an active leader in the early 1970s.[9] In "Under *Albany*," Silliman recalls that in the 1970s he "was still wary of any organizations with a specific ideological line," finding them "manipulative in their use of people and issues almost invariably counterproductive to the building of a larger Left coalition" (333–4). To new leftists like Silliman, the SLA must have seemed like a combination of farce and nightmare: propelled by racial politics (the group was nominally headed by two black men, though nearly all its members were white radicals), adopting an incoherent mix of socialist and Third World rhetorics, and willing to turn the language of revolution into a violent reality.

What's distinctive about Silliman's diagnosis of new left fragmentation is his emphasis on the failure of leftist language. The madness of the SLA, Silliman suggests, lay not in its ideology or its identity politics but in its development of a language that had lost touch with reality. But most striking is Silliman's assertion that such a language's own logic, "the syntax itself," might determine the group's action. Nor would such a phenomenon be limited to a tiny group: as Silliman's reference to Hitler suggests, a government or an entire society might find itself propelled toward atrocity by language. Silliman's thirty-first proposition provides two Vietnam-era American examples, quoting phrases widely attributed to the U.S. military: "'Terminate with extreme prejudice.' That meant kill. Or 'we had to destroy the village in order to save it'" (46). Such formulations, like the official political speech Allen Ginsberg rails against in "Wichita Vortex Sutra" ("McNamara made a 'bad guess'"), not only hide the truth but can themselves serve to justify further violence, dehumanizing the enemy and blithely contradicting themselves. Whereas Ginsberg attempts to supplant official language with his own authentic language, Silliman—writing not in 1967 but 1974—displays a post–new left skepticism about these kinds of substitutions, arguing that the left, as the SLA shows, is just as capable of creating destructive language as its opponents.

By the time he began work on "The Chinese Notebook" and *Ketjak*, Silliman had already published three books of poetry: *Crow* (1971), *Mohawk*

(1973), and *Nox* (1974). Silliman seems largely to regard the first two books as juvenilia. In the Marshall-Vogler interview, he describes his writing during the period of *Crow* as "post-Williams, post-Creeley, post-Olson kind of lyrics," while registering the strong influence of Robert Grenier's minimalist writing, and he remarks that *Mohawk* "reads like [Clark] Coolidgeana to me now" ("Marshall" 11–12). The pieces in *Nox* do not, on the surface, read that much differently than the Grenier-influenced poems in *Crow*. Silliman's innovation in this text is not verbal but structural: each page is divided into four quadrants, separated by lines, with a poem in each quadrant. For Charles Bernstein, this is "a highly schematic prototype of the work to come" in Silliman's oeuvre: "By not homogenizing the text into a single voice or syntax, the separate elements are able to interconnect with each other through the readers' mediation" (*Dream* 314).

Ketjak, composed from June to November 1974, continues this concern with large-scale structure, but its breakthrough move is its turn to prose, and specifically to the style of what Silliman will come to call "the new sentence":

> To keep warm burn the news. The type of old man who wears his white hair in a crewcut and keeps small, fat dogs. Terms imply domains. Art as a habit merges with the renewal of solutions which constitute it. It was only when the trash bag crashed into the middle of the kitchen that we realized it bore the weight of ants. (27)

In her essay "Language Poetry and the Lyric Subject," Marjorie Perloff provides a pithy summary of the theory of the new sentence: "The 'new sentence' is conceived as an independent unit, neither causally nor temporally related to the sentences that precede and follow it. Like a line in poetry, its length is operative, and its meaning depends on the larger paragraph as an organizing system" (414–5). Bob Perelman writes in *The Marginalization of Poetry* that "[a] new sentence is more or less ordinary itself, but gains its effect by being placed next to another sentence to which it has tangential relevance. . . . Parataxis is crucial: the autonomous meaning of a sentence is heightened, questioned, and changed by the degree of separation or connection that the reader perceives with regard to the surrounding sentences" (61).

In his own 1979 talk on the concept, reprinted in *The New Sentence*, Silliman asserts that unlike a conventional paragraph, a paragraph in a new-sentence work has "no specific referential focus. The paragraph here is a unit of measure," like a stanza (89). What has happened, Silliman argues, is that "poetic form has moved into the interiors of prose. . . . The torquing which is normally triggered by linebreaks, the function of which is to enhance ambiguity and polysemy, has moved directly into the grammar of the sentence" (90). One of the most important effects of this method is, according to Silliman, the disruption of the "syllogistic" function of sentences, the logical chains by which sentences form linear arguments or coherent descriptions. Yet it is equally important that the arrangement of sentences not be random. Crucial to the new sentence is its use of "methods for enabling *secondary* syllogistic movement to create or convey an overall impression of unity, without which the systematic blocking of the integration of sentences to one another through *primary* syllogistic movement . . . would be trivial, without tension" (92). *Ketjak* itself employs such a method: its first paragraph contains one sentence; its second paragraph contains that first sentence plus another; its third paragraph contains both lines of the second paragraph plus two more; and so on, doubling each time and repeating the entirety of the previous paragraph (with important variations) each time:

Revolving door.

Revolving door. A sequence of objects which to him appears to be a caravan of fellaheen, a circus, begins a slow migration to the right vanishing point on the horizon line.

Revolving door. Fountains of the financial district. Houseboats beached at the point of low tide, only to float again when the sunset is reflected in the water. A sequence of objects which to him appears to be a caravan of fellaheen, a circus, camels pulling wagons of bear cages, tamed ostriches in toy hats, begins a slow migration to the right vanishing point on the horizon line. (3)

The theory of the new sentence has been further elaborated by others, but for the moment I wish to focus on the argument that Silliman and other Language writers make for the political significance of this aesthetic device. Why is it important, at this historical moment, to insist on a "blocking of the integration of sentences . . . through primary syllogistic movement"? Silliman's justification in *The New Sentence* is largely theoretical, beginning from the claim that linguists and philosophers have failed to generate a coherent theory of the sentence. Silliman argues that the failure to find the boundaries of the sentence, related to a failure to distinguish between speech and writing, results in a failure to recognize the way language actually operates. By disrupting the usual syllogistic logic of sentences, the new sentence brings us toward "the recognition of language" and its workings, because it "limits the reader's ability to get away from the language itself" (82–3)—an echo of the desire to "experience language directly" in "The Chinese Notebook." This foregrounding of the aesthetic device is traced by several Language poets to Russian formalism, and is claimed elsewhere in *The New Sentence* as a means of resisting the commodification of language in late capitalism.[10]

The new sentence, however, also has a more specific political function for Silliman: its "increased sensitivity to syllogistic movement endows works of the new sentence with a much greater capacity to incorporate ordinary sentences of the material world" (90). Since a new sentence on its own need have no particular "poetic" value, but gains its significance in its ambiguous relations to the sentences that surround it, new-sentence writing can be "realistic" in ways conventional poems cannot be. Silliman's writing includes overheard phrases, advertising copy, recipes, and found text that would usually be rejected as too banal to be included in an artwork. Ultimately, Silliman argues, the new sentence is a comprehensive and integrative form, "the first method capable of incorporating all the levels of language" (93). Bob Perelman is even more direct in extrapolating the political implications of this method: the new sentence represents an "egalitarian politics" in which apparently insignificant observations coexist with grand theoretical statements. Silliman's work is, Perelman suggests, a real and material depiction of our social world, "an exemplary guide to contemporary urban life" (67). Yet it also refuses to present a single view of this world: "Its shifts break up attempts at the natural reading of universal, authentic statements; instead they encourage attention to the act of writing and to the writer's multiple and mediated positions within larger social frames" (65).

Perelman's last remark begins to move us from the abstract politics of Language writing to a consideration of how that politics is located in a historical moment. Silliman, Perelman, and other Language writers have constructed genealogies that give Language poetry an aesthetic history, from Russian formalism and Gertrude Stein to Louis Zukofsky and Clark Coolidge. But what were the more immediate and local concerns that shaped the politics of Silliman's writing? As I have already suggested, Silliman's work emerges in the context of the fragmentation of the new left and the subsequent rise of groups based on ethnic, gender, and sexual identity, many of which produced new literary formations. In fact, Silliman's essays, in their justification of the politics of Language writing, often display a tension between the universal and the particular—a tension, as I have argued, central to the avant-garde project itself. Is the new sentence simply a historically necessary development, born from the contradictions of language under late capitalism? Or is it to be understood as the writing of a particular community, one defined not only as an aesthetic group (the "Language poets") but often as white and male?

We can see suggestions of this latter perspective in the *Quarry West* interview, when Silliman describes the genesis of the lecture series organized by Bob Perelman and later collected in the volume *Writing/Talks*: "For awhile, there were 'men's group' sessions at our [Silliman's and Barrett Watten's] flat that were vague prototypes of what would, under Bob's hand, turn out to be talks. We consumed enormous amounts of whiskey and thought very hard about just how to conduct a revolution in poetry" ("Marshall" 13). Although there is some self-mockery here, the "men's group" was a real feature of the 1970s, as the rise of the women's movement and its "consciousness-raising" groups led men, uncertain of their own position in a politically gendered landscape, to form their own groups in response. Indeed, labeling Language poetry as a "men's group" would not surprise the many women experimental poets who, as Ann Vickery has meticulously shown, felt excluded from the male-dominated discourse of Language poetry.[11]

A more explicit discussion of this issue appears in Silliman's essay "The Political Economy of Poetry," collected in *The New Sentence*, which takes the question of audience as primary to the politics of poetry:

> What can be communicated through a literary production depends on which codes are shared with its audience. . . . The social composition of its audience is the primary context of any writing. Context determines (and is determined by) both the motives of the readers and their experience, their history, i.e. their particular set of possible codes. Context determines the actual, real-life consumption of the literary product, without which communication of a message (formal, substantive, ideological) cannot occur. (25)

The political value of a poem, then, "lies not in its explicit content, political though that may be, but in the *attitude toward reception* it demands of the reader" (31). Reading elsewhere in Silliman's essays, we can conclude that Language poetry answers this demand by increasing the reader's awareness of the work of reception, by making the "attitude toward reception" an explicit element of the composition. But if the "social composition" of an audience determines the reception of a poem, two questions arise. First, what is the social composition of the audience to which Language poetry speaks? Second, how is it possible to construct a poem that escapes such determination, that generates an awareness of the ideological constraints of reception?

To approach these issues, Silliman provides a quotation from a talk given by writer Robert Glück at 80 Langton Street, a leading San Francisco space for avant-garde writing and art at which many Language writers gave readings and lectures. Glück was thus, to some degree, part of the same larger San Francisco writing community that Silliman was.[12] Silliman quotes Glück's account of the different reactions to his work from different audiences:

> At several movement readings I was interested to see members of the audience come up afterwards and say where the writer had got it right (yes, that's my life) and where the writer had got it wrong. I want to contrast this with the audience that admires writing as if it were a piece of Georgian silver, goods to be consumed. Of course this depends on an identification with a community, a shared ideology. For example, I read a story at a gay reading about being "queer-bashed." The audience responded throughout with shouts of encouragement and acknowledgement. Afterwards people told me I got it right. I read the same story to an appreciative and polite university audience, and afterwards people told me they admired my transitions. To a certain extent, my story registered only in terms of form. (Silliman *Sentence* 24)[13]

Silliman takes Glück's observations, to some degree, as evidence for his own point about the determining force of audiences and shared codes. In fact, Silliman takes the point far beyond Glück, making the case for an almost total balkanization of audiences: "The work of Clark Coolidge, for example, might seem opaque and forbidding at a gay reading, for the same reason that a Japanese speaker cannot communicate with an Italian: no codes are shared from which to translate word to meaning" (25). This essentializing view—gays and academics as different nationalities speaking mutually incomprehensible languages—can be read as yet another expression of anxiety over left fragmentation, with identity-based political groups seen as radically separatist.

Surprisingly, though, Silliman's primary move is to criticize Glück for the way he "dismisses" the academic audience and insists on the "correctness" of gay readers' interpretation. Even if this were not a divergence from what Glück actually seems to be saying, the idea that only gay readers "correctly" read the codes of Glück's story would seem to be consonant with Silliman's earlier, deterministic claims. But Silliman's goal seems actually to be to defend the formalist response of the "academic" audience. He rejects Glück's characterization of such readers as "consumers," arguing instead that "consumption *for further production* is a moment of production itself—it *is* action. It is through the question of transitions, for example, that the 'seamlessness' . . . of perceived reality . . . might be revealed as the affect [*sic*] of a partisan ideological construct" (31). Such an insight is, of course, precisely the kind that is meant to be generated by the new sentence, and it does not take much effort to recognize that Silliman is identifying himself and other Language writers with these formalist, academic readers.

What, then, is the social composition of this formalist audience? Silliman provides a remarkable answer that seeks to locate Language writing as a social formation with respect to other social and political groupings:

> It is . . . a major characteristic of the social codes of just those formations most often apt to attend a college reading not to know or speak their own name. . . . This self-invisibility has parallels throughout contemporary life. It has only been through the struggle of non-whites, of women and of gays that the white male heterosexual has come into recognition of his own, pervasive presence. In poetry, there continues to be a radical break between those networks and scenes which are organized by and around the codes of oppressed peoples, and those other "purely aesthetic" schools. In fact, the aesthetics of those latter schools is a direct result of ideological struggle. . . . It is characteristic of the class situation of those schools that this struggle is carried on *in other (aesthetic) terms.* (30–1)

The "social codes" that guide the reception of Language writing, then, would seem to be those of the white male heterosexual: for he is the one excluded from the codes of "oppressed peoples," who have developed a language all their own. This formulation, which appears numerous times in Silliman's work, can be and has been interpreted in at least two ways: as an honest, descriptive assessment of the historical and personal forces that seem to have given rise to Language writing (which is how Silliman likely intends it), or as an exclusionary, prescriptive formula that suggests women and minorities do not or cannot engage in experimental writing. But there can be no doubt that Silliman is making an analogy between such categories as "women's writing," "black writing," and "Language writing"—understood as "white male heterosexual writing."

There is, of course, one absolutely crucial difference between these categories. Silliman deems experimental writing utterly opaque to, for example, a gay audience. Yet he defends the right of straight white male readers to give a formalist reading to the work of a gay writer. This is the inevitable effect of declaring that the ideological struggle of experimental writers is conducted "in other (aesthetic) terms": such writers are granted access to, and indeed a monopoly over, the universalizing category of "the aesthetic," whereas women, minority, and gay writers are excluded from that category. And this is, finally, one of the more powerful, and unsettling, aspects of Silliman's claim that the new sentence is "capable of incorporating all the levels of language." Language poetry now appears as the *re*integrative force that brings together the shattered discourses of the new left. It arrogates to itself the ability to provide a total view of society and culture, while limiting the work of "oppressed peoples" to communication within the codes of a circumscribed community. Silliman claims his own position as particular *and* universal, capable of registering class, race, gender, and sexuality while simultaneously transcending their limits.

It is this subjectivity that Silliman strives to develop in *Ketjak*, his first major work using the new sentence. Through its foregrounding of its formal devices, *Ketjak* works to critique the general structures of contemporary narrative and language, resisting the transparent representation of social reality. Yet *Ketjak*'s content—ostensibly made irrelevant by its focus on form—marks it as emanating from a particular historical and political moment and location. How do we understand the authorial subjectivity of this text? Does it succeed in its integrative goals, or does it remain circumscribed, marked indelibly as a "white male heterosexual" work? And how does it register the presence of those other discourses, the "struggle of nonwhites, of women and of gays," in its apparent politics of form?

To ask these questions is, in part, to ask what the name "Language poetry" signifies. It is now widely used to refer to a poetic avant-garde or school, in the way that one might refer to surrealist or Beat writers. But those writers identified with Language writing, although acknowledging their participation in a community of poets, have always been leery of group identification. Silliman perhaps best embodies this paradox; he has been both the most tireless supporter, promoter, and anthologizer of Language writing and the most furious critic of those outsiders who would presume to use that label. Even Silliman's first gathering of Language writing, "The Dwelling Place: 9 Poets," published in *Alcheringa* in 1975, insists that the anthology represents "[n]ot a group but a tendency in the work of many" (104). What is the source of this anxiety about group identification, even from the writer who seems most invested in promoting that group?

Part of the answer may be found in Silliman's voluminous correspondence, now in the Archive for New Poetry at the University of California, San Diego, which is an impressive testament to his energies as literary impresario. His letters show him offering generous praise and stringent critique of his friends' work, putting far-flung writers in touch with each other, organizing publications and anthologies—all with a clear sense of his own aesthetic direction and ambitions. They also show him to be a ruthless policer of the boundaries of what he would call in one letter "'my kind' of poetry" (Letter to Hagedorn, 8/19/86),[14] engaging in outraged and occasionally vicious polemics against critics of Language writing, while showing a remarkably nuanced sense of the politics of group identification in poetry.

One of the most telling discussions is that around the founding of the journal $L=A=N=G=U=A=G=E$, edited by Bruce Andrews and Charles Bernstein and published from 1978 to 1981. The journal became a primary organ for letters, reviews, and essays by Language writers and helped raise the group's critical profile—while cementing, through its title, the label "Language poetry." In a letter of February 14, 1977, found in Bernstein's papers, also at the Archive for New Poetry, Bernstein makes the initial proposal for the magazine, which would be "committed to publishing the kind of work publ in [Silliman's magazine] Tottels & bruces Toothpick issue," but which would also put a strong emphasis on nonpoetic texts—letters, visual work, critical writing; in practice, these latter modes of writing would come to dominate the journal. Bernstein also proposes that each issue have a "special focus" and lists some possibilities: "visual oriented wrtng," "sexuality," "politics," "abstraction (or lnge centerd wrtng) & women (ed by a woman, of course)" (Letter to Silliman, 2/14/77).[15] Expressing concern, however, that "the quality of some performance text and conceptual documents often is not in the wrtng itself but in the 'idea' to be 'done' somewhere outside the page," Bernstein insists that the major criterion for inclusion should simply be "that we stand fully behind the quality of the actual writing in every single piece we publish . . . as a fully realized thing . . . as writing, there, in this magazine."

The remainder of the letter consists largely of lists of potential contributors, organized under Bernstein's proposed topics. Many of those listed are writers who would become strongly identified with Language writing—Lyn Hejinian, Michael Palmer, Ray DiPalma, Steve McCaffery—whereas others, such as Larry Eigner and Clark Coolidge, would come to be acknowledged as important influences. But Bernstein's sprawling list suggests the difficulty of identifying any clear group of writers or any coherent aesthetic that the magazine could be said to represent—a gesture similar to that made by Silliman in his introduction to *In the American Tree*, which lists several dozen writers not included in the anthology but whose work could be collected to create an anthology of "absolutely comparable worth" (xx). At the same time, the letter does display a sense of what "our" aesthetic might be, though perhaps only in anxieties over how that aesthetic might be compromised. This is most evident in Bernstein's list of contributors for the "sexuality" issue—which includes Kathy Acker, Michael Lally, Hannah Weiner, and Helen Adam—of which Bernstein writes: "perhaps here we cld involve people not central to our effort." Is it not possible to construct an issue about sexuality within the boundaries of writers "central to our effort"? Does the introduction of thematics, subject matter, identity threaten to disrupt the magazine's aesthetic coherence?

Silliman and Andrews both responded in some detail to these questions, though taking rather different tacks. In a letter of February 17, Silliman restates the magazine's focus as "writing as a coherent part of the whole of human experience." He agrees with Bernstein's reservations about including writing whose value might be found "somewhere outside the page," but then adds a lengthy qualification:

> [W]e run the risk of leaving a blind spot in our approach if we don't recognize a certain legitimacy to work wch isnt "a fully realized thing, in itself, as writing, there, in the magazine" (my sense of language centered writing is that it is the progressive writing of the industrializd tradition, & that excluded groups—including women whove done more w/ the diary than any other form, as well as the oralism of 3rd world groups—have pgressive writing, wch we ought to include, but wch is not necessarily language centered or even text centered). (Letter to Bernstein, 2/17/77)

Here we find again the tension evident in Silliman's essay "The Political Economy of Poetry," in which Language writing is held to be both particular and universal, emanating from a circumscribed social position— that of straight white men—yet still (by virtue of its immersion in the aesthetic) capable of incorporating all other discourses. In this context, however, Silliman is more circumspect in his claims for his own mode of writing. Bernstein's rhetoric of "fully realized" writing is an appeal to the aesthetic that Silliman particularizes, correctly seeing in it not a general category ("good" writing) but a coded reference to the kind of writing he and Bernstein practice, that which might be referred to as "language centered." By characterizing Language writing as "the progressive writing of the industrializd [*sic*] tradition" ("industrialized" here seeming to stand for the dominant aesthetic modes of the industrialized nations of the West, presumably practiced by white men), Silliman acknowledges that however "progressive" Language writing may seem with regard to mainstream American writing, it is still, like mainstream writing, grounded in the exclusion of women and writers of color from its practices.

Thus Silliman recognizes a moral imperative (a "blind spot" that "ought" to be filled) that requires him and his colleagues to take the writing of women and minorities into account. At the same time, he contains the threat posed by such writing by essentializing it: the diary as the primary site of women's writing, the fundamentally oral nature of nonwhite literature. Both these categories seem more restricted than the "language-centered" and "text-centered" practice of white men, shading back toward the aesthetic judgment that characterizes Bernstein's initial formulation.

Nor is the method by which women and minority writers are to be included at all clear. Later in his letter, Silliman critiques Bernstein's proposal for a "sexuality" issue:

> on sexuality i note that what you do is print list of folks w/ different libido orientation than you or i, we need a deeper idea than that w/ wch to proceed (my idea for next tottels by the way is a simple collection of work by hejinian, r waldrop, dreyer, acker, child, weiner, but not to be identified as a womans issue, perhaps rae [Armantrout] & carla harryman as well, dont know. (Letter to Bernstein, 2/17/77)

While feeling a need to include, say, women writers in the journal, Silliman is uncomfortable with the explicit use of identity categories as an organizing

principle, though what a "deeper idea" for inclusion might be is not immediately offered. Silliman does provide one suggestion: "a feature on simon
j. ortiz, the pueblo poet."

Silliman's discomfort with such use of identity categories is amplified
in Andrews's response of February 26. Although Silliman, for all his reservations, is relatively comfortable identifying with the "progressive writing
of the industrialized tradition," Andrews is less secure both about his own
position and about the positions of those other, excluded groups. In what
becomes a defense of Bernstein's demand for writing that is "fully realized,"
Andrews warns against the use of identity categories:

> In fact, if we don't use language as [our] criteria, we are *left* with purely &
> complacently political criteria as our choice-point: as if we could transfer
> this tradition of letters by picking another class stance, like that of the work-
> ing class. I dont really think at this juncture in America that we can do that,
> especially given who we *are* . . . neither an unfocussed *nor* a class-stanced
> tradition of letters is enough. . . . I wonder what you [Silliman] suggest
> by "wch means perhaps special #s of specifically working class materials &
> orientation" or to talk about our need to include the "progressive writing"
> of "excluded groups." . . . My immediate reaction was to think that the
> effort to accord "a certain legitimacy to work which isn't 'a fully realized
> thing,' in itself, as writing, there, in the magazine" is *not* our place. . . . It's
> one thing to talk of "atextualization" as a response to exclusion, as in the
> oral tradition, but it's another to state with any precision what the source of
> our shared interest is expected to be in the face of *texts* that embody specifi-
> cally working class or 3rd World material. . . . Otherwise we end up with
> the "quota-liberal" tendencies of the recent attack on the American Poetry
> Review or on WBAI.[16]

Andrews's sense that it is "*not* our place" to attempt to include working-class
and minority writing, "given who we *are*," is typical of the white male new
leftist's sense of disempowerment in the face of identity politics (and divergent from Silliman's impulse, at least here, to embrace the contradictions of
that position). The "language-centered," aesthetic stance is presented as the
only refuge from the "purely & complacently political criteria" of identity categories, governed by a quota system for various ethnic groups. Andrews seems
to fear that any open attempt to include working-class and minority writers
would be viewed as politically dishonest, since what unifies him with Silliman
and Bernstein is not primarily a political but an aesthetic orientation.[17]

Bernstein's response, in a letter of March 7, echoes Andrews's concerns but in a context of more personal anxieties. Bernstein notes that his original conception of the magazine was simply "a personal selection of what i thought wld be the best/most interesting &c writing" but then realized the greater appeal of a collectively edited journal that would "include a variety of concerns, perspectives, &c" (Letter to Silliman, 3/7/77). To Bernstein, this variety is a way of fending off a certain kind of elitism or egotism, "the SoHo atmosphere of self preoccupation and self importance as reflected in a recent Christopher Street article . . . wch set out to name & photograph the new New York 200—ie the 200 key SoHo ites, leaders of tmrw & glamour of today." What Bernstein proposes instead is "a kind of modesty," a denial that any single group should be located at the cultural or aesthetic center:

> i think all of us operate some of the time out of a sense of trying to locate, or trying to be inside, some central place & often this ends up with defining ourselves as the center & oftimes it ends up a feeling left out of some center & defining it as a cohesive thing wch has an inside & trying to get into it or being resentful that we can't or being disappointed in it when we arrive there and find it was no center at all but just another grouping. (Letter to Silliman, 3/7/77)

This desire for centrality combined with a mistrust of groups is a theme of Bernstein's work, memorably treated in such essays as "The Conspiracy of 'Us'" in *Content's Dream*, and resonates with his colleagues' suspicions about group identification.

Bernstein thus endorses, to a limited extent, Silliman's desire to incorporate the work of excluded groups into the journal. He even suggests (following Silliman's lead) that language-centered writing ought to be placed alongside the writing of women and minorities as forms of "underdeveloped" writing, with a clear allusion to the gap between "developed" and "developing" nations. Yet he also worries, like Andrews, that such inclusion might mean a lowering of the magazine's ultimately aesthetic standards:

> now i'm not, lest there be concern, suggesting we print bad poetry or anything that smacks of quota liberalism, but rather am suggesting we look into various modes that for reasons of preserving their own political/sexual/ethnic integrity & tradition have not entered into the "mainstream" (a choice wch has generally meant becoming academic, incidentally) . . . part of my concern . . . is that i don't really know right now what exists in the

area & feel the possibility that it does get off into a kind of theoretical issue
that ends up with concerns over equal representation & the BAI analogy is
much to the pt. (Letter to Silliman, 3/7/77)

Bernstein attempts to relativize his own position by acknowledging the
distinctiveness of other traditions of writing; yet the very need of such
traditions to maintain their "integrity," apart from the mainstream, ren-
ders them inaccessible to readers outside those traditions. In judging such
"underdeveloped" work, how does one distinguish what is distinctive from
what is simply "bad poetry"?

Indeed, all three poets imply that much of what is presented under the
categories of women's or Third World writing is simply bad, and that finding
work that both represents those other traditions and still meets their standards is difficult. This is the paradox inherent in the poets' use of identity categories; their political positions require them to consider the writing of those
affected by racism and sexism, but their aesthetic positions prevent them
from choosing such work based on its explicit content. As Bernstein puts it:

> [M]y own first section to Three or Four Things is an attempt to get at the
> experience of the workplace . . . but the question to me is exactly what kind
> of wrtng exists that comes out of the working class life—we don't want
> stuff *abt* the life (ie social realism or look back in anger or death of a sales-
> man). maybe diaries, journals, etc exist, maybe documents from the work-
> place. (Letter to Silliman, 3/7/77)

Silliman, finally, in a March 28 letter, tries to put the topic to rest by arguing
that the journal can have it both ways, incorporating such work without
altering its aesthetic orientation:

> likewise i agree we must avoid the quota-liberal or what you call Progres-
> sive Labor mystifications of working class or 3rd World peoples. . . . i dont
> think we need to be paternalistic abt such projects, as i do think there is
> work there wch does in fact stand up. . . . i agree that we have to have a
> sense that we are not simply The Center (here is where Bruce's uneasi-
> ness w/ say 3rd World materials is to me too ethnocentric—i'd have no
> problem w/ materials by Lorenzo Thomas, Piedro Petri,[18] any # of such
> people (or such britishers as [Tom] Raworth or Allen Fischer . . .). . . .
> here of course is where the idea of each issue singly structured . . . wld al-
> low such things to occur, but w/o the problem of lowering standards (wch
> *are* ethnocentric ones, the page, as such, is a white boozhy standard & has

no special sanction, tho the proposition of a mag is, in fact, the proposition of the page—we have to keep these problematics in mind!). (Letter to Bernstein, 3/28/77)

Silliman does a remarkable job of tacking across Andrews's and Bernstein's positions here, seeming at first to endorse their concerns about lowering standards; his response is to argue, simply (and in the face of apparent doubts), that there *is* good writing by writers of color. What this seems to mean is that there are nonwhite writers—Simon Ortiz, Lorenzo Thomas—whose work is recognizably "language-centered" and who thus could be safely incorporated into the journal. But in what sense, then, can such writers be said to represent the "integrity" of a different tradition? They become, in essence, Language writers who "happen" to be African American or Native American. Silliman's solution smacks of tokenism, and Silliman knows it—which is why he immediately tries to distinguish his position from that of Andrews, whose doubts about Third World writing he characterizes as racist. Yet in his final statement Silliman brings down the whole house of cards, declaring that the "standards" that seem so much at stake are themselves ethnocentric, particular and not universal. If Andrews's and Bernstein's attitude toward the standards of language-centered aesthetics might be described as one of guilty attachment—defending them even though their politics seem to tell them better—Silliman seems willing both to embrace aesthetic standards and to acknowledge their potentially exclusionary specificity, without embarrassment.

Silliman's position at the end of this exchange seems to be an attempt to strike a balance between the particular and the universal, reading the apparently universalist aesthetic aspirations of Language writing as the form of social struggle native to white men trained in the "industrialized" tradition—struggle "in other (aesthetic) terms," as he puts it in "The Political Economy of Poetry." In the mid-1980s, however, these issues reappear in more explosive form. The publication of $L=A=N=G=U=A=G=E$ was only one of many factors that raised the public profile of Language writing, and by 1986 two competing anthologies of Language writing had appeared: *"Language" Poetries*, edited by Douglas Messerli and published by New Directions, and Silliman's own *In the American Tree*. One effect of this increased prominence was a hardening of the label "Language poetry," increasingly seen as a group or school, in contrast to earlier attempts by the poets to keep affiliations loose. During this time, Silliman mounted often withering attacks on those he saw as perpetuating caricatured notions of Language writing—attacks that at the same time seemed to confirm Language poetry's status as a particular and socially identified, rather than universal, project.

In June 1986, Silliman sent an angry letter to New Directions denying permission to use his work in Messerli's *"Language" Poetries* anthology; he sent copies of this letter to Bernstein, Lyn Hejinian, and Bob Perelman, with an attached note describing his sense of "personal betrayal" over the anthology. In his letter to Bernstein, dated June 9, Silliman writes:

> I think Douglas' book is the singlemost destructive act of opportunism that I have seen in 20 years on the literary scene. Imagine Ezra Pound editing *The Big Jewish Book* (he was, after all, given his editing skills and relation to Oppen as well as Zukofsky, *more qualified* than the present editor—and his take on the subject hardly more curious). If his failure to respond to issues did not demonstrate an active bad faith, Douglas' title certainly does.
>
> To the degree that you have made his book possible—indeed, to the degree that Douglas is simply a creation of your own literary maneuvers—you have damaged the community. Permanently and perhaps beyond repair. (Letter to Bernstein, 6/9/86)

Even more inflammatory, however, was Silliman's attached letter, addressed to Peter Glassgold of New Directions:

> I am not a language poet.
>
> I hope, in choosing your title, that you are aware of the comparability of the phrase "language poetry" to epithets such as nigger, cunt, kike or faggot.
>
> Certainly reviewers can be expected to note this. (Letter to Glassgold, 6/9/86)

Silliman is claiming that "language poetry" is a term of abuse and derision, unfairly used to associate and stigmatize a certain group of writers. But the real moral charge—and the offensiveness—of Silliman's formulation lies in his implication that he and his colleagues are the equivalent of an oppressed social group—like women, African Americans, Jews, or gays—and that the term "Language poet" is an offensive slur, as unacceptable as any of the other epithets Silliman lists.

Silliman's equation seems, on its face, absurd, and Bernstein and Hejinian say as much in their enraged responses. In a June 13 letter, Bernstein declares, "I am shocked, angered, and saddened by your self-righteous and hostile letter," and finds Silliman's comparison to be offensive:

> It is weird for someone who edited an anthology of—according to the spine—"'Language' Writing" to complain about a title such as *'Language' Poetries* on the basis that the title is derogatory. But even if such terms were generally taken to be negative—*and they are not*—it would in no way be comparable to terms associated with rape, murder, and genocide—anymore than calling someone an egghead poet is comparable to racial and sexual slurs. This problem is compounded by your comparison of Messerli editing *Language Poetries* to Pound editing *A Big Jewish Book*. If you can't see that Pound's Holocaust-era fascism has no relation to your aesthetic and political disagreements with Messerli . . . I won't argue it out for you. If this is just to be taken as exaggeration or escalation of rhetoric, I find it distasteful and to show an appalling insensitivity to the real-life brutality of racial, sexual, and ethnic persecution. (Letter to Silliman, 6/13/86)

Hejinian's response echoes Bernstein's objections and charges that Silliman's true motives are self-interested, driven by a desire to destroy Messerli's anthology.

Both Bernstein and Hejinian reject Silliman's formulation by positing an incommensurability between sociopolitical and aesthetic categories: to call someone a lousy poet, Bernstein argues, is in no way comparable to using a racial slur against the person. Indeed, Hejinian asserts that to conflate the two is literally crazy. Bernstein's and Hejinian's rebuttals do seem eminently reasonable in the face of Silliman's inflammatory rhetoric.

Yet it is also true that the equation of Language writers with a racial or gender grouping flows logically out of Silliman's earlier pronouncements on poetry and politics—pronouncements that other poets like Bernstein and Andrews at least in part endorsed. If language-centered writing is, as Silliman argues in his earlier letters, a form of poetry just as "underdeveloped" as the writing of women or Third World writers, and if its social origin ("progressive" white male writers of the "industrialized" tradition) is just as particular and marginalized, why should a caricature of such writing not be as offensive as racist or sexist caricature, since both rely on the same logic of social marginalization? Here the particularity of Language poetry is paramount, since if it could make any claims to universality, it could hardly claim marginal status.

By insisting that Language poetry is an aesthetic category, Bernstein denies Silliman's claim to particularity. But even though the appeal to the aesthetic, as we see in the discussion around $L=A=N=G=U=A=G=E$, can be universalizing, it also removes poetry from the realm of "real-life brutality," limiting Language writers to an oblique position of critique, giving them little social traction (recall Andrews's concerns about passing judgment on the work of others, "especially given who we *are*"). Bernstein himself has been ambivalent on this point, at times seeing Language writing as political allegory, at others—as in the introduction to *A Poetics*—regarding it as an authentic social position of dissent, comparable to the positions of women and minorities (though in much less strident terms than Silliman).[19] Silliman's powerful, possibly offensive, equation of "Language poetry" with racial slurs suggests the bluntest version of this latter position: "Language poet" is not simply an aesthetic but a social identity. Ultimately, this ethnicization of Language writing can be seen as an attempt to reclaim the moral authority extended to the writing of women and minorities—a kind of redemption of white new left discourse.

If, after developing this context, we return to *Ketjak*, we can now see that the driving force behind the text is less an abstract formal principle than the very problem of locating the social identity of the Language poet. In part this may simply mean that with the fading of Language writing's original polemical impact, its historical and social context and origin are becoming more visible. As Marjorie Perloff observes in "Language Poetry and the Lyric Subject," since some of Language poetry's more general critiques—the "demise of the transcendental ego, of the authentic self, of the poet as a lonely genius, of a unique artistic style"—are now "taken as something of a given" (409), the "differences among the various poets now strike us as more significant than similarities or group labels" (410). Perloff takes Silliman's "Albany" as a case in point, arguing that Silliman's individual style is immediately recognizable and cataloging the particularities of Silliman's position:

> There is . . . not the slightest doubt that "Albany" is a man's poem, a man aware of the sexual needs of the women in his life but centrally caught up in the political. . . . These "casual" sentences point to an author who is matter-of-fact, streetwise, and largely self-educated; his is the discourse of a working-class man. . . . Pain, violence, and injustice are the facts of his life. . . . Yet . . . his "voice" emerges as sprightly, engaged, curious, fun-loving, energetic. (416–7)

Such a reading locates Silliman in a "working-class male" subject position, one that might seem analogous to the position of those "oppressed peoples" from whose writing Silliman distinguishes Language poetry. Silliman's style, in short, has not allowed him to escape class and gender. Perloff reinforces this point through a comparison to Leslie Scalapino, who describes a woman on a bus as having a "snout": "Silliman would never describe a woman as having a snout; indeed, his eyes would barely take in her person and quickly, impatiently, move on to something else—a memory, perhaps, of what *he* did with *her*, or a description of a boarding house, or an amusing pun that occurs to him" (419).

Perloff does not explicitly label this a "sexist" or "male" gaze, but that a Language poet might be anxious about such an interpretation is evident from Perelman's oddly genteel reading, in *The Marginalization of Poetry*, of a line in *Ketjak*, "She was a unit in a bum space, she was a damaged child": "But we don't focus on the girl . . . she is not singled out for novelistic treatment. There's a dimension of tact involved: she's not representative of the wrongs done to children, but she's not given the brushoff either" (67). Since "tact" is a term that hardly seems applicable to Silliman's writing—either to his polemical essays or to the pointed artifices of his poetry—I think we can read Perelman's gloss as an attempt to deflect an analysis of the gendering of Silliman's gaze.

Ketjak is, in fact, culturally marked from the outset by its name, which refers to a form of Balinese dance. The *ketjak*, as Thomas C. Marshall writes, "incorporates both a recitative of formalized textual narrative and a texture of repeated phrasings emptied nearly to the point of pure gesture by chanting recitation" (58). *Ketjak* is thus one of several Silliman works given an Asian label—from the contemporaneous "Chinese Notebook" to the 1981 work *Tjanting*, named for an instrument used in Javanese batik work. In a blog entry of September 20, 2003, Silliman describes his discovery of the *ketjak* and its influence on his work:

> I first discovered [the *ketjak*] on a recording made by David Lewiston entitled *Golden Rain*, first released by Nonesuch Records in 1969. I'd bought the album for its gamelan music. . . . I'd discovered that for me at least gamelan—the Balinese word for orchestra—was more than just another mode of music.
>
> But it was the oral chant of *Golden Rain*'s "B" side, 200 men participating in what Lewiston's notes characterized as the Ramayana Monkey Chant, that mesmerized me. At 22:08 minutes, it was—still is—the most amazing oral performance I have ever heard. In *Ketjak* . . . the effects of accumulation,

reiteration & collaboration are instantly available to any ear. It was those aspects that I had in mind when I chose to name my evolving non-narrative prose poem *Ketjak*. (Silliman "Blog")

Although Silliman does not seem to have explicitly modeled the text on the structure of the *ketjak*, he does note in his blog entry that the title "gave me permission in terms of my following a structure that had more to do with music than exposition or narrative." In "Under *Albany*," Silliman reports that it was, in fact, another musical work that inspired the formal structure of *Ketjak*; it was at a performance of Steve Reich's *Drumming*, Silliman writes, that "I began to sense, for the first time, exactly what the formal structure of *Ketjak* would be" (332). But these influences are actually not so far apart. Reich, like other minimalist composers, drew on Asian music and rhythms as an alternative to the Western classical tradition; like Silliman, Reich found in Balinese gamelan a particularly rich inspiration.

Indeed, it could be argued that minimalist music offers a particularly apt parallel to the structures of Silliman's work.[20] As practiced by Reich, Terry Riley, Philip Glass, and others in the 1960s and 1970s, minimalism employed a radically reduced musical palette, often using repetitive patterns to emphasize music as process rather than as expressive medium. Reich's *Drumming*, which suggested to Silliman a formal model for his poem, employs multiple percussionists engaging in what Reich calls "rhythmic construction": starting with a single beat per measure and gradually replacing rests with beats as the measure is repeated, musicians create complex patterns that overlap and move in and out of phase with each other. The result is a work in which the individual voice is decentered in favor of the textures and patterns inherent in the work's formal structures. We can certainly see a parallel here to the form of *Ketjak*, with its repetition and doubling of lines, and to the way in which Silliman's work seeks to decenter the author's own social position.

This decentering takes place within a cultural sphere strongly marked by Asian and other non-Western influences. In his *Writings on Music*, Reich notes that he composed *Drumming* shortly after returning from studying African drumming in Ghana, and he later engaged in intensive study of Balinese gamelan (69). While he resisted incorporating merely "exotic" sounds into his work, he sought to compose "in the light of one's knowledge of non-Western *structures*" (71), seeking not "to *sound* Balinese" but "to *think* Balinese" (148).

Minimalist music was hardly the only aspect of American culture of the period to reflect Asian influence. In the 1960s and 1970s, Asian culture held a particular pull for Americans, particularly those who identified with the new left or the counterculture; although this interest in Asian culture is certainly familiar from the Beats in the 1950s, in the 1960s it took on a political edge with American involvement in Vietnam. As Todd Gitlin notes in *The Sixties*, opposition to the American war in Vietnam often had as its corollary an iden- tification with the Vietnamese revolutionaries, and with the Chinese Cultural Revolution the ideas of Mao gained ascendance among American leftists seek- ing an alternative to Soviet communism. Language writing was no exception: the representative status of Bob Perelman's poem "China" is due largely to Fredric Jameson's somewhat notorious discussion of it in *Postmodernism*, but it is hardly an anomaly. Just as Silliman's "Chinese" notebook represented a ninety-degree "turn" from American writing and culture, naming *Ketjak* after a Balinese dance allows the white American writer to move outside his own subject position, to a critical location outside white America.[21]

Indeed, that sense of being outside is crucial to *Ketjak*, for this is above all a poem of observation, of documentation and detail. Around this time, Silliman began writing regularly while riding public transportation; he notes in "Under *Albany*" that significant parts of *Ketjak* were written while riding transit and "The Chinese Notebook" was written entirely on Golden Gate Transit buses (312). In this context, Silliman's prose poems can come to seem like field notes—glimpses of individuals and interactions, overheard conver- sations, news and advertising—but with a keen awareness of the juxtaposi- tion of social markers that occurs on a crowded bus or train, as Silliman remarks in the *Quarry West* interview:

> Public transportation is . . . a form of tremendous theater in our society. It is one of the few places where different people stand or sit literally touching one another. . . . Riding public transportation was and is also a profoundly classed (and thus for me *class conscious*) experience. Who sits where, how people interact, who's missing—all are heavily predetermined by those socio- economic codes that constrain us all as actors. . . . A lot of what occurs in my writing in transit is close to pure description, but with the class codes turned up to a level of maximum sensitivity. (26)

Silliman's notion of a "pure description" of travel is reminiscent of Allen Ginsberg's tape poems, in that both seek to provide a highly accurate recording of experience. But Ginsberg seeks a transcription of *his own* consciousness, one that is constantly receiving visual and auditory inputs and producing a linear stream of speech. His poetry is written from the perspective of the automobile—of an individual traveling in isolation through a degraded landscape. Silliman's writing, in contrast, attempts to reproduce the experience of public, *collective* transportation by declining to provide a coherent perspective; it's worth noting that *Ketjak* contains many descriptions of people but contains very few descriptions of things that one might see out the window.

How does Silliman's method of description work? Perhaps the most distinctive thing about Silliman's recording of observations is that no observation will appear just once, as it would in a conventional narrative or stream of consciousness. Instead, because of the form of *Ketjak*, any sentence that appears in a given paragraph should be repeated in every subsequent paragraph, occupying a shifting place in a gradually accumulating structure. Moreover, many of these sentences are varied or expanded as they are repeated. One example, which most explicitly registers the bus as a location of writing, first appears in the fifth paragraph and is gradually expanded in succeeding paragraphs:

> The nurse, by a subtle shift of weight, moves in front of the student to more rapidly board the bus. (4)

> The nurse, by a subtle redistribution of weight, shift of gravity's center, moves in front of the student of oriental porcelain in order to more rapidly board the bus. (5)

> The young nurse in sunglasses, by a subtle redistribution of weight, shift of gravity's center, moves in front of the black student of oriental porcelain in order to more rapidly board the bus home, before all the seats are taken. (6)

> The young nurse in blue sunglasses, by a subtle redistribution of weight, shift of gravity's center, moves in front of the black lanky graduate student of oriental porcelain in order to more rapidly board the bus, before all of the seats are taken. (8)

> [repeated identically in several sections]

> The young nurse in sunglasses, by a subtle redistribution of weight, gravity's center, moves in front of the Black student of oriental porcelain in order to more rapidly board the bus home, before all the seats are taken. (63)

These multiple versions of a single, banal event bring us a long way from Ginsberg's assertion in "Howl": "this actually happened." Given Silliman's compositional method, it is likely that the sentence's first appearance represents an actual observation at the time of writing. But in subsequent sections Silliman is presumably not reexperiencing this moment; instead, he is quite literally turning back to an earlier section of his notebook and copying out his previous sentence. Memory, if we can call it that, is textualized and formalized; the observation recurs not because it plays a role in a conventional reminiscence (which would then be tied to some current thought of the author's) but because its recurrence is prescribed by an impersonal pattern.

What, then, do we make of the variations? For even though we might expect the details of a memory to fade with time, in this textual recurrence Silliman actually adds information with each iteration. The process that Silliman seems to enact here is the layering of social markers that characterizes any social interaction; the addition of markers of occupation, age, and race gives precisely the "subtle shift of weight" that shifts the meaning of this encounter. The event is viewed through an increasingly complex social matrix that cannot be merely personal: whereas a casual observer could certainly know the race and approximate age of the individuals, the observer could not know for certain that one was a student of "oriental porcelain" or that the other was trying to get home. These are hypotheses, possible explanations for what we might sense as the social valence of an encounter. Is it simply an instance of a tired worker doing what's necessary to get a seat? Does this incident have racial overtones?

But any sense that Silliman is building to a definitive social analysis is dispelled by the final iteration of this incident, which actually reduces the amount of information provided: the adjectives *blue* and *lanky* are dropped, as is the phrase "shift of." To be sure, this is in part an inevitable result of *Ketjak*'s form. As Silliman puts it at one point: "How will I know when I make a mistake" (5). The labor of copying, and of keeping track of which sentences have and have not been repeated, is arduous, particularly in the later sections, which include hundreds of sentences; it seems that in the final section Silliman may have copied the shorter version of this sentence that appears in the third paragraph. In the overall arc of the text, however, this reduction of information suggests that our social perceptions may not always be stable and are always subject to revision; it may even cast doubt on the idea that we can truly know the social actors who surround us in the public spaces we move through every day.

It is the structure of public space that is, I believe, the largest theme of *Ketjak*, and in particular how that space is structured by capitalism. The first phrase of *Ketjak*, "Revolving door," gives us an image of controlled public space, compartmentalizing and separating individuals. Silliman notes in "Under *Albany*" that the door in question was at the San Francisco headquarters of the Bank of America (332), and the text is filled with similar images, from financial power—"Fountains of the financial district" (3)—to government authority—"The bear flag in the plaza" (4). But Silliman's approach is not simply to catalog the contents of such public spaces, as Ginsberg does in his cross-country travels. Instead, Silliman's sentences often juxtapose public and private spaces, and the progress of the sequence continually reconfigures the relations between the two. Public and private interpenetrate in surprising and subversive ways, illustrating the classic new left maxim "The personal is the political" while showing that this relation operates in both directions. Consider, for example, the following section from early in *Ketjak*:

> Portrait of the best worker in auto plant 7. Fountains of the financial district spout soft water in a hard wind. Repeating on paper that stanza one hundred times, each with a new pen, watching how the width of the ink's path shifted the weight and intention of reference, penumbra of signification, from act to act. Little moons of my thumbnail grow. I see that young woman each morning as she jogs in a blue sweatsuit, trailed by her four small dogs. In a far room of the apartment I can hear music and a hammer. The asymmetry in any face. Grey clouds to give the sky weight. Layers of bandage about the ankle. The bear flag in the black marble plaza. Roundness is an ideal embodied in the nostril. A white bowl of split pea soup is set upon the table. It's cold. Rapid transit information. Doors open, footsteps, faucets, people are waking up. Those curtains which I like above the kitchen sink. Stood there broke and rapidly becoming hungry, staring at nickels and pennies at the bottom of the fountain. (10)

We can identify various levels of language at work here. There are observations of *public*, often administered, space, as in the first two sentences. Individuals in these settings are types—the "portrait of the best worker" is gestured to but never revealed—and observation is impersonal. Then there are observations of *private*, domestic space, as in "Those curtains which I like above the kitchen sink"; these often feature an observing subject, an "I." But then there are a number of other kinds of remarks: *bodily* observations, often focused on a particular body part ("bandage about the ankle," "embodied in the nostril"); *found text* ("Rapid transit information"); and perhaps most strikingly, *self-reflexive* statements about writing, which appear throughout the text and which often seem to be reflections on *Ketjak* itself: "Repeating on paper that stanza one hundred times." Does it make sense to think of these as "public" or "private" spaces? What kinds of connections does Silliman's method make between these realms?

It might seem at first that Silliman makes no connections at all between his observations, but it would be more accurate to say that he makes no suggestion of natural or narrative connections. If *Ketjak* is, as Silliman puts it, "only dailiness" (48), Silliman declines to give his account of a day a conventional structure. We can certainly recognize elements of such a structure: waking up in the morning ("Doors open, footsteps, faucets"), going to work (the financial district, the auto plant), returning home and making dinner (the split pea soup, the kitchen sink), perhaps even doing some writing ("Repeating on paper"). But such a narrative arc—beginning from the private, going out into the public, and returning to the private—allows public and private to remain as radically divorced from each other as they seem to be in real life, while allowing the private sphere to remain the telos of everyday living. Silliman denies this division by shoving the public and private up against one another, like passengers on a bus, forcing the reader to see public and private as part of a larger system mediated by language. The "worker-of-the-month" picture and the financial-district fountain, which might be seen as attempts to humanize the workplace, are shown up by their juxtaposition as ineffectual and absurd, "soft water in a hard wind." The remarkable and rapid cross-cutting between bodily images and visual observations ("The asymmetry in any face. Grey clouds to give the sky weight. Layers of bandage about the ankle. The bear flag on the black marble plaza. Roundness is an ideal embodied in the nostril") makes even the body, that most private of sites, a public and general construction. Indeed, the repetitive and accumulative structures of *Ketjak* itself are likened to a bodily process: "Little moons of my thumbnail grow." And finally, the cozy domestic scene of soup and curtains is rudely juxtaposed with a scene of poverty, of a bereft public space that ironically echoes the "soft" fountains of the second line.

One result of Silliman's method, then, is to produce a map of social space that is not solely grounded in the private, which does not simply proceed from the perspective of a single consciousness. But what kind of subjectivity, then, is represented? *Ketjak* cannot be characterized as a polyvocal text in the same way that, say, Pound's *Cantos* or Eliot's *Waste Land* might be. Although the perspective and location of the different observations may shift, nearly every statement in the text with an identifiable speaker can be usefully read as emanating from Silliman's authorial position. The four first-person statements that appear in the previous quotation can easily be attributed to the same male apartment-dwelling urbanite, and the text is peppered with autobiographical details, many of which appear again in "Under *Albany*." Although quoted material does appear in the text, it is usually clearly quoted from a written source—it simply does not sound like the rest of the text.[22] Silliman never allows his consciousness to cohere into a single voice or narrative and constantly breaks up and rearranges his perspectives. But they are unquestionably, even flamboyantly, all *his* perspectives.

This is nowhere more evident than when the text turns its attention to women—which often means, to sex. A taste for sexual innuendo, often of an aggressive nature, is evident throughout Silliman's work, giving what might seem like formal exercises a visceral edge. "Sunset Debris," composed shortly after *Ketjak* and published in *The Age of Huts*, consists entirely of questions, most of which are double entendres: "Can you feel it? Does it hurt? Is this too soft? Do you like it? Do you like this? Is this how you like it? Is it alright? Is he there? Is he breathing? Is it him? Is it near? Is it hard?" (11). One might easily respond to this with a line from *Ketjak*: "You use, she said, rising up from the bed angry, sex as a weapon" (83). Observations of women in *Ketjak* can seem at times to be a case study in the male gaze and in male-dominated sexuality:

She had only the slightest pubic hair. (6)

She threw her legs back, up, over my shoulders, and with my ass I shoved in. (19)

Watching her hand to see if there is a ring amid long, thin fingers. (11)

How, between tongue and lips, she took my foreskin, licking. (68)

She liked to lower herself on top of him. (76)

In the middle of a blow job, she puked. (84)

Wiggled two fingers deep in her cunt. (86)

She loves to give head. (91)

When the male body is represented, it is with an almost parodic focus on the phallus and phallic anxiety:

Then we found the testes in the scrotal sac. (14)

A procedure by which they stick a metal device up one's prick. (19)

Sperm count. (30)

Bruised cock. (80)

The tenor sax is a toy. (7)

The tenor sax is a weapon. (73)

The tenor sax is a phallus or cross. (92)

The very crudeness of some of these images might be read as an embattled masculinity struggling to reassert itself in the face of changing gender roles: "That he was not brutal enough for her confused him" (18). And in fragments scattered through the text, Silliman gives us glimpses of the origins and traumas of his own male working-class identifications, suggesting an interest in exploring the roots of masculinity later fleshed out in "Under *Albany*":

Men eating burgers in silence, at a drugstore counter, wearing t-shirts and short hair, staring at their food. (20)

The boys play at war atop washers, amid dryers. (28)

He stood over them, alternately shouting and drinking from a bottle of bourbon. (29)

Hotels for old single men. (31)

Grandfather robed in white, horizontal in grey-green shadows of Intensive Care, would not look up, tubes in nose, waiting. (47)

Early memory of sensation, being picked up by father, first recognition of height, absorbed later into dreams where I just float off of earth's surface, slow, uncontrollable, weightless flight. (67)

Collecting these passages together gives us a very different *Ketjak*, one that seems to correspond more closely to the discourse of the "men's group."

Silliman puts on display an aggressive masculinity, while also delving into the biographical and class origins of that position. Yet read this way, *Ketjak* hardly seems like a progressive political poem; it seems all too trapped within the perspective of the white male (albeit working-class) writer.

But the sentences gathered together here are actually scattered throughout the text, constantly recontextualized through Silliman's repetitions. They retain some of their elemental charge but can never accumulate together to the level of a "masculine" structure of feeling. ("Ideological basis of sleep. She loves to give head. A pleasure and discomfort in the knowledge of having become, by the fact of your absence, the focal point" [91].) The method of *Ketjak* may be a way of "opening" the poem to the world, but not to other consciousnesses; rather, it is a way for Silliman to provide a buffer against *his own* consciousness in order that its structures—of gender, of sexuality—not come to rule the piece. Indeed, Silliman seems to hope that the poem's public spaces will allow an erosion of those social roles that can be oppressive even to those whom they benefit, a blurring of the gender opposition that lurks in the work: "The feminine way men fold their hands when, say, they ride the bus" (31).

It is Silliman's hope that the method of the new sentence deployed in *Ketjak* will provide a realistic and documentary language that manages to escape the boundaries of his own (straight white male) perspective, with all its limits. Although all the elements of this masculinist perspective are present within *Ketjak*, they are dismantled and scattered; they are made public through their interweaving with a wide range of materials; and they are governed not by a submerged psyche but by an artificial, impersonal, foregrounded structure. But can the products of Silliman's gaze be redeemed by simple rearrangement? Does *Ketjak* earn its status as a total poem, incorporating all levels of language and social experience? Silliman's utopian gamble, and the gamble of all Language writing, is that experimental techniques can render the Language poem both particular *and* universal—much like the utopian vision of Ginsberg's "Howl," albeit with a much stronger and perhaps more realistic sense of the force of social divisions. Language poetry, in Silliman's imagination, is both a delimited community and an aesthetic through which social markers might be transcended: "On a warm night, browsing from bookstore to bookstore, wandering from café to tavern to café, the conversation of women and men was the life I'd imagined" (80).

If Silliman's essays and letters describe a social landscape rigidly divided by lines of race, gender, sexuality, and class, his poetry can be read as a utopian attempt to transgress these divisions. Yet we cannot read this as a simple desire for transcendence, which would seek to subsume social differences in the beauties of lyric poetry. Instead, the techniques of the new sentence— ideally—allow social identities to retain their integrity while allowing none to gain dominance. Silliman's identity as a straight white man from a working-class background—and its concomitant perspectives and prejudices—is everywhere in evidence in *Ketjak*, often in observations that may disturb or offend. But the technique of parataxis, of following one sentence with another that is apparently unrelated, refuses to allow that perspective to cohere—serving, in essence, as the author's bulwark against himself.

The techniques of *Ketjak* allow Silliman to extend Ginsberg's vision of a documentary poetry, one that attempts a comprehensive recording of social data while guarding against the excess of subjectivity that threatens to make Ginsberg's poetry a mirror image of the powers it opposes. With the fragmentation of the left in the 1970s, Silliman's desire for this kind of "realism" is threatened not only by the limits of individual subjectivity but by that of group subjectivity—the new awareness of how perspectives can be limited by boundaries of race, gender, and sexuality.

Silliman adapts to this new social landscape by ethnicizing the avant-garde, positing Language writing not simply as an aesthetic movement but as a social identity. By the 1980s, "Language writing" would thus become a category equivalent to "black writing" or "women's writing," and potentially as restrictive. At the same time, Silliman wants to retain the idea of Language writing as an aesthetic category, one capable of achieving a comprehensive view of the social landscape—an aesthetic evident in *Ketjak*. This tension is apparent not only in Silliman's own writings but in the more ambivalent pronouncements of Silliman's peers.

It might be argued, then, that Silliman's ostensibly progressive project has a reactionary element to it, responding to the threat posed by the growing moral and political authority ascribed to the writing of women and minorities in the wake of the 1960s. If white new leftists ultimately felt compelled to cede moral authority to racial minorities, Silliman attempts to reclaim it through a corollary exploration of the social identity of the avant-garde, positioning his own writing as just as "marginal," and hence politically oppositional, as any other. At the same time he hopes his writing will serve a universalizing and integrative function lost with the collapse of the new left. The unease with which Silliman's colleagues have greeted such pronouncements, and the critiques by those who have called Silliman's formulations exclusionary, are a sign of how difficult it has been to breach this barrier between the aesthetic and the social.[23] Perhaps the best way to understand *Ketjak* is to see it as a testament to this struggle: it is both a convincing but decentered map of our contemporary social landscape and an often uncomfortable exploration of white male consciousness—a sensibility, as Silliman puts it elsewhere, awkwardly aware of its own "pervasive presence."

THREE

Inventing a Culture

Asian American Poetry in the 1970s

In what sense can Asian American poets be said to form an avant-garde? Although it is frequently acknowledged that there are a certain number of Asian American poets who now write in recognizably "experimental" styles, including John Yau, Myung Mi Kim, and Tan Lin, such writing is often regarded as a recent development in Asian American literature, a departure from the familiar Asian American literary modes of autobiographical lyric and narratives of family history. What I argue in this chapter is that from its inception in the 1970s, Asian American poetry as a whole was an avant-garde, a grouping that defined itself not just through race but through bold experiments with form and style in the search for an Asian American aesthetic. If white avant-gardists such as the Language poets were compelled to "ethnicize" their writing, it was in part because of an awareness that emerging categories like "Asian American writing" were taking their place alongside those groups traditionally labeled "avant-garde."

The image of Asian American poetry familiar to most readers is a product of the 1980s, which saw the rise to prominence of poets like Li-Young Lee, Cathy Song, David Mura, and Marilyn Chin. Like many of their non–Asian American peers, these poets were largely trained in poetry workshops and are now often professors of creative writing themselves; their work fits comfortably into what some critics have called the "MFA mainstream" of the 1980s and 1990s, with its emphasis on personal voice, epiphanic insight, and loose verse form.[1] This formal consonance has allowed Asian American poetry to become an acceptable part of the multicultural curriculum, a transparent conduit for those neglected stories that some have asserted it is the job of minority literature to tell.

But if we return to the scene of Asian American literature's emergence in the 1970s, in the ephemeral newspapers, journals, and anthologies of that period, we get a very different image of Asian American poetry, one that is not so easy to place in the mainstream of American poetry. The poems in publications like *Gidra*, *Aion*, and *Bridge* are politically charged and direct, angry and passionate, frequently reaching for a populist aesthetic. Their authors—Fay Chiang, George Leong, Ron Tanaka, Francis Oka— are absent from recent anthologies of Asian American writing; only Janice Mirikitani and Lawson Fusao Inada continue to be read. And the influences on and directions of this work are much more diverse than the canon of the 1980s and 1990s, with Beat, jazz, and Asian influences reflecting an interest in aesthetic as well as political vanguardism. Indeed, the poetry of writers like Lee, Song, and Mura may eventually come to be seen as an anomaly within the development of an Asian American poetry whose allegiances are much more appropriately placed with the avant-garde. Walter K. Lew's anthology *Premonitions*, which places writers of the 1970s like Inada and Mirikitani alongside experimental writers of the 1990s like Kim and Lin, is one of the most striking statements of the continuity of the Asian American avant-garde.

Perhaps most remarkable of all, though, is just how central a role poetry seems to have played in the politics of the early Asian American movement. Each issue of the seminal monthly *Gidra*, for example, included a section called "The People"—a full-page selection of poems written by readers. The groundbreaking 1971 anthology *Roots: An Asian American Reader* contains over twenty pages of poetry—and no fiction. Its 1976 sequel, *Counterpoint*, contains a section on "Literature" of over one hundred pages, with more than thirty poems. It is hard to imagine a recent political movement giving such a central place to poetry. Why, in the early 1970s, did poetry seem vital to the Asian American political project?

To answer that question, we must acknowledge that the early Asian American movement was as much a cultural revolution as a social one—a purposeful phrasing that evokes many Asian American activists' attraction to Maoism and the example of Chinese communism. Asian American manifestos of this period emphasize education, historical and cultural awareness, the establishment of Asian American publications and ethnic studies programs, and the rejection of "Oriental" stereotypes, all in the name of claiming an authentically Asian American identity.

Asian American poetry of the 1970s shared the documentary impulse central to political poetry of the period and found, in its different ways, in the work of Allen Ginsberg and Ron Silliman. Moreover, Asian American writers shared the desire of Ginsberg's "Howl" to portray the life of a community. But this should not be taken to mean that Asian American poetry is a poetry of pure content, one that transparently represents Asian American subjectivities and communities. In fact, the 1970s witnessed a long and politically charged negotiation of the forms that Asian American poetry would take, a negotiation that took place, like the emergence of Language poetics, in a post–new left political and aesthetic context.

Although it would be simplistic to choose a single origin for the Asian American movement,[2] the student strike of 1968–9 at San Francisco State was perhaps its most important catalyst. Central to the strikers' demands was the establishment of a department of ethnic studies that would focus on the identities, histories, and communities of students of color. The most immediate model for this kind of cultural nationalism was the Black Power movement, embodied in the Bay Area by the Black Panther Party, whose rise was one of Silliman's markers for the demise of a unified, multiracial new left.

Events like the rise of Black Power and the San Francisco State strike may have served to make white radicals feel marginalized. But that does not mean that the conversion of Asian Americans into authentic revolutionary "Third World" subjects was an automatic or natural process. Just as the new left's adoption of the black civil rights movement led to a kind of imitative anxiety, with white activists "borrowing" the authentically revolutionary rhetoric of African Americans, Asian Americans in the 1970s found the rhetoric of black identity both exemplary and chastening. It provided a model for an Asian American identity but at the same time suggested, at least to some writers, how far Asian Americans had to go in defining their own racial consciousness.

In his introductory essay to the recent collection *Asian Americans: The Movement and the Moment*, Steve Louie debunks the suggestion that young Chinese Americans were honoring their heritage in taking up the ideas of Mao: "I heard about Mao's ideas from the Black Panther Party. The Panthers introduced the Red Book to the American movement" (Louie and Omatsu xxii). This idea—that Asian Americans were coming to consciousness in part through the structures of black identity—was not limited to the realm of politics but extended to culture and aesthetics, though in this latter realm the point is tinged with anxiety. Many of the writings on literature in the early issues of *Bridge*, one of the most prominent Asian American journals of the 1970s, lament the relative paucity of Asian American writers; an essay in the September/October 1972 issue asked, "Why Are There So Few Sansei Writers?"—a point sometimes contrasted with the plethora of African American writers. In a panel discussion published in *Bridge's* third issue, one speaker, Bill Ling, noted of Asian Americans, "There aren't any people who are willing to write a book and get it published and publicized throughout this whole damn place. . . . There are no playwrights like LeRoi Jones to put it as it is" ("What Interests Chinatown Is $, Not China!" 29). Ling's explanation for this is a harbinger of discussions throughout the 1970s of Asian American culture:

> One thing that I can see is the Chinese have a culture, and if you dig hard enough it's there, but blacks have had a terrible time identifying with the African culture so they have developed a subculture in the United States: black literature, black playwrights. They are creating something for a good foundation to get back on, and develop their own economic ways. I don't know whether it is going to be attached to the Establishment in the U.S. or separate. (29)

African Americans, Ling argues, have developed a distinctive African American culture in the face of racism and cultural holocaust—an ethnic culture internal to the United States but still possibly oppositional to it. Chinese Americans, in contrast, have a culture still continuous with that of China; yet this has had the paradoxical effect of stifling their ability to construct an ethnic subculture in the United States. The culture of Chinese Americans in the United States, unlike that of African Americans, still remains to be formed.

Although Frank Chin has made a career of criticizing those, like Ling, who suggest a continuity between Chinese and Chinese American culture, Chin's own writings display a similar unease in the face of the distinct cultural identity claimed by African Americans. One of Chin's best-known essays, "Confessions of a Chinatown Cowboy," is motivated in part by admiration of what he calls the "badass" image of African Americans, in contrast to the "kissass" stereotype of Asian Americans.[3] It is a concern shared by

Chin's audience as well: in a review of Chin's play *The Chickencoop China-man* in the July/August 1972 issue of *Bridge*, William Wong writes, "The play confronts the issue of the self-contempt we all feel at one time or an-other. . . . Our self-contempt is also evidenced in our language—or our lack of one. The language of both Tam and Kenji is laced throughout with black jargon, and other American subcultural dialects that aren't really their own" (26). Just as some white radicals saw black language as an authentic speech they could only imitate, Wong worries that Chin's attempt to discover an Asian American language is parasitic, doomed to a kind of parody of Afri-can American vernacular.

The larger point here is that the example of black cultural nationalism, and the politics of identity to which it gave rise, could be just as discomfit-ing to Asian American writers as to white leftist writers like Ron Silliman. For all the talk of roots, history, and Asian cultural heritage, many Asian American writers confronted what they saw as the task of building a culture from the ground up with whatever tools were at their disposal. The task could not simply be one of filling extant cultural forms with Asian Ameri-can content; the struggle to describe an Asian American consciousness was also a struggle to find appropriate and distinctive forms for that conscious-ness, one that led Asian American poets to draw from a wide range of styles and traditions throughout the 1970s.

It is generally acknowledged that the first Asian American literary maga-zine was *Aion*, which published its two issues in San Francisco in 1970.[4] The journal grew directly out of the San Francisco State strike, and its chief edi-tor was Janice Mirikitani, a master's student in creative writing during the strike who would become one of the best-known Asian American poets of the period.

Aion's two issues were substantial—the first issue contained more than sixty pages, the second, more than one hundred—and included poetry, short stories, photography, drawings, and essays. Even between these two issues, however, the distribution of material shifted. In the first issue, it is not immediately clear to a reader that *Aion* is a literary magazine per se; the opening editorial describes it as "a forum for Asian American self-definition and expression on issues relevant to problems and needs of our communi-ties" (5). The journal's cardstock cover and heft make it resemble a periodi-cal like the later *Bridge*, and the number of pages devoted to political essays and journalism—including such pieces as "The Need for a United Asian

American Front," "On the Containment of China," and an interview with Alex Hing, minister of information for the Red Guard Party—far outweigh those devoted to poems. But by the second issue the journal's literary task has become explicit: its self-declared role is as both a community forum and a place "for the self-definition of Asian artists and writers." And poems now outnumber essays by more than two to one.

Aion, then, is a kind of microcosm of how Asian American poetry emerged in the context of the radical Asian American politics of the early 1970s. It provides a glimpse into the theory and practice of Asian American writing, while also showing Asian American literature in the process of becoming a category relatively autonomous from political rhetoric.

The editorial that opens the first issue gives what would become a standard argument for the need to construct an Asian American culture, centered around negative stereotypes of Asians in America:

> As Asian Americans, we have been conditioned by stereotypes imposed upon us by the white middle class and have internalized the consequent insecurity and confusion. Dependency upon these values and standards has caused an absence of self-knowledge and its complementary fear and paralysis.
>
> Our continued complacency within this racist society will bring about our cultural destruction. We must join the international movement to end the exploitation of all Third World peoples and work to create our own revolutionary culture in this country. ("Editorial" 5)

Like nearly all Asian American writings of this period, the editorial characterizes anti-Asian stereotypes as a scourge that oppresses—and potentially unifies—Asian Americans across ethnic lines. But the focus on stereotype also shifts the battleground from politics or economics to culture, and to an emphasis on the way in which racism can be "internalized" by Asian Americans. Stating the challenge to Asian Americans in these terms also dictates the solution: to "create our own revolutionary culture," one opposed to the racist culture that currently traps Asian Americans. But there is an ambiguity here as well in the dynamic between "cultural destruction" and cultural creation. Is the culture of Asian Americans something already present but submerged, something that needs to be celebrated and preserved from destruction? Or is it something that does not yet exist and needs to be created?

This tension is evident as well in the dominant political presence in *Aion*'s first issue: Alex Hing, who contributes both an opening essay and an interview. Hing was "minister of information" for the Red Guard, a group modeled on the Black Panthers that became one of the best-known Asian American revolutionary groups.[5] Hing's essay "The Need for a United Asian-American Front" captures some of the issues that will become central in debates about Asian American culture:

> The most politically aware of the Asians in America are usually those who have reached a high level of assimilation into the White Mother Country's culture. . . .
> Most of the politically aware Asians are students who are undergoing identity crises. They realize that they cannot fit into White society, yet at the same time they are also rebelling against the strict, Confucian ideas instilled into them by their parents. The contradiction caused by trying to assimilate into two cultures at one time can be resolved not by rejecting one and assimilating more into the other, but by rejecting the bad elements in both cultures and building a revolutionary culture from the best elements of both. (9)

Hing acknowledges that political consciousness is culturally mediated—a nod to the fact that Asian American activism, like much activism of the late 1960s, was centered around universities. Hing portrays the Asian American as caught between cultures (an image Frank Chin and others will roundly critique over the course of the decade) and describes the Asian American cultural task as a kind of bricolage, an active construction drawing on both white American and Asian cultures.

Hing expands on this task, and the Red Guard Party's role in it, in an interview with Neil Gotanda later in the issue:

> The Red Guard is part of the Cultural Revolution that's going down in the United States. Most of us are Asian Americans who were born here and we spent most of our lives trying to assimilate into the culture. And, you know, we can't relate to that because they won't let us anyway. . . .
> And there are cultural things and hang-ups in most American people that makes it hard to reach them, so what we're trying to do is set up an alternative—an alternative for the people to groove on, and that is to edu-cate the people—Third World and White—to the fact that we're all people struggling to live normal, comfortable lives. Chinese people shouldn't try to be white, because we're not, and that we have to identify with what we are

and make it all work out so that we don't think we have to throw away our culture to live and be comfortable. (32)

The goal of activism, then, is from the beginning cultural, aesthetic—to create a different "groove"—but also ultimately didactic. Here, though, the emphasis is on cultural recovery rather than on creation, the need not to "throw away *our* culture" and to "identify with what *we are*." But Hing gets into a final rhetorical wrinkle when he talks about struggling to bridge the gap between American-born Asians and immigrants:

> [W]e American born Chinese tried to be Americans and found that we couldn't do that. And by doing that, we've divorced ourselves from the people, the immigrants—the people who think Chinese and speak Chinese. Those are the people we want to relate to and like *we're going to have to learn to speak our language*. So we're starting to educate ourselves, politically and scholastically so we can get back to our people. (33, emphasis added)

"We" has become a divided entity; "we" American-born Chinese have become estranged from a language that is "ours" but that we do not know how to speak. This, in a nutshell, is the paradox in which Asian American writers of this moment find themselves: faced with a culture that is somehow felt to be naturally "theirs" and in need of recovery and telling, yet having to learn how to describe that culture, to find or create appropriate aesthetic forms for it. Like Allen Ginsberg, whose most spontaneous work required the maximum amount of technological intervention, Asian American writers needed to draw on a wide range of artifices to construct a writing that was somehow distinctively Asian American.

Perhaps the most interesting presence in the pages of *Aion* is that of Miri-kitani's co-editor, the Japanese-born Francis Naohiko Oka, whose writing combines the didactic impulse of many of the other poems with an irreverent "groove" that seems reminiscent of Beat writers like Ginsberg. Oka is listed as co-editor on the masthead of *Aion*'s first issue but was killed in a motorcycle accident in June 1970 at the age of twenty-four; *Aion*'s second issue is dedicated to his memory and contains a selection of his poems.[6] Given the sensibility evidenced in those poems, it seems likely that Oka had a hand in the witty list that follows the very serious opening editorial in *Aion* 1.1. The list notes that the magazine is "dedicated to" all those "who made this magazine necessary," and includes S. I. Hayakawa, Dean Rusk, William Randolph Hearst, Charlie Chan, Commodore Perry, "R. Mill-house

Nixon," "'Fat Jap' Agnew," the Ku Klux Klan, and the Chevron Island Girl.[7]
The list moves cleverly from historical and contemporary political figures to
American cultural icons, suggesting a seamless link between American im-
perialism and American culture.

Oka's poems show plenty of political awareness and fire but also a with-
drawal from and ironizing of politics, a trait his work shares with Ginsberg's.
Oka's poem in the first *Aion* juxtaposes public and private, using the image
of the "cell" as both a place of resistance and a domestic space, but ambiguous on whether the personal or the political is meant to be seen as the real:

> We spoke of politics—
> our love-making
> a reflection
> in revolutionary posters
> hanging as spectres
> on our bedroom walls.

> ("Cell" 12)

The most striking poems by Oka in the second *Aion* explicitly state their
Beat origins; one, an apostrophe to "America," evokes Ginsberg's poem
of the same name; two others are marked as being written at City Lights
Bookstore, the Beat mecca in San Francisco's North Beach.[8]

Oka's "America," like Ginsberg's, is an ironized and even agonized paean
that condemns America's failings even as it acknowledges the speaker's own
complicity in and attraction to America and its culture:

> America,
> I could have loved you
> with your T.V. sets blinking across a mindless eye
> and your automated forests recoiling in horror
> at the christening of your newest campsite.
>
>   .   .   .
>
> I've seen the final analysis of your culture
> and have grown to accept roast beef
> and have come to like your money being
> greener than your forests
> and redundant to my tastes.

(7)

Oka's City Lights poems move into another realm explored by Ginsberg: that of the bodily grotesque, a radical awareness of the physical that undermines the pretensions of the powerful.[9] The anaphoric "Reagan Poem" mocks the then-governor of California in a style reminiscent of the "Moloch" section of Ginsberg's "Howl." But whereas Ginsberg's anaphora is centripetal, creating a kind of constellation around the figure of Moloch—"Moloch the incomprehensible prison! Moloch the crossbone soulless jailhouse and Congress of sorrows! Moloch whose buildings are judgment! Moloch the vast stone of war!" (*Poems* 131)—Oka's is centrifugal. Rather than coming together into a condemnation or demonization of Ronald Reagan, Oka's caricatures turn "Ronald" into a free-floating signifier, of which "Ronald is Governor of California" is only one aspect.

The poem's humor is gleefully juvenile; even those characterizations of Reagan that are ostensibly political quickly veer into the comic or grotesque: "Ronald is a reactionary paper tiger pissing in his pants . . . Ronald is John Birch turned conservative . . . Ronald is Hitler's left ball castrated" ("Reagan Poem" 8). Indeed, many of the images crudely perform this "castration" of Reagan: "Ronald is finger nail polish on a dyke / Ronald is long hair on girls pubes . . . Ronald's cunt grows mildew." But perhaps the poem's most interesting gesture is to move—or rather, to return—Reagan, the former actor, to the realm of culture: "Ronald is Donald Duck in 'Gone with the Wind' / Ronald is Joey Bishop's hairstylist . . . Ronald is Ringo Starr's drumstick." There's even an attempt to equate Reagan with stereotyped (and false) images of Asian Americans: "Ronald is the I-Ching in paperback by Dell publishers . . . Ronald is psychedelic fried Won Ton with pineapple sauce." "Ronald" has become a monstrous cultural-political amalgam, identified with those specifically cultural forces that oppress Asian Americans. But putting Reagan in this realm also opens up the possibility of a cultural response, as the poem's conclusion shows:

> Ronald is the Confederate General from Big Sur in disguise
> Ronald is all watched over by machines of loving grace
> Ronald is against interpretation
> Ronald doesn't want to relate to me.

> (8)

The first two lines allude to titles of books by Richard Brautigan, a Beat-affiliated writer whose novel *Trout Fishing in America* made him a cult figure in the late 1960s. The surreal blend of casual speech, romance, and the grotesque in Brautigan's poetry seems to have influenced Oka's style. Brautigan's poem "All Watched Over by Machines of Loving Grace" imagines a strange utopia that is both natural and technological, a "cybernetic ecology" in which we are "joined back to nature" while being "watched over / by machines of loving grace" (1). This intertext gives a surprisingly optimistic turn to the poem's conclusion, as does Oka's identification of Reagan with Susan Sontag's *Against Interpretation*—we might well expect Reagan to be identified with the philistines of interpretation rather than with the aesthetes of formal appreciation. But the last line makes clear that these identifications are against the subject's will. Governor Reagan would not willingly have anything to do with a young, radical, Asian American poet, but Oka's poem has forced "Ronald" into a relationship with him on the ground of culture, engaging an out-of-reach political figure in a strange kind of dialogue.

If "Ronald" is hard to pin down in this poem, so is the "me," a figure defined only by how he "relates" to the other cultural icons cited in the poem. Though Oka may draw techniques from Ginsberg, his "I" is not Ginsberg's bardic speaker or even Brautigan's self-deprecating romantic; he shares Silliman's post–new left skepticism about the individual voice and perspective. Oka's more personal poems in *Aion* 1.2 are vexed by the self's inadequacy to the outward-looking political vision of works like "Reagan Poem"; the poet worries that "I am too far drawn / within myself" ("Shades Drawn Tight" 4). Yet Oka does retain a sense of a private self that he is wary of politicizing and labeling Asian American:

> The pale yellow composition is not my skin;
>> it is only what my brothers would have me believe,
> though they mean well
>>> my skin is not yellow . . .
> My skin is skinny (no pun intended) or arrogant,
>> clear and without doubt a complexion acquired
>> thru the meager trials I've faced in my life.
>
> ("Blue Crayon" 5)

Oka displays a keen awareness of Asian American identity as a composition rather than a biological or biographical fact. The perceived gap between that identity and the self of personal experience gives a post-Ginsbergian pathos to Oka's work.

Another possible direction for Asian American writing appears in the work of perhaps the most established writer who appears in *Aion*, Lawson Fusao Inada. Inada's first collection of poems, *Before the War: Poems As They Happened*, would be published the following year by William Morrow. In a contributor's note for the special "Asian American Poetry 1976" issue of *Bridge* in October 1976, Inada writes that *Before the War* was "probably" the first book of poems published by a Japanese American; he also notes that he (as well as Frank Chin) attended the prestigious Writers' Workshop at the University of Iowa in the early 1960s and "knows a thing or two about jazz" ("Asian American Poetry" 61). In a limited sense, Inada might be seen as a model for those Asian American poets who would come to prominence in the 1980s. Writing in a polished style, with skills honed in a university creative writing program, Inada was a professional writer years before the advent of the Asian American movement—unlike most of the poets in early Asian American publications, who came to writing largely through activism. But Inada's position "before" the upheaval of the Asian American movement means that the lack of models for Asian American writing is starkly evident in his writing.

For Inada, as for Frank Chin, a similarly situated writer, African American culture, especially jazz, becomes the touchstone for his writing; jazz is a source of inspiration that Inada shares with American avant-gardists of all stripes, from the Beats to the Black Mountain poets to the Black Arts movement. But just as the example of black activism seems double-edged for many Asian Americans in this period, the African American cultural example is hardly a "natural" fit for Inada, as the opening poem of *Before the War*, "Plucking Out a Rhythm," shows:

> Start with a simple room—
> a dullish color—
> and draw the shade down.
> Hot plate. Bed.
> Little phonograph in a corner.
>
> Put in a single figure—
> medium weight and height—
> but oversize, as a child might.
>
> The features must be Japanese.
>
> Then stack a black pompadour on,
> and let the eyes

slide behind a night of glass.

The figure is in disguise:

slim green suit
for posturing on a bandstand,
the turned-up shoes of Harlem . . .

Then start the music playing—
thick jazz, strong jazz—

and notice that the figure
comes to life:

(13)[10]

The poem's title suggests jazz improvisation, but also the piecemeal, almost Frankenstein-like manner in which the poem's subject is constructed. The figure's race is not a natural trait, but a conscious, even forced identification: "The features *must* be Japanese," not "are." The body's building is described in mechanical terms, "stack" and "slide," delivered in the imperative, as if in an instruction manual. But perhaps the most striking statement is the claim that the figure is "in disguise"—a phrase that surely would have conjured up to the reader Daniel Okimoto's autobiographical *American in Disguise*, published in the same year. Inada, Chin, and the other editors of *Aiiieeeee!* would later characterize Okimoto's book as a case study in Asian American self-loathing, with its dominant image of Asianness as a mask obscuring the true American beneath.[11] But in this poem Inada's figure dons a mask marked as African American, "posturing on a bandstand" in "the turned-up shoes of Harlem."

It is music—the jazz of the poem—that animates this patchwork creature. But it is hard to say whether Inada means this to unify these complex identifications. The poem's conclusion shows the figure's life to be fleeting:

Then have the shade flap up
and daylight catch him
frozen in that pose

as it starts to snow—
thick snow, strong snow—

blowing in the window
while the music quiets,
the room is slowly covered,

and the figure is completely
out of sight.

(14)

The layers of Japanese and black masks are covered by another layer—one
that is, disturbingly, white, though the word never appears—and ultimately
erased. Inada gives us no sense of an authentic racial or even personal
identity; the Japanese American jazz his construction produces is unstable,
audible only for a brief interval.

Inada's poem in *Aion* 1.1, "Father of My Father," is much less abstract and
more explicitly biographical, foreshadowing the almost exclusive focus on
personal history that will come to characterize Asian American writing by
the 1980s. But even in this poem racial identification is unstable:

Have you ever seen
blue eyes in a Japanese face?

That is the main thing I remember . . .

Have you ever been
wakened by blue eyes shining into your face?

You wondered who you were.

You couldn't move.

(45)

The conjunction of blue eyes and Japanese features, like the conjunction of
Japanese features and the "Harlem" suit, throws the identity of both viewed
and viewer into doubt. This doubt seems to contaminate memory itself, as
Inada writes toward the poem's end: "[W]hat comes second-hand / is not
the same. // Something is missing." In Inada's work, neither the example
of black identity nor the details of personal history are sufficient to ground
the Asian American subject.

Oka's and Inada's styles ultimately prove, for the 1970s at least, to be out-
liers, moments that show Asian American writers working within or borrowing from established traditions in American poetry and culture. It is,
instead, the work of Janice Mirikitani that proves to be, among *Aion's* writers, paradigmatic for the period. Mirikitani epitomizes the activist, populist
poet: her direct and explicitly political writing is matched by her commitment to political activism and community work, and her work as an editor

has included Third World, feminist, and Japanese American anthologies. Her style and credentials would seem to place her in opposition to university-trained professionals like Inada and make her less uncertain about the solidity of Asian American identity.

But even Mirikitani's work is much more complex than this, still vexed in its approach to Asian American writing. These tensions are evident in a 1976 interview in the *Asian American Review*, published out of the Ethnic Studies program at the University of California, Berkeley. The interviewer, Teri Lee, gives us the standard image of Mirikitani's work as a direct and raw poetry of protest:

> Her poetry speaks from a Third World perspective. Her images can be often savage, as she mourns the effects of the internment experience on the Japanese American self-image, attacks the war on Vietnam, screams at liberated White women who do not see the racist undercurrents in their own behavior. Her poetry also speaks joyfully of unity in struggle of Third World people. (36)[12]

Mirikitani in part supports this image, noting that "when you read poetry you spill your guts" (34), and argues for the need for writers of color to fight stereotypes and speak for themselves:

> Others are constantly trying to study, talk, *write* about us, resulting in distortions, myths, and lies about Third World people. . . . Even the well-meaning outside of the Third World cannot express the soul of it because they have not "lived in the house," and do not speak the depth of the language. (37)

But what is this "language" that Third World writers are to speak? Like other Asian American writers, Mirikitani is only able to say with certainty what this language is not:

> Now, Japan is part of the (Japanese American culture), but it is not *us*. We are a unique culture, authentic to us. . . . The Issei had a unique experience in this predominately White culture. Our experience in this White culture has GOT to be different from the White experience. And our experience has got to be different from the Asian experience. (38)

Remarkably enough, this question of cultural distinction, one that continues to haunt Asian American writers, turns out to be in part a question of poetic form. This may seem especially surprising given Mirikitani's own claims elsewhere in the interview that writers of color "don't have the luxury at this time" of concerning themselves with aesthetics; Lee writes, "Jan contends that Third World poetry must transcend the pure aesthetic and deal with concrete social and political issues" (38). But the "pure aesthetic" seems to be more an issue of content—poems, as Mirikitani puts it, "about bees, or birds, or nature." Poetic form, on the other hand, seems absolutely crucial to staking out a distinctive Asian American culture:

> For instance, I can't write haiku. And I feel that haikus written in English [are] a prostitution of the form, since it's a form specifically meant to be used in the Japanese language. But the feeling of the haiku—the cleanliness, the simplicity of the feeling, is something I can incorporate into MY language and MY style. Yet I have no desire to *copy* haiku. See what I mean? (38)

The haiku, as a poetic form, is a synecdoche for Japanese culture, but Mirikitani argues that the importation of the haiku's mere numerical pattern into English misses the essence of that form. One task of an Asian American writing, then, might be to discover an equivalent form in English that would capture the sensibility of the haiku without imitating it—an analogy for the Asian American subject herself.

Mirikitani's rejection of the "aesthetic" might also seem to place her in opposition to the Anglo-American canon. Yet her position turns out to be much more ambivalent than this. To label her anti-academic would be simplistic; she has, after all, done graduate work in creative writing, albeit at San Francisco State rather than at Iowa. Although it seems at times that it is only Third World writing that deserves the label "political," Mirikitani ultimately thinks better of this position:

> "When you pick up a Third World anthology, you don't want to read about bees, or birds, or nature, but you want to read about what experiences have made us suffer, what we have enjoyed, what makes us love. I mean, if you want to read something like 'Ash Wednesday', or 'Prufrock—'"
>
> She stops suddenly, hand arched in midair, and cocks her head to her side, eyelashes fluttering in thought. "But then, Prufrock is a political poem," she says aloud to herself. Her eyebrows furrow as she admits abstractedly, "Okay, Shakespeare's political too," but then she immediately hits the table with her fingers and says, "But that's Shakespeare's perspective. I want to hear Third World problems. From the people who can talk about it firsthand."

"I don't read poetry to escape. I want reality. That's what poetry should be. I'm very opinionated about that. I really am." (38)

Mirikitani begins to dismiss Eliot and Shakespeare—two pillars of the canon—as irrelevant, but realizes that the question of their relevance is not the same as asking whether or not they are "political." Her subsequent assertion that they *are* political may seem somewhat surprising; to argue that "The Love Song of J. Alfred Prufrock" is political is to expand one's sense of the political beyond the explicit assertion of a political position or the articulation of a dissident viewpoint. Instead, Mirikitani concludes that the political poetry that interests her can be measured by two traits: its *perspective* and the *reality* it portrays. A Third World poetry has to emerge, she suggests, from an alignment of these two elements: the realities of ethnic minority life in the United States told from a distinctively minority perspective—a unity, we might say, of content and form, if we understand form to include the sensibility or "feeling" of haiku that Mirikitani describes.

It should not surprise us, then, that the poems of Mirikitani's that appear in *Aion* are much less direct, much less easily read, than Lee's initial characterization might lead us to believe. The interview hints at this in discussing Mirikitani's attitude toward personal experience—in particular, her family's experience of being interned at the Tule Lake internment camp during World War II:

> Jan's own family was sent to Tule Lake, a desolate community on the California-Oregon border. She was too young to remember the camp experience, and her family is reluctant to discuss that time with her. Many of her internment poems are about her relatives. . . . Even in such mentally searing works, Jan is painstakingly careful to keep her voice separate from the other voices in her poems. "I write about my experience with that person—it's not fair to project myself and write as if I *am* that person." (40)

This indirectness or distance is evident in a poem by Mirikitani from *Aion* 1.1, written to accompany a photo-essay documenting conditions in San Francisco's Chinatown. The poem appears below a photograph of people walking through a rainy alley.

Broken alleys
clutching my
broken doorway

Rain
like nails
making a splintered wall
                    against my face

It pains me, too
that my umbrella is old

and my room
                empty.

                ("Broken" 15)

Mirikitani does, in fact, speak in the voice of a Chinatown resident here,
but the voice is quite different from that in some of her other works—the
line breaks more severe, the images concrete, the voice subdued. In fact, the
form and sensibility are quite close to what Mirikitani describes as emerging
from the haiku. Mirikitani represents but does not presume to speak for this
person; only "It pains me" is a direct expression of emotion, and even that
is ambiguous, displaced onto an arrangement of objects in the room.

Mirikitani's more characteristic voice is what might be called archetypal.
Her other poem in *Aion* 1.1, "Poem to the Alien/Native," presents a female
speaker in a dreamlike state who seems to move through all phases of wom-
anhood, from childhood to motherhood to old age:

I watched a child sleep
dreaming away her age
and we woke to the sound of
a woman dying.

    The old woman said:

    "A tree sprang from the belly of stone
    We bled for many days, I and the stone—
    The tree darkened.

    Worms choose my leaves
    to spin their graves.

    Moths die when born
    I was born old before beautiful."

                        (28–9)

The breaks are less charged than in the earlier poem, generally corresponding to the beginnings and ends of phrases, giving a more "natural" feel to
the lines. The diction tends toward the aphoristic or gnomic, the imagery
toward the elemental (stone, tree, leaves). This may, perhaps, be Mirikitani's
attempt to render a "Third World" consciousness. But it is less clear that
this poem presents the "realities" faced by U.S. minorities or that a peculiarly Asian American sensibility can be found within it.

The second issue of *Aion* contains two more Mirikitani poems that pull
her aesthetic in very different directions. "The Time Is Now" is her most
explicitly political poem, accompanying photographs of internment camps.
It is a model for those many Asian American historical poems that take
internment as a unifying experience for Asian American politics, linking
World War II–era racism to the war in Vietnam:

> You have seen the towers
> guarded in your bowels,
> Miniature high rise
> monuments to the white man's dream.
>
> > Amerika.
>
> Slow motion dust storms
> mushroom.
> And yellow skin sheds
> like pitiful leaves
> on burning trees.
>
> > Manzanar.
>
> > (99)

But Mirikitani's juxtaposition is far more indirect than another accompanying poem by Pat Sumi, "Tule Lake":

> TULE LAKE!
> You are the history we seek
> the defiance always there!
> You are the pride of our people
> the ancestor spirit of our movement!
> You are the otochan and okachan of us now.
>
> > (100)

Sumi's poem takes the form of revolutionary song or rallying call, address-ing itself directly to her "Brothers and Sisters" and anthropomorphizing the camp as a symbol. It is a public, not a personal response. Compare this to Mirikitani's other poem in the issue, "Tansaku":

A time too worn
by ghosts

Sometimes I am that spectre
seeking a refracted self
in language

Kotoba
Kagami—
soretomo tansaku   ka . . .

Language to fracture or mend.

There is less of me now
than when I began.

(57)

The ostensible subject is one raised in Mirikitani's interview: the Japanese American's alienated relation to the Japanese language. But perhaps more disturbing is the sense of how the self is "refracted," and perhaps even dis-sipated, in the poem, rather than that self's identification being confirmed or shored up. The ghostly, undefined quality of the Asian American self is thus evident in the work of writers as different as Mirikitani and Inada.

For poets of the 1970s, defining an Asian American perspective is thus a self-conscious and self-critical project, one that cannot take for granted the poetic form that is most appropriate for Asian American content. Indeed, the acknowledgment of the fragmentation of the Asian American self, and of the artifice necessary to articulate that self, is reminiscent of Language writer Ron Silliman's interest in presenting a "white male" perspective that is simultaneously broken up and undermined. In this sense, both Language and Asian American writing participate in a distinctively post-1970 avant-gardism, which openly acknowledges the social location of its emergence while using formal gestures that acknowledge the limits of that location.

If *Aion* shows a snapshot of Asian American poetics at the beginning of the 1970s, *Bridge*, one of the best-known Asian American publications of the period, can give us a good sense of its development over the decade. Published by the Basement Workshop, an Asian American arts and community organization in New York's Chinatown, *Bridge* began publishing in mid-1971 and continued through the mid-1980s.[13] It began as a Chinese American publication whose stated goal was to bridge the gap between immigrants and American-born Chinese, but it rapidly became a multiethnic Asian American publication. Although, like *Gidra*, it carried Asian American news, it adhered more to the format of a magazine, with theme issues, long articles, and interviews. It always published poems, but its commitment to literature gradually increased; by 1975 it was publishing a pull-out insert called "Poetry: An Asian American Perspective," and in October 1976 it published a special number, "Asian American Poetry 1976," with the work of over thirty poets. What *Bridge* illustrates is the gradual waning of avant-gardism in Asian American writing, characterized by a growing divide between Asian American aesthetics and Asian American politics, and culminating in a turn toward the personal lyric as the dominant paradigm of Asian American poetry.

Bridge lacks the consistently radical political program of *Aion*, a fact visible in its poetry as well as its prose. Even though Mirikitani rejects the poetry of "bees, birds, or nature" as apolitical, a poem in *Bridge*'s first issue by Eleanor S. Yung might well be characterized in that way:

And I heard your voice   in the green wilderness, like a stream
of sunlight coming through the sheltering of the leafy branches
And the shattering coolness is sprinkled by the songs of the birds

(19)

If poetry and politics are seen as continuous in *Aion*, in *Bridge* they are often an opposition to be carefully negotiated. By 1974 the journal is proposing "a series of annual awards for the best literary work published in these pages each year." In 1975 frequent contributor Fay Chiang publishes a poem called "For Those Who Runaway from the Movement." A report on the 1975 Asian American Writers Conference by Dale Yu Nee notes, apparently approvingly, that "there was a complete absence of any discussion of Imperialism, Indochina, Struggle, REVOLUTION. . . . This conference wasn't going to be any One Struggle Many Fronts Movement" (42).

Like *Aion*, *Bridge* published a number of articles on the question of Asian American culture and its relation to politics. Because of its interest in engaging with immigrants, *Bridge* did not share the position held by Mirikitani, Chin, and others that Asian American culture had to be understood

as radically separate from Asian culture. Its sense of possible continuities inflected its attempts to articulate what an Asian American culture might be.

The second issue opens with an editorial by Frank Ching, "American
in Disguise," which encourages the Chinese American to respond to the
"search for identity" with a "turn inward, seeking emotional security and
personal identity in his family and his parents' ancestral homeland" (4).
This turn to Asia is evident in the wide range of translated and Asian-
themed materials in *Bridge*, many of which serve to complicate the voice
of Asian American writing emerging from the magazine. *Bridge* 1.2 includes
Lo Yen's "Moon and Old Folks," translated by Wan Kin-lau, which employs
a style of juxtaposition of words borrowed by American modernist poets;
Bridge 1.4 publishes excerpts from a 1960 Chinese collection of songs and
poetry by Chinese laborers in the United States. And *Bridge* published a
number of installments from a martial arts novel, *Flying Fox of Snow Mountain*, translated from the Chinese.

Ching's assertion that Asian Americans could access Asia simply by turning inward, however, did not go unchallenged. The difficulty of "Japanese"
identification, and its potential toll on the self, is evident in Mirikitani's
and Inada's work. In *Bridge*, the challenge came in an exchange of letters
between Ching and Frank Chin, who would edit the groundbreaking anthology *Aiiieeeee!* and who was then coming into prominence as the author
of the play *The Chickencoop Chinaman*.

The initial part of the exchange was published in the December 1972
Bridge (2.2) as "Who's Afraid of Frank Chin, or Is It Ching?" The debate
took place around a discussion between Ching and Chin about publishing
part of *Chickencoop Chinaman* in *Bridge*. Ching had questioned Chin's rejection of connections with Chinese immigrants, and Chin responded with
a blistering attack on *Bridge*'s aesthetic:

> Your notion behind BRIDGE to appeal to both the immigrants and the
> American-born leaves me cold. . . . FLYING FOX OF SNOW MOUN-
> TAIN is a piece of shit. The writing is embarrassingly out of touch with
> any language any sensibility and wit. . . . There's no excuse for bad writing.
> . . . If the purpose of BRIDGE is to bind me to the immigrants, I'm not
> interested in being bound. If it is to acquaint me with immigrant thought,
> I find it dull and tediously working hard to be hip and/or intellectual/
> scholarly following white rules of language, argot, slang and grammar and,
> like Charlie Chan's Number One Son, fucking it all up badly and yet admi-
> rably. (Chin and Ching 31)

Chin here articulates his now-famous argument that Chinese American culture and sensibility are entirely distinct from either Chinese or white American culture and grounded in the historical experience of Chinese in America. But his rage is as much aesthetic as ideological: his major complaint is simply that *Bridge* is full of bad writing.

Chin's disagreements with other Asian American writers have often been understood as matters of political dogma—cultural nationalism, masculinity, an American-born sensibility. This exchange, however, shows us Chin as champion of aesthetics and the literary against the political, narrowly understood—a writer opposed to the kind of continuity between politics, culture, and writing that Mirikitani endorses. Chin reproaches Ching not merely for having the wrong political opinions but for neglecting Chin's achievements as a professional writer:

> [W]e do and should continue to work the way we know how. . . . For me that means practicing my trade and working my badmouth out into the open where it'll be heard, get all kinds of people mad, uptight, happy, thinking and told off. . . . Badmouth is my practice I like to work in the open and make them pay for. My plays, stories and novels are my work and have been working for me since 1962. Neither you nor Ralph Blumenthal ever heard of my literary motion before the 70's . . . but then, I'm not surprised. Why should you know anything about Chinese-American writing? (32)

Indeed, the only writer that Chin recommends to Ching is one whose politics he finds loathsome, Diana Chang. Chin endorses her on purely aesthetic grounds, as someone "whose work I respect and find fucked up as a thinker. . . . She fails to come to grips with her Chinese-American identity, but does repeat the clichés and racist stereotype with a certain style and an occasional nice line" (32).

Rather than defend himself by critiquing Chin's division of politics and literature, Ching surprisingly endorses it, apologizing for the poor quality of the writing in *Bridge* and adopting Chin's rhetoric of the "professional" writer:

> [Y]ou feel the quality of the writing is low. I readily concede that much of Bridge can be dull and uninspiring. That is because there are few professional Asian writers. Moreover, the Asian-American movement itself is so new that much of the literature that reflects and explains it is coming out of the universities, in the way of term papers, theses, etc. (34)

In this account, the rough, raw quality of Asian American writing is not, as Mirikitani might argue, the sign of a dissident sensibility; it is merely an effect of apprenticeship, one that will presumably disappear as Asian American writers mature.

By mid-decade, however, individualism was prevailing in the *Bridge* aesthetic. Although the journal continued to publish work by populist poets such as Mirikitani and Fay Chiang, more representative of the period's mood was the work of Alan Chong Lau. Lau did not lack activist credentials; Dale Yu Nee, in his report on the Asian American Writers Conference, describes him as "one of the most popular poets at San Francisco State before and during the Strike" (44). But his work displays a certain skepticism toward communal and activist projects, preferring to register the impact of historical and contemporary events on a sensitive individual consciousness.

Lau's first poem in *Bridge*, "my ship does not need a helmsman," appears in the February 1974 issue. According to Lau, however, the poem was written much earlier, during the San Francisco State strike:

> i was going to san francisco state university during the strike when [S. I.] hayakawa was president. we met in classes off campus with teachers who honored the strike and taught in their homes. in the evenings we would go into chinatown and volunteer to tutor kids at commodore stockton school and help out with their home work. i wanted to see this changing dynamic sweeping through chinatown through the eyes of an old-timer, a first generation member of the bachelor society who might be just a little confused and puzzled at the rapid changes going on right before his eyes. (E-mail)

The poem earns a mention from Garrett Hongo in his introduction to his 1993 anthology *The Open Boat*, a book that marked the full mainstreaming of Asian American poetry; Hongo writes that when he was handed the poem by a friend in Kyoto in 1973, "it was the most moving thing I'd yet read by anyone of my generation" (xxvii). What Hongo does not say is that what made the poem "moving" was also what made it a challenge to the politicized Asian American poetry of that moment. Although the poem in *Bridge* does not have an epigraph, in Lau's 1980 book *Songs for Jadina* an epigraph has been added that explains the title's punch:

> "a ship depends upon
> its helmsman for direction
> the great ship china
> is guided by mao tse tung"
> —as seen on the entrance to one of
> the floors of the people's republic

of china department store—
kowloon, hong kong[14]

Given the attraction of many radical Asian American groups to Maoism, Lau's declaration that "my ship does not need a helmsman" might well have read as a pointed critique of that brand of radical politics. The poem's speaker is an elderly immigrant living in poverty in Chinatown:

here i lie in chinatown
coughing into my mattress
soaked with the odors
of salted fishes
dark years old

home is not,
never was
this graygreased
smoke filled room

the walls smell the same
as the rotting wood crates
from china
that lie piled
with my memories
buried under old papers
scented with mothballs

(30)

He is precisely of that immigrant generation that *Bridge* is designed to link to younger activists. But the speaker rejects this mission, turning away activists' attempts to "organize" him with resignation:

the young barbarians
urge me to protest
in a western style,
this gray life

they thrust
red books in my face
but I see nothing
except the pigeons
leaving droppings
on my bench

> they do not realize
> i would rather
> withdraw from what
> i have never belonged to
> than to embrace it

(31)

The speaker does ultimately, as Frank Ching would put it, turn inward, but what he finds there is not political and cultural empowerment but the sadness of memory, "the bones / and ashes of my wife / who died waiting / in the home / of my province." The speaker's imagined refuge is not in politics but in privacy, in a longing for a lost domesticity:

> a ship does not need
> a helmsman
> only a woman
> who strokes my brow
> and laughs
> at the moon
> when it is full

(31)

It may be that the political power of this poem is in its pathos—its moving picture of a life lost to history, which might spur a reader into compassion and action. But there can be no question that its emotional effect derives directly from its explicit turn away from politics, from the "helmsmen" of the public world, whether they be statesmen or community organizers. Although Lau usefully points to the political context of the work's composition, the poem would seem to cast a skeptical eye on the activists with whom Lau identifies himself. If this poem, for writers like Hongo, is Asian American poetry coming into its maturity, it does so by separating the public and private and questioning poetry's explicit links to politics.

That Hongo chooses "my ship does not need a helmsman" as paradigmatic is no accident. For by the time of the publication of *The Open Boat* in the early 1990s, individualism and privacy had resoundingly prevailed in Asian American poetry. Hongo's anthology contained no poems by writers such as Fay Chiang, Francis Oka, or Pat Sumi; instead, it was dominated by poets like Lau, Cathy Song, David Mura, and Hongo himself, whose work focused on personal reflection and family history and declined to speak openly in a broader political dialect. By 1993, Hongo could, in his introduction, give this arch description of a "seventies" vision of "what the Asian American writer was supposed to be":

> [T]he Asian American writer was an urban, homophobic male educated at a California state university who identified with Black power and ethnic movements in general; he wrote from the perspective of a political and ethnic consciousness raised in the late sixties; he was macho; he was crusading; he professed community roots and allegiances; he mocked Eurocentrism and eschewed traditional literary forms and diction in favor of innovation and an exclusively colloquial style; and, though celebrated in the Asian American "movement," his work was widely unrecognized by "the mainstream." (xxxi)

It is easy enough to recognize this as a caricature of Frank Chin. But what Hongo does not acknowledge is that Chin was already, in the mid-1970s, advocating the individualist and professional approach that would allow Hongo to call for a rejection of political dogma in favor of "diversity, intellectual passion, and an appreciation of verbal beauty" (xxxvii). What has been erased by the 1990s is precisely the communal urge that characterized Asian American poetry at its outset, and the unease that accompanied its search for a distinctively Asian American voice. The avant-gardism of Asian American poetry would "disappear" for over a decade; it would be reclaimed again only in the mid-1990s, in the wake of radical shifts in the reception of Asian American and experimental writing.

FOUR

Audience Distant Relative

Reading Theresa Hak Kyung Cha

By the close of the 1970s, Language poetry and Asian American poetry had achieved a degree of success. Each now possessed a thriving community of writers with a sense of participation in a shared political and aesthetic project. Each had developed its own institutions of production and reception, from journals to reading series to anthologies, through which writing could be circulated and dialogues opened. And each had produced exciting, innovative work that pushed beyond what had been thought permissible or possible in previous American poetry, struggling to find appropriate poetic forms for the emerging social identities of the contemporary period. In short, Asian American poetry and Language poetry were now established avant-gardes, linking their existence as social groups to their aesthetic projects.

This did not mean, however, that either Asian American or Language writers had succeeded in reaching a wider literary audience. The successes both groups of writers enjoyed in the 1970s were very much in line with the avant-garde aspirations of that decade. Rather than producing great individual writers whose work would be praised according to widely accepted literary standards, Asian American and Language writing had established parallel channels in which such conventional standards did not apply and in which work that actively rebelled against those standards could flourish. These alternative channels themselves, as much as any individual poem that appeared within them, formed that critique of the dominant institutions of art that Peter Bürger finds characteristic of the avant-garde. And the very nature of such channels, with their restricted resources and audiences, meant that the work circulated through them would rarely reach readers beyond a tightly knit, like-minded community.

Yet avant-gardes, as Bürger also points out, can become victims of their own success. Although many journals of the 1970s were short-lived, some, like the Asian American publication *Bridge*, continued to publish regularly well into the 1980s, providing a stable forum in which poetry could be read by insiders and outsiders alike. It is no coincidence that Cathy Song, who became the first Asian American poet to gain mainstream poetic recognition when her 1982 book *Picture Bride* was selected for the Yale Younger Poets series, had one of her first major publications in *Bridge*. Meanwhile, the journal *L=A=N=G=U=A=G=E* played much the same role for Language writing, providing both a focal point for the movement and a means by which a wider audience could become familiar with the arguments underlying the Language project. In short, both groups' success in creating alternatives to mainstream writing had the paradoxical effect of attracting attention from the mainstream itself. When, as Bürger puts it, the avant-garde provocation becomes accepted *as art*, it can lose its critical potential, absorbed into the mainstream on the mainstream's own terms.

This mainstreaming of previously avant-garde work might best be described as a shift from a paradigm of writing to one of reading. The label "avant-garde" initially describes a distinctive context of artistic production: a small group of like-minded artists devising their own channels for the creation and distribution of unconventional work, with an audience largely limited to other members of the group, sympathetic peers, and a few mainstream readers whose sensibilities the work is in part designed to shock. Definitions of membership and aesthetics are often fluid, unnecessary for writers and readers who share the same social milieu. But as the work of the avant-garde begins to reach readers who are distant from the context of production, group labels come to function for such readers as new modes of reading, initiated by the original context of avant-garde production but often encompassing writers far removed from the founding group. Thus Sau-ling C. Wong's *Reading Asian American Literature*, published some two decades after the birth of Asian American writing, conceptualizes Asian American literature not as a body of work produced by a particular group of authors but as a "textual coalition" held together by similar themes and tropes (9). And as Language writing began to gain critical attention in the mid-1980s, readers came to see "Language poetry" as a broader category that included not only founding avant-gardists, like Ron Silliman and Charles Bernstein, but also writers only loosely affiliated with the movement, such as Susan Howe and Michael Palmer. Indeed, by the 1990s the label "Language poetry" itself had been subsumed by blanket terms such as "experimental" or "innovative" poetry, categories that encompassed writers from Jackson Mac Low to Jorie Graham and that were based not on avant-garde communities but on perceived stylistic deviations from the mainstream of American poetry.

As Asian American and Language writing drew attention from the mainstream, each became detached from its original social context and came to be perceived through more conventional categories. The understated, first-person lyrics of a poet like Cathy Song were consonant with the "workshop" style coming to dominate American poetry, helping to secure an image of Asian American poetry as a body of work that diverged from mainstream writing only in its overt themes, not in its politics or style. This interpretation was abetted by the paradigms that dominated the nascent field of Asian American literary criticism in the 1980s, with its emphasis—following Elaine Kim's groundbreaking 1982 study *Asian American Literature: An Introduction to the Writings and Their Social Context*—on the ways in which literature revealed the social history of Asian Americans. Language writing, in contrast, came to a wider audience through the critical work of *L=A=N=G=U=A=G=E* and the attention of academic critics, cementing its reputation as a poetry motivated primarily by theoretical and formal concerns. The result was a sharp divide along the lines of content and form—corresponding to the divide between different schools of critics—and a sense of experimental and ethnic writing not as analogous avant-garde formations but as separate projects with separate means and goals.

I explore this shift in our understandings of Asian American and Language writing through an examination of Theresa Hak Kyung Cha's book *Dictée*, which over the course of the 1980s went from an obscure text known only by Cha's white avant-gardist peers to a central document in the Asian American canon. Cha was neglected by Asian American critics through most of the decade in large part because a text with so many "experimental" features could not be understood as Asian American in its concerns—even though Cha's race helped ground *Dictée*'s appeal to its few white readers. Asian American readers' embrace of *Dictée* at the beginning of the 1990s was thus portrayed as a breakthrough, an opening up of Asian American writing to formal innovation and to transnational perspectives. But in practice the divide between Asian American and experimental paradigms remained intact, with Asian American critics focusing on *Dictée*'s narrative elements at the expense of its more abstract sections.

The paradoxical effect of *Dictée*'s canonization—and its presentation as a work that unified experimental forms and Asian American content—was to obscure the much more complex history of avant-gardism from which *Dictée* emerges, and to which *Dictée* itself is an eloquent testament. For *Dictée* is ultimately, I would argue, a divided text, one in which paradigms for reading Asian American and experimental writing are made visible and even, at times, brought into conflict with one another. The strange history of *Dictée*'s reception—from experimental to Asian American and perhaps back again—reveals the limits of our dominant paradigms of reading and forces us to return to the wider avant-garde contexts from which both Asian American and experimental writing emerge.

The poetic mainstream with which Language poetry and Asian American poetry engaged in the 1980s was dominated by the well-crafted, understated first-person lyric, whose aesthetic Charles Altieri labels the "scenic mode":

> Craft must be made unobtrusive so that the work appears spoken in a natural voice; there must be a sense of urgency and immediacy to this "affected naturalness" so as to make it appear that one is reexperiencing the original event; there must be a "studied artlessness" that gives a sense of spontaneous personal sincerity; and there must be a strong movement toward emphatic closure, a movement carried on primarily by the poet's manipulation of narrative structure. (10)

Vernon Shetley links the rise of this aesthetic with the rise of the creative writing workshop as a dominant force in contemporary poetry, labeling this dominant style the "MFA mainstream" (20). Language writer Charles Bernstein has even more forcefully argued for the institutional power of mainstream style by calling it, in his collection *Content's Dream*, a product of "official verse culture" (247)—a constellation that includes publications from the *New Yorker* to *Poetry* and the major trade and university publishers. The intertwining of institutions and aesthetics makes it difficult for new approaches to gain traction with mainstream readers and admits new authors only insofar as they can be adapted to the dominant paradigm of the lyric.

What happens when avant-garde discourses such as those of Language and Asian American writing encounter the mainstream is evident from the shifts in discussions of race and aesthetics among both groups during the 1980s. In the case of Asian American poetry, the success of Cathy Song's work not only set an example for mainstream readers, most of whom had likely never read poetry by an Asian American before, but also shifted the center of gravity within Asian American writing itself. Well-known writers of the 1970s, such as Lawson Fusao Inada and Janice Mirikitani, were eclipsed in favor of younger writers more consonant with the lyric mainstream, such as Song, David Mura, and Li-Young Lee. As I suggested at the end of the last chapter, Garrett Hongo's 1993 anthology *The Open Boat: Poems from Asian America* is the definitive statement of this shift, replacing the avant-garde, highly political paradigm of the 1970s with a focus on individual, lyric subjectivity.[1]

The Open Boat was the first anthology of Asian American poetry edited by an Asian American.[2] In his introduction, Hongo explicitly repudiates the image of the Asian American poet as politicized avant-gardist, labeling it an "older, culturally biased model of the Asian American writer," viewed as a remnant of "a political and ethnic consciousness raised in the late sixties." He criticizes the "vulgar few" who would still demand that Asian American literature be representative on the basis of "professed community loyalties" (xxxi–xxxii). Instead, Hongo advocates a poetics of the individual lyric voice: "It is perhaps difficult to make a poetry from that emotional catch in the throat, that which compels us to speak when so much passion swells that, out of pride, the act of speaking is what we might fear the most. But our poets speak anyway" (xl). The 1970s debates over the forms of Asian American expression have been replaced by a focus on pure content: "We write about violence to women, about the paintings of Utamaro and Willem de Kooning, about plantation workers and picture brides, about factory work and the pleasures/dangers of sex. We write about our Eurasian children" (xix). Asian American identity, for Hongo, is refigured in institutional and academic terms. Hongo's introduction opens with an account of the meeting of the Asian American Literature Study Group at the 1990 MLA conference—a meeting at which "a new community was in the process of bringing itself together" (xvii).

Hongo's rejection of politicized, avant-garde rhetoric in favor of a naturalized conception of poetic art—"We lift our voices, bodies from the sand, and call" (xlii)—suggests how effectively Asian American poetry, by the early 1990s, has aligned itself with a mainstream aesthetic, as does his catalog of Asian American writers' success in the elite realms of academia, publishing, and government.[3] The selections in *The Open Boat* reflect this new alignment, emphasizing younger writers of first-person, autobiographical lyrics, while including relatively little work by such major 1970s poets as Lawson Fusao Inada and Janice Mirikitani and neglecting other significant Asian American poets of the 1970s entirely. But Hongo's anthology, and the aesthetic that it represents, has come to be the face of Asian American poetry for most non–Asian American readers. And reading through the pages of *The Open Boat*—which includes only two poets, John Yau and Mei-mei Berssenbrugge, whose work had previously been recognized as having experimentalist tendencies—it is not difficult to understand why many readers would characterize ethnic writing as conventional in form, focused purely on the telling of personal stories, and radically separate from the practice of white language-oriented poets.

It is this literary landscape—apparently divided between an "experimental" poetry of form and an "ethnic" writing of pure content—that guided the reception of Theresa Hak Kyung Cha's *Dictée* through the 1980s and into the 1990s. Published in 1982, *Dictée* spent most of its first decade in obscurity, read only by a few critics and ignored by Asian American readers. Yet by the mid-1990s, *Dictée* occupied a secure place in the Asian American canon. It was the subject of an influential collection of essays by prominent Asian American critics; it was the centerpiece of Lisa Lowe's paradigm-shifting 1996 study *Immigrant Acts*; and it had become a staple of Asian American literature syllabi. *Dictée*'s unlikely history of reception—and its continuing ability to trouble settled modes of reading—provides a map of the conflicts between the paradigms established for reading experimental and Asian American writing and forces us to return to the more complex history of both as avant-gardes.

The recent apotheosis of *Dictée* is all the more striking given Asian American readers' strong resistance to the text during the 1980s. Elaine Kim, whose 1982 study *Asian American Literature* was the first major work of Asian American literary criticism, opens the 1994 collection *Writing Self, Writing Nation* with the admission that she initially found Cha's work completely alienating: "The first time I glanced at *Dictée*, I was put off by the book. I thought that Theresa Cha was talking not to me but rather to someone so remote from myself that I could not recognize 'him'" (Kim and Alarcón 3).

In her contribution to the collection, L. Hyun Yi Kang writes, "I found myself literally yelling at the book. . . . It angered me that the text was not always accessible, that it seemed to speak to a highly literate, theoretically sophisticated audience that I did not identify with. Most of all, Cha herself remained elusive" (Kim and Alarcón 75–6). How did such an opaque, difficult, infuriating text come to be a cornerstone of Asian American literature? What made *Dictée* illegible in 1982 and legible in 1994—and, in particular, legible as an Asian American text?

Cha's art of the 1970s displays her deep engagement with language itself. Personal and historical relationships become, in her work, linguistic ones; persons become understood as positions within language. Cha's interest in, and rewriting of, the work of Beckett demonstrates her turn away from narrative and identification and toward the exploration of linguistic structures, an impulse toward abstraction that also animates *Dictée*. It was through such concerns, with their feminist and psychoanalytic underpinnings, that Cha's work was understood during the 1980s. Cha's peers, and her readers, located the political power of her work in her critique of dominant historical narratives, evident in her juxtaposition of photographs, historical documents, and personal reflections.

Although Cha's identity as Asian American seemed absent from this avant-garde discourse—a discourse dominated by white artists and critics—her race remained covertly present through a form of orientalism, which we might call American postmodern orientalism. Whereas American modernist orientalism, exemplified by the work of Ezra Pound and Marianne Moore, might have been defined by ideograms and chinoiserie, postmodern orientalism is defined by the catastrophe of the war in Vietnam. The desire to understand and even identify with the East, as epitomized in the Buddhism of poets like Allen Ginsberg and Gary Snyder, can be understood as a critique of American national culture. Yet insofar as it becomes a regime for the production of "authentic" knowledge of Asia that can be incorporated into American discourse, it takes on an orientalizing function. White avant-garde discourse understood Cha not as American ethnic but as orientalized other, whose work could be read as part of a discourse animated by resistance to U.S. wars in Asia. In a curious doubling, Cha's formal innovations were understood as both the product of American avant-garde training and as a marker of racial and national difference, a fact that gave Cha's work an authenticity not allowed to white avant-gardists.

It was precisely the experimental style of *Dictée* that made it unreadable to Asian American criticism—or, at least, Asian American criticism of the late 1970s onward, which largely overlooked Asian American poetic experiments in favor of the autobiographical narrative. The telling of Asian American stories through such narratives—forms that were, not coincidentally, consonant with those Asian American works finding the greatest mainstream success—was at the core of the "cultural nationalism" of the 1970s and 1980s; it was the questioning of this paradigm in the early 1990s that opened the door for Asian American readings of *Dictée*. But *Dictée* assumed a paradoxical role as both effect and cause of the paradigm shift— most notably in the work of Lisa Lowe, who found in *Dictée* a model of a newly heterogeneous and hybrid Asian American culture.

Reclaiming *Dictée* as an Asian American work, in the face of competing claims by white avant-garde critics, meant reinterpreting Cha's "experimental" techniques as somehow distinctively Asian American. But the reception of *Dictée* by Asian American critics shows that reconciling Cha's writing with the perceived political foundations of Asian American criticism proved a difficult task. In order to claim the text as Asian American, readers continue to fall back on biographical and narrative markers, neglecting those parts of *Dictée* that aim precisely to question such identifications. Insisting that *Dictée* is an Asian American text may very well mean questioning whether the "Asian American," as understood through narrative, can continue to have any coherence at all.

Dictée itself, I argue, can offer us a trajectory through these political and critical battles, although its vision unsettles our received understandings of both experimental and Asian American perspectives. *Dictée's* multiple structures of organization—mythic, historical, biographical, linguistic—are often at odds with one another, undermining any single paradigm of reading. Although most Asian American critics focus on the treatment of Korean history in the text's early sections, the great theme of the book is in fact the paralysis caused by historical and mythical thinking. The book's critically neglected second half is an attempt to move toward an abstraction of historical and personal relationships, a move anticipated in Cha's visual art; it is also, finally, an embrace of writing itself as the master discourse that moves out into agency from the stasis of history.

Dictée is truly a divided text. Cha insists that the book's first half— whose historical and biographical impulses we might ally with the Asian

American—must be followed by the "experimental" and abstracting turn of the second half, in order to return to a "home" that can only be located in writing. The mainstream Asian American paradigm ultimately proves inadequate to *Dictée*'s task. But the text also questions whether the white avant-garde from which *Dictée* springs has a place for history and race that is no longer understood in terms of orientalism and otherness. As a limit case for both Asian American and experimental writing, *Dictée* illustrates the aesthetic and political contradictions of each category, posing crucial questions for the politics of contemporary literature and criticism, and returning us to the idea of an avant-garde of which experimental and Asian American poetics are different but linked expressions.

Upon its publication in 1982, *Dictée* went largely unnoticed. Apart from a brief, though positive, review by Donald Richie in the *Japan Times*, *Dictée* received no serious critical attention until 1986, when Michael Stephens gave it a substantial treatment in his book *The Dramaturgy of Style*. Two further discussions of *Dictée* appeared in the later 1980s: Stephen-Paul Martin devoted a chapter to Cha in his *Open Form and the Feminine Imagination* (1988), and Robert Siegle discussed *Dictée* in his chapter on Tanam Press in *Suburban Ambush* (1989). All three of these critics read Cha as part of what can be broadly called experimental contemporary writing, associating her with writers like Gilbert Sorrentino, Kathy Acker, Susan Howe, and Ron Silliman; they see some feminist themes in Cha's work, but they do not, by and large, discuss her as an American minority writer.

That Cha is not, in the 1980s, discussed as an Asian American writer cannot be understood simply, as Elaine Kim claims in *Writing Self, Writing Nation*, as neglect of the book's engagement with Korea and Korean history (Kim and Alarcón ix). In fact, Richie, Stephens, and Siegle all dwell quite extensively on Cha's reexamination of Korean colonial history. Nor can it be attributed to a reading of Cha as merely a "writer," without regard to race; Stephens clearly understands Cha as fundamentally a Korean artist, while Siegle displays a nuanced awareness of race in his discussion of other writers. Instead, what is at issue is a phenomenon diagnosed by Asian American writers and critics in the 1970s: the Asian American writer continues to be regarded by the white American reader as remaining fundamentally Asian in outlook and temperament, unalterably foreign. The insistence by activists, writers, and scholars on the integrity of the category "Asian American" was an attempt to create an identity that was neither simply Asian nor equivalent to that of white America. But for many critics, Cha's formal difference was sometimes easily read as cultural difference, as foreignness—a slippage that haunts not only white critics but later Asian American critics as well.

Michael Stephens's *Dramaturgy of Style*, which provides the first substantial critical account of *Dictée*, surveys an eclectic and international collection of writers, beginning with such figures as Beckett, Kafka, and Borges. The core of his study is, though, American writers of the 1960s—Paul Blackburn, Joel Oppenheimer, Gilbert Sorrentino. Stephens's chapter on *Dictée* is titled "Korea: Theresa Hak Kyung Cha," demonstrating that nation and national culture are crucial to Stephens's understanding of authorship and voice: Beckett, for example, is a fundamentally "Irish" writer, a fact that determines the rest of his work. But when Stephens writes elsewhere of "the fiction of Vietnam," he does not mean the work of Vietnamese writers but the writing of Americans about Vietnam, defined entirely by the Vietnam War. This imbalance—West as subject, East as object—is, of course, the fundamental insight of Said's *Orientalism*, but it has a peculiar twist in the American context, given the history of American intervention in Asia in the twentieth century; "Vietnam" and "Korea" signify not only nations in Southeast and East Asia but sites in American history and culture. Stephens's reading of *Dictée* is thus framed by an orientalism that is not only peculiarly American but distinctively postmodern, defined by the Vietnam War and resistance to that war. The American engagement with Asian culture in the wake of the 1960s, from the Buddhism of poets Gary Snyder and Allen Ginsberg to Stephens's own interest in the samurai ethic, can be understood as the flip side of American imperialism in Asia—a critical response to that imperialism that can itself become a form of appropriation.

Like Elaine Kim and L. Hyun Yi Kang, Stephens finds himself nearly defeated by the difficulty of Cha's formal techniques, prefacing his chapter on Cha with a section titled "Notes from an Abandoned Work." Frustrated in his attempts to write about *Dictée*, Stephens travels to Korea to visit his wife's family, hoping that a walk through the landscape of Cha's country of origin will illuminate the text:

> It was that old thing about experiencing Korea through your thighs and calves, and I thought maybe this walk would clear my head about *Dictée*. . . . [I]t is this landscape of mountains and rivers without end, which has to be evoked to understand the roots of Theresa Cha's voice. . . . Beauty and sadness, they seesaw in my mind, placing one foot on one stone, the

other foot on the next stone, feeling Korea, as I say, in my legs, ascending this mountain path. (188–90)

This equation of Cha's voice with the landscape of Korea allows Stephens to understand Cha as an essentially Korean subject, uncontaminated by immigration or Americanization. And in this guise, Cha is a presence Stephens can literally feel, unmediated by language—in contrast to the difficulties of her text. More important, by translating Cha into the landscape of Korea, Stephens is able to incorporate Cha—and by extension, Korea itself—into his own body, "feeling Korea . . . in *my* legs." This cultural identification proves to be Stephens's key to *Dictée*, allowing him to see the text, despite its difficulty, as a transparently autobiographical work. Cha herself becomes a "kindred spirit," a person who "would have been one of my good friends . . . we would have gotten along very well" (188).

Robert Siegle's *Suburban Ambush* provides a more nuanced treatment of Cha's work; yet Siegle, like Stephens, is willing to regard Cha as "other," as outside the ideology that constrains white artists. Siegle focuses his attention on what he regards as a single, relatively coherent artistic scene, "a concentration of talent and productivity in the region stretching from Tribeca to the Lower East Side in New York" (xi). Writers such as Kathy Acker, Constance DeJong, and Lynne Tillman, Siegle argues, "connect their reflexive analysis of the possibilities of narrative with an equally penetrating awareness of the social realities beyond the realm of art. . . . [E]nergetic reflexivity inevitably takes one deep into a critical engagement with the social, political, and economic structures of the culture" (xii–xiii). The major target of this work is the commodification of culture, particularly through the mass media.

Siegle describes the artists he studies as inhabiting the margins of society, the interstices of downtown New York; this position makes it possible for them to speak in a "nonhegemonic tongue," and their "best work gives voice to a lost Other" (7). However, Siegle is quite astute about the ways in which the marginalization of these "city-dwelling suburban exiles and fortunate urbanites of the postmodern persuasion" may be analogous to, but not identical to, that of "their black, Hispanic, or immigrant neighbors" (8). Although the "Other" for which this art speaks may be "one shaped by race, or class, or gender, or belief" (7), the actual artists that Siegle describes are nearly all white. "Otherness" is universalized, not particularized, in ways that raise the specter of race without addressing it in any concrete way.

This paradoxical position of privileged/marginalized white urbanite gives these artists, Siegle suggests, a particular awareness that their voices are constantly being co-opted: "[I]t does not expect of itself the pure voice of the Other—it knows its own language is divided against itself, its every move a contradiction that marks the position of the speaking subject at the end of the twentieth century" (4). No speech is uncontaminated, no gesture of opposition immune to assimilation. Yet in Siegle's account, outside this system there does seem to remain some residue of opposition, in actual communities of social marginalization—those working-class and minority communities for which the art community is only an analogy, and occasionally an adversary. Siegle discusses the work of Latino writers such as Bimbo Rivas and Miguel Piñero in relation to, but never as part of, the community of white artists; Rivas and Piñero are representative of those who "have lived through *real* revolutions," not just artistic ones (8). Rivas is "[a]n Other to any conceivable home," and Piñero is "someone used to telling it like it really is," to whom white Lower East Side artists "turn for inspiration" (9). This self-conscious and cynical art world thus does have its own romance with the Other, an Other defined by race.

In the case of Cha, the vesting of authenticity in the nonwhite subject intersects with American orientalism. Identifying with the Asian other becomes a way to escape from the boundaries of nation, opposing American identity by identifying with a culture whose foreignness is inassimilable, irreducible. And it is in these terms, I suggest, that we can understand the interest in Asian culture and mysticism present not only in many of the artists Siegle examines, but in the Bay Area art scene from which Cha emerged. The name of Tanam Press, the publisher of *Dictée* and one of the groupings Siegle discusses, is drawn from Sanskrit (meaning "endless, thou"), and Tanam Press publisher Reese Williams's own work takes as its end point what Siegle calls "Eastern meditations" or "Zenlike states" that Williams himself describes in terms of yin and yang. Such gestures are part and parcel of a political sensibility shaped by resistance to the war in Vietnam; Eastern mysticism becomes, for these writers, a means of identifying with and incorporating the Asian other who is the victim of American power.

It is in this context, I would argue, that Cha's work, and her race, would have been received by her peers in the Bay Area and New York art worlds—as consonant with the mysticism and orientalism already present in those circles. Whereas Siegle, for instance, quite consciously distinguishes the work of his white artists from the discourse of Latinos or African Americans, he seems not to register that several of the artists he discusses, including Cha and video artist Nam June Paik, are Asian American—a fact that would be less surprising if Siegle did not draw such attention to race elsewhere. Although such a silent assimilation would seem to be quite the opposite of Stephens's positioning of Cha as Korean and foreign, I would suggest that Stephens and Siegle represent flip sides of a single position present in the avant-garde art world of the 1970s and 1980s, one based on an orientalized gesture of identification. Stephens sets Cha up as Asian and foreign and then proceeds to identify with her; Siegle understands the Asian as already identified with the American, through Vietnam and mysticism, and seamlessly absorbs Cha as a representative of these tendencies.

Siegle's reading of *Dictée* itself is persuasive, though brief, doing justice to the book's complexities and various layers of organization. He does not exoticize Cha's work, nor does he question her status as an accomplished American artist. Siegle does, however, signal that Cha is primarily to be read through the discourse of resistance to U.S. war in Asia. His focus is on *Dictée*'s critique of the "official historian," whose reliance on "automatic word choice, prefabricated syntax, and conventionalized rhetoric" is obviously linked to U.S. war reportage, a paradigm of the media culture examined by other artists in Siegle's book. And although Siegle resists the urge to reduce Cha's work to autobiography, he does place a greater emphasis than he does for other writers on Cha's "struggling for speech," calling *Dictée* "its narrator's effort to open a cultural window in order to ring out the full resonance of the voice of her personal, family, national, racial, and gender histories" (242). For other artists, "there is no outside" to the system, as Siegle notes later in the book; in Cha's case, however, it does seem possible to escape, to gain "some measure of individual identity" (238), to give voice to otherness. I think the only explanation for Siegle's optimism here—though he never states it—is that Cha is a racialized, foreign subject, outside the commodified national culture and hence closer to some form of authenticity.

These early readings of Cha suggest the limits of simply seeing *Dictée* as an "avant-garde" work in some general sense. Although Stephens and Siegle both seek to link Cha to other white experimental writers, race is always covertly present as a determining factor. Yet the experimentalist aesthetic offers no way to account for the impact of race on the work beyond the lens of orientalism. A full account of *Dictée*, then, would seem to require reading

Cha's avant-gardism through an Asian American paradigm. Although this reclaiming of Cha as Asian American writer would be taken up by Asian American critics in the 1990s, such critics would also have to grapple with Cha's isolation from any extant Asian American community, making a reading of racial themes in her work challenging indeed.

The efforts by Elaine Kim and other Asian American critics to claim *Dictée* as an Asian American text in the early 1990s were explicitly intended as a response to readings such as those by Stephens and Siegle. They were necessary, Kim and her colleagues suggested, because these readings had been insufficiently political or materialist—a claim that later Asian American critics have largely accepted.[4] But as we have seen, white critics did find great political value in Cha's work and, in particular, in the forms of *Dictée*. Kim's claim on the politics of *Dictée* must be understood not simply as a corrective but as an attempt to shift the ground of literary-political value within Asian American criticism itself.

Although the project of *Writing Self, Writing Nation* was begun in 1991, the first significant published notice of *Dictée* by an Asian American critic was by Kim in her foreword to the 1992 collection *Reading the Literatures of Asian America*, edited by Shirley Lim and Amy Ling. Lim and Ling's collection was one of a number of books of the early 1990s that sought to shift the terms of Asian American studies away from what was coming to be called the "cultural nationalist" paradigm of the 1970s and 1980s. In the narrative told by these revisionist critics, cultural nationalism, modeled on black nationalism and other ethnic-consciousness movements of the late 1960s, sought to define and express an essential "Asian American" identity that was absolutely separate from either Asian or white American identities. Its primary expositors on the cultural front were held to be the editors of the 1974 anthology *Aiiieeeee!* and in particular the prominent essayist, playwright, and novelist Frank Chin, but pioneering works of Asian American criticism such as Kim's *Asian American Literature* were understood to have been written under the aegis of cultural nationalism. This early work in Asian American studies focused primarily on the two largest ethnic groups, Chinese Americans and Japanese Americans, and tended, as Kim's work did, to see literature as a window into the social history and personal experience of Asian Americans.

Even though Asian American critics of the 1990s acknowledged the political necessity of insisting on a coherent Asian American cultural identity in the 1970s, they argued that such cultural nationalism had become both ideologically and historically problematic. Cultural nationalism, they argued, was exclusionary, not only because of its use of Chinese and Japanese Americans as a stand-in for all Asian Americans but because of the masculinism of Chin and the other *Aiiieeeee!* editors, who took the reclaiming of Asian American manhood as one of their primary goals and frequently criticized female Asian American writers as sellouts. Moreover, revisionist critics claimed that cultural nationalism was an idea whose historical moment had passed, particularly given the emergence of newer immigrant groups from South and Southeast Asia who complicated any unitary notion of Asian American identity.

The new paradigm these critics offered would perhaps be best captured by Lisa Lowe at mid-decade: "hybridity, heterogeneity, multiplicity." Asian American identity was acknowledged to be not a single experience but many experiences, complicated not only by diverse ethnicities but by crosscutting categories of gender, class, and sexuality. Asian American studies also needed to respond to a globalizing world by shifting from a U.S.-centered to a transnational paradigm, one that acknowledged movements of persons and capital back and forth between Asia and America and that did not ignore the continuing cultural and economic linkages between Asia and Asian diasporic communities in the United States.

Some books of the late 1990s, particularly those by Jinqi Ling and Rachel Lee, have raised questions about this wholesale rejection of cultural nationalism, arguing for the continued importance of "America" as a rubric for Asian American studies and suggesting that "cultural nationalism" caricatures the complicated negotiations of Asian American critics in the 1970s. Nonetheless, in the early 1990s—the moment when *Dictée* appeared in Asian American critical discourse—the consensus was that a new paradigm was needed. But how would work under such a paradigm differ from work under cultural nationalism? And—perhaps the most insistent and difficult of all—what would be the political grounding of the new Asian American studies, if cultural nationalism had formerly provided that grounding?

It is these questions that are raised by the reception of *Dictée*; in fact, as Kim's foreword to *Reading* shows, *Dictée* presents itself at the precise point of rupture between the old and new paradigms, both as cause and effect of this paradigm shift. Kim begins her foreword with an account of cultural nationalism, which "has been so crucial in Asian Americans' struggle for self-determination: insisting on a unitary identity seemed the only effective means of opposing and defending oneself against marginalization" (Lim and Ling xi). Such an identity, although politically expedient, "was necessarily exclusive rather than inclusive, leveling such critical differences as gender, nationality, and class" (xii). But shifting historical conditions, including wider reading of Asian American texts and increased mobility between Asia and America (making the line between the two "increasingly . . . blurred" [xiii]), have created the possibility of a new "cultural pluralism," which celebrates difference and "the dynamic nature of our communities" (xiv–xv), moving beyond the exclusions of cultural nationalism.

On the surface, Kim's suggestions do not appear radical; it would seem that her goals could be achieved through a broadening of the scope of the older paradigm. But Kim's choice of *Dictée* as her example of a text that "brings us vivid new ways of thinking about Asian Americans, culture, and identity" (xv) suggests that a true rupture has occurred within Asian American literature. Kim here makes the remarks about being "put off" by the book with which she later opens *Writing Self, Writing Nation*, and which I have discussed above. What Kim foregrounds is her initial failure to identify with the book, a failure so extreme that she cannot even imagine sharing the same gender with Cha's assumed reader: "[S]he was addressing her haunting prose to someone so distant from myself that I could not recognize 'him'" (xv). The experience of reading *Dictée*, Kim writes, at first seemed incompatible with her struggles "to recuperate what I thought was 'my' Korean American identity" (xv). Kim here distances and ironizes her gestures of ownership and identification, suggesting the ways in which *Dictée* consistently blocks such strategies of reading.

Ultimately, however, Kim does return to identification to approach *Dictée*, an approach most evident in her contribution to the 1994 collection *Writing Self, Writing Nation*. The collection is itself methodologically split: Kim and L. Hyun Yi Kang seek to personalize *Dictée*, bringing it into line with earlier paradigms for Asian American writing, while Lisa Lowe and Shelley Sunn Wong hail *Dictée* as a work that opens up Asian American identity, exposing its multiple and shifting forms. Yet Lowe and Wong also seek to find in *Dictée* a new grounding for Asian American identity, one that may not fully acknowledge the radical potential of *Dictée* to transform Asian American literature.

Both Kim and Kang foreground their personal investments in and response to the book, framing their essays in terms of their own histories.

Kim narrates her own frustrations in traveling to Korea, and facing Korean gender expectations, to open an account of how Cha creates "a space where 'woman' and 'Korean' might work together" (Kim and Alarcón 7). Kang also writes that her initial encounter with *Dictée* was a frustrating one, but she was eventually able to appreciate how Cha's linguistic experiments do, indeed, mirror Kang's own "multiple relations to language" as "a bilingual Korean immigrant" (Kim and Alarcón 73).

It is identification that allows Kim and Kang to make their surprising leap, from their resistance to *Dictée* to the claim that *Dictée* is a distinctively Korean American work. Although *Dictée* does not provide a recognizable autobiographical narrative, Kim and Kang focus on those elements of the text that seem most autobiographical, and read those elements as a narrative of Cha's experience—in contrast to the text's own nonnarrative impulses. The stories that are thus extracted from *Dictée* are then paralleled to Kim and Kang's own personal stories, creating a narrative identification that produces a filiative sense of Korean American identity. Kim's identification of "the daughter" as a unitary protagonist in *Dictée*, and her reading of this protagonist's narrative in terms of generational conflict,[5] presents *Dictée* as a classic narrative of Asian American identity, one consonant with the concerns of cultural nationalism.

The other two essays in the collection, in contrast to Kim's and Kang's, acknowledge the more radical possibility that the reading of *Dictée* as an Asian American text marks a true rupture in the very concept of the Asian American. In their contributions, Lisa Lowe and Shelley Sunn Wong reject the idea that *Dictée* can be absorbed into an expanded notion of the Asian American. Instead, they place *Dictée* at the divide between an older model of cultural nationalism and an emergent paradigm of hybridity, multiplicity, and difference. But these readings, in their anxiety about the move away from cultural nationalism, do not give a full account of Cha's formal strategies and their potentially subversive effects. Lowe, while emphasizing *Dictée*'s antirealist and antiessentialist elements, understands *Dictée* in essentially narrative terms. It is Wong who comes closest to a full reading of the politics of *Dictée*'s form, in part because she is willing to read *Dictée* as a poetic rather than narrative text; and it is in Wong's essay that the category of "Asian American" comes most into doubt as an adequate rubric for understanding Cha's writing.

Lowe's "Unfaithful to the Original: The Subject of *Dictée*" is perhaps the most influential essay written on Cha's work, not least because it forms the centerpiece of Lowe's seminal 1996 book *Immigrant Acts*. For Lowe, *Dictée* is the text that best embodies her notion of an Asian American culture that is hybrid, heterogeneous, and multiple, offering a site of resistance to American discourses of abstract citizenship and nationalism. *Dictée*, in Lowe's theoretically sophisticated reading, evokes a writing subject that is not determined by any single national, linguistic, or racial identification but that instead emerges in the "confluences and disjunctions" of such identities, a process demonstrated by a text that "repeatedly calls attention to the varied locations of its writing" (Kim and Alarcón 36). *Dictée*, Lowe argues, opens up "a dialectic between the politics of identity and the politics of difference," suggesting the possibility of an Asian American writing that "engages with rather than suppressing heterogeneities of gender, class, sexuality, race and nation" while still "maintain[ing] and extend[ing] the forms of unity which make common struggle possible" (63–4). In this last sentiment, Lowe curiously echoes the sentiments of Elaine Kim, who sees in *Dictée* a text in which "we can 'have it all'" (Lim and Ling xvi). But Lowe's own reading, focusing on the critical rather than constructive elements of Cha's work, on difference rather than identity, raises the question of how *Dictée*, after dismantling the foundations of identity, gives us a means to begin building again.

Lowe's confidence in *Dictée*'s potential may be grounded in her close readings of *Dictée*, which ultimately join those of Kim and Kang in reading the text in terms of narrative content and "voice." Lowe argues that *Dictée* is not a developmental narrative of individual self-realization—a rejection of the terms underlying Kim's and Kang's readings of the text. Yet Lowe also speaks of the text in terms of a single "narrator," a consistent presence from section to section whose connection to the material is biographical; the student doing dictation exercises at the book's opening is understood to be the same person who tells her mother's story in "Calliope." Lowe further reads the book as a process of this protagonist's coming into "voice," albeit a "hybrid, nuanced, 'unfaithful' voice" (47).

Lowe's interpretation of *Dictée* in terms of an individual's coming to voice allows her to maintain the unity of the Asian American subject in the face of multiplicity. But such an approach may give insufficient weight to the resistance in Cha's work to the voicing of personal narrative, even as biographical elements inform the work. How, in Lowe's reading, are we to understand sections like "Erato," which gives third-person cinematic and religious vignettes on facing pages, or "Thalia," which includes a facsimile of a 1915 letter to "Laura Claxton" from "H. J. Small"—both unidentified?

Indeed, it could be argued that what is distinctive in *Dictée* is its pronounced *lack* of narrative content, its refusal to provide the full facts of its stories. "Melpomene," for example, offers us several different elements that do not seem to add up to an extractable narrative of incorporation. It opens with a map of a divided Korea, followed by a third-person vignette that seems to describe a woman sitting in a cinema, followed by a letter, headed "Dear Mother," that moves between the 1950s, 1960s, and the present, describing protests and soldiers at their posts. The events recounted in the letter are ambiguous enough that some readers have assumed Cha's own brother was killed in a Korean student protest. Cha does not provide a historical narrative to contextualize these events, nor does she identify the significance of the specific dates that she gives. Whatever Cha's contribution is, it is not in providing counternarratives to dominant historical narratives; any full account of her work must ask why she declines to tell not just the conventional story but any "story" at all.

Of the four contributors to *Writing Self*, only Shelley Sunn Wong focuses on the ways in which *Dictée* does *not* tell stories, understanding the fundamental principle of *Dictée* as poetic rather than narrative. Wong's connection of *Dictée* to concerns in contemporary poetry, particularly those around the concept of the lyric "I," acknowledges the consonance of Cha's writing with other avant-garde and poststructuralist concerns. Wong notes that "*Dictée*'s insistence on multiple subjectivities would seem to contradict any effort to enshrine a mode of literary production traditionally premised on a single, unified, autonomous consciousness or identity—that of the lyric 'I'" (Kim and Alarcón 117). Given this "instability and unsettledness of subject positions" in *Dictée*—an instability present even in *Dictée*'s shifting use of grammatical persons—Wong notes that reading Cha raises the paradoxical possibility that "if there is a foundational moment for minority discourse, it is to be located . . . within the anti-foundational moment and space of dictation" (120).

Wong's acknowledgment of *Dictée*'s unstable subject positions is not without consequences; her refusal to read *Dictée* as a narrative emanating from a unified "I" raises the question of whether *Dictée* should be read as an Asian American text at all. Thus Wong is the only critic explicitly to incorporate and rebut white experimentalist readings of Cha, since such readings are particularly perilous for her claims that *Dictée* is distinctively Asian American. Wong closes her essay by decrying "appropriations" of *Dictée* by critics who neglect specific issues of race and nationality. She cites Stephen-Paul Martin, whose reduction of *Dictée* to "feminist experimental writing" effectively "neutralizes" its multivalent critique of race and nation, as well as Priscilla Wald, whose discussion of *Dictée* in general terms of "hybridity" and "alterity" neglects "the specific and material social conditions out of which Cha attempted to speak the difference of the Korean American immigrant woman" (135). But Wong's ammunition against these positions is limited by her acknowledgment that the "Korean American immigrant woman" is a position to which *Dictée* itself refuses to give any determinate content. The ground for claiming *Dictée* as an Asian American text remains very much in question.

Although the four readings in *Writing Self* present *Dictée* as marking a shift in Asian American critical paradigms, all ultimately pull back from the most radical difficulties of reading this text as Asian American. All four critics suggest to varying degrees that Cha does not allow the unitary subject and narrative that traditionally ground Asian American reading. Yet three of the four implicitly return to such a narrative subject, whether through identification with their own personal narratives (Kim and Kang) or through the identification of a single narrator who relates historical narratives (Lowe). Wong goes a step further, recognizing that *Dictée* does not present a coherent narrative or lyric subjectivity; but having conceded this, she finds her reading threatened by interpretations that do not recognize the text as Asian American at all. If the establishment of a narrative subject whom we can identify as Asian American is the foundation of Asian American reading, then can a text like *Dictée* truly be claimed as Asian American?

If *Writing Self, Writing Nation* did not fully answer such questions, it did succeed in its more pragmatic goal of inserting *Dictée* into Asian American critical discourse, an achievement that has also helped raise Cha's profile for a wider audience. *Dictée* has increasingly found its way onto Asian American literature syllabi and has been the subject of an increasing number of articles by Asian American critics. This rapid embrace of Cha by Asian Americanists, however, has left open the question of how a text like *Dictée* comes to be labeled and functions as Asian American literature. The radical break in Asian American critical paradigms heralded by Lowe, Wong, and others has in practice amounted to little more than thematic pluralism, an expansion of cultural nationalism rather than a critical examination of its underpinnings. Although much ink has been spilled over the shift to a new "transnational" paradigm in Asian American studies, the major practical effect on Asian American literary criticism, both in print and in the classroom, has simply been a shift toward works that thematize transnational movement or postcoloniality, particularly toward South Asian American texts like Bharati Mukherjee's *Jasmine*.[6]

Meanwhile, increased attention by Asian American critics has also expanded the mainstream readership for Cha's writing and art. The Asian American intervention has meant that whereas gender was the primary category through which Cha's work was understood in the 1970s and 1980s, race has become primary for critics in the 1990s, and Cha's work has increasingly been included in exhibitions and articles under a multicultural rubric. But the orientalism present in criticism of Cha by white avant-garde critics in the 1980s continues relatively unabated, a testament not only to the durability of orientalist assumptions in avant-garde American aesthetics but to the ways in which Asian American critics have failed to make a firm case for Cha's status as Asian American artist.

A 2001 exhibition of Cha's work, *The Dream of the Audience*, while extraordinarily valuable in bringing Cha's work to a wider public, demonstrates the limited reach of Asian American readings of Cha. Lawrence Rinder, a former curator at the Berkeley Art Museum who oversaw the acquisition of Cha's archive there and who has been a tireless advocate of Cha's work since the late 1980s, suggests in the exhibition catalog that Cha remains a fundamentally Korean artist whose work attempts to enact a return to "her lost homeland" (Lewallen 15). Rinder notes that many of Cha's "forms, motifs, and themes [are] borrowed from traditional Korean culture" (17) and repeats a conventional piety of American orientalist criticism by connecting Cha's sensibility to Confucianism, which he argues "serves as the model for Cha's recurring invocation of filial connection" (18). The terms "Asian American" and "Korean American" do not appear in Rinder's essay.

In the past few years a new approach has emerged that attempts to fuse avant-garde and identity paradigms, often through the study of minority experimental writers such as Cha, Myung Mi Kim, and Harryette Mullen. This approach is evident in the work of Juliana Spahr and Brian Kim Stefans, younger poets writing in the wake of Language poetry and its paradigms for politics in poetry. Spahr argues that *Dictée* "decolonizes" reading, "destabilizing reading practices that seek to conquer or master" by the way it "calls attention to . . . all that is least assimilable about a reader's connection to a work" ("Postmodernism" 24). Spahr acknowledges that her "decolonization" is a metaphor borrowed from Cha's discussion of Japanese colonization of Korea, making Spahr vulnerable to Wong's charge that poststructuralist readings can generalize away the specificity of *Dictée*'s Asian American origin—a risk of which Spahr is keenly aware, and that her work carefully tries to negotiate.

Spahr seeks to combine Asian American and experimental reading positions by insisting on the unity of content and form: just as *Dictée* thematizes decolonization through its depiction of Korean history, it enacts decolonization through the reading processes its form encourages. The two modes of reading can thus, Spahr hopes, be consonant. But while she continuously notes that *Dictée* emerges from an immigrant, minority, racially marked position, she simultaneously suggests its true contribution is the way it transcends that position, questioning any and all modes of categorization. In *Everybody's Autonomy*, Spahr argues that debates internal to minority or postcolonial discourse—for example, calls for a return to a native language versus embrace of the oppositional possibilities of the colonial language—are dead ends, and that the only way out is to reject such categories as "native" and "colonial" altogether: "If we are truly looking for a work that reconfigures and challenges the conventions of colonial thinking, then we need to examine works that challenge how we read to categorize, conquer, penetrate, and settle" (127). In the encounter between experimental and minority discourses, Spahr arguably allows the former to trump the latter.

Spahr's unease with the category of the Asian American is certainly due in part to the scope of her project, which includes Lyn Hejinian, Bruce Andrews, and Harryette Mullen as well as Cha. But this same questioning of categories is evident in Brian Kim Stefans's essay "Remote Parsee: An Alternative Grammar to Asian North American Poetry," which takes the articulation of an Asian American poetics as its explicit goal. Stefans suggests that he is presenting an alternative to "mainstream" or "movement" theories of Asian American literature but is reticent about what relationship his alternative canon has to that mainstream. Formal innovation in Asian American poetry has "probably" been limited by its status as one of the "oppositional 'movement' literatures," Stefans writes, but the details are "too deep to go into here" (67). Instead, Stefans simply seeks to describe an alternative tradition of Asian American poetry, one centered around more experimental writers such as Cha, John Yau, and Mei-mei Berssenbrugge, and offers insightful discussions of a number of poets.

Stefans argues that to connect the poets he discusses in some unified or narrative way would be a "suturing, politically mollifying project" that would undermine the very formal strategies exemplified by this poetry (43), but the resulting lack of connection between the writers he catalogs opens the question of what "Asian American poetry" signifies in his analysis. In his conclusion, Stefans asks whether Asian American literature has any remaining function as a category at all, claiming that "there is no longer a single thread of discourse that an Asian American writer feels obliged to confirm or argue" (70) and suggesting that Asian American identification has become little more than "a vague sense of membership in a racially defined community" (72). Although the Asian American remains Stefans's ostensible principle of organization, in practice the poets' orientation toward an experimentalist aesthetic seems more relevant than their participation in a discourse of race.

In turning, finally, to *Dictée* itself, I want to suggest that what *Dictée* provides is neither a means of choosing between experimental and Asian American methods of reading and writing nor a synthesis of the two. Rather, in its multiple and often clashing structures of organization—linguistic, poetic, mythical, historical, personal—*Dictée* shows us a way of keeping these two paradigms in productive tension, always visible but never resolved. If *Dictée* is representative of a new political and aesthetic moment, it is not a moment where we can, as Kim suggests, have it all, but rather one where we must constantly weigh the strengths and weaknesses of different modes of literary and political affiliation. It is an avant-garde text that engages two divergent avant-garde modes—those represented by Asian American and Language poetry—and reflects upon their sometimes conflicting history.

Establishing the subject of *Dictée*—both who speaks it and what it is about—has been the starting point for nearly all readings of the book and is the key to struggles over its classification. These two tasks are inseparable: marking the speaker of *Dictée* as "female" or "Korean" or "Asian American" is necessary to identifying *Dictée* as a narrative about gender, history and nation, or immigration and race. Even the most sophisticated recent interpretations, such as that of Anne Cheng in *The Melancholy of Race*, reflect this need to fix *Dictée*'s subject. Although Cheng skillfully negotiates the poles of postmodern and Asian American reading, she does not question the "generally accepted" reading of *Dictée* as "Cha's autobiography" (140). She also takes for granted the claim that the text is "profoundly interested in the processes of *identification*" (141)—specifically, of racial identification—and that it is "preoccupied with history" (142). While Cheng acknowledges that we cannot locate a stable "political subject" to whom we could ascribe didactic intentions, it is precisely her firm identification of *Dictée's* "subject," in this broader sense, that allows her to read the text as an intervention into American racial discourse.

I would argue that it is not so easy to establish either the who or the what of *Dictée*. Perhaps the most telling sign is that almost all critics focus on the book's first half, particularly the opening and the "Clio/History" and "Calliope/Epic Poetry" sections. These are the sections with the most obvious "content"; they thematize language learning and colonialism and explicitly incorporate historical materials. Yet most critics entirely ignore the book's second half, in which Korea largely falls away as an explicit topic and the writing becomes much more abstract, archetypal, and stylized. Whereas the book's early sections give critics a ground on which to identify *Dictée's* subject and mark its author's race and nationality, these later sections seem to undermine such efforts. But they are also where Cha attempts to move beyond the paralysis and repetition that seem to characterize historical experience, evoking a much more abstract notion of subjectivity that does not precede writing but emerges from it. The critical inability to reconcile these competing tendencies within *Dictée* again suggests that its most radical implications for our current modes of reading have not yet been understood. Although parts of *Dictée* can be understood as "Korean" or "Asian American," parts of it, as the dearth of Asian American criticism on the book's second half shows, apparently cannot. What kind of political and aesthetic contribution can be made by a text that is thus divided?

Even if parts of *Dictée* can be understood in narrative terms, the text displays a number of competing modes of organization, modes that often cannot be reconciled. The most obvious framework is Cha's labeling of the book's nine major sections with the names of the nine Muses. Such a "mythic method" is, of course, a paradigmatic modernist technique, one that, as T. S. Eliot writes in "*Ulysses*, Order, and Myth," provides an alternative to the exhausted narrative method of the novel. Joyce's use of myth, "in manipulating a continuous parallel between contemporaneity and antiquity," is, Eliot argues, "simply a way of controlling, of ordering, of giving a shape and a significance to the immense panorama of futility and anarchy which is contemporary history" (177). Cha's use of archetypal female martyrs—Joan of Arc, St. Thérèse of Lisieux, Yu Guan Soon—also recalls Pound's notion of the "subject-rhyme," which links disparate cultures and historical periods through similarities in mythic motifs.

Joyce's method, of course, does provide a kind of narrative scaffolding, since he has chosen a classical source—the *Odyssey*—that itself has a narrative structure. Cha's postmodern move is to reject even this remnant of narrative, choosing a structure that is much more schematic and abstract. The list of Muses is presented in the text as a table of elements whose logic of order and precise relation to each other are unclear:

CLIO	HISTORY
CALLIOPE	EPIC POETRY
URANIA	ASTRONOMY
MELPOMENE	TRAGEDY
ERATO	LOVE POETRY
ELITERE	LYRIC POETRY
THALIA	COMEDY
TERPSICHORE	CHORAL DANCE
POLYMNIA	SACRED POETRY[7]

This list suggests no narrative, nor does it seem to imply a hierarchy. Indeed, Cha's text continually flirts with the idea that this schema has no particular relevance and grants no particular authority to the work; the sections do not correspond in any obvious way to the modes with which they are labeled.[8]

But the list does suggest a kind of progress, one that is not narrative, but rather that tracks a shift in the orientation toward narrative itself. Those genres that lend themselves most to narrative and story—history, epic poetry, tragedy—are concentrated at the beginning of the text; those that seem least adapted to narrative—dance, religious poetry—come at the end. The text enacts its resistance to narrative not by relating counternarratives but by its very structure, suggesting a model of change that is neither narrative nor biographical.

Perhaps Cha's most striking subversion of the mythic method, though, is her sense that myth can be both a redemptive, empowering force and a kind of stasis, a freezing of the terms of life and discourse that can preclude individual agency. Most critics have tried to read the archetypal women of

Dictée thematically, either as attempts to articulate a feminine voice in opposition to the male discourse of nationalism or as indices of the repressive
strictures of patriarchy, which force woman into the position of martyr. But
what Cha actually demonstrates is an ambivalence toward the very structure
of myth, suggesting that the mythic method organizing her own text cannot
be regarded as final.

Cha's ambivalence toward myth is perhaps most evident in her treatment of Korean nationalist heroine Yu Guan Soon in the "Clio/History"
section.[9] Many critics have read Cha's inclusion of Yu as a feminist gesture
of "telling the women's stories," claiming an active role for women in a
previously male-dominated narrative of nationalism. In *Writing Self, Writing Nation*, Elaine Kim argues that Cha "reclaims Yu's story from official
Korean History . . . by emphasizing . . . Yu's agency" rather than focusing on
her martyrdom, converting her from a symbol of female self-sacrifice to an
image of heroism (Kim and Alarcón 16). But to suggest that Cha does this
by presenting an alternate narrative of Yu's life would be misleading; Cha
explicitly narrates Yu's experience in only two paragraphs of a fifteen-page
section. What Cha seems most concerned with is Yu's conversion into a
mythical, archetypal figure—the process by which she is "rendered inces-
sant, obsessive myth" (Cha 28). Cha acknowledges that "official" historical
discourse is the primary force behind this mythification: "History records
the biography of her short and intensely-lived existence. . . . The identity of
such a path is exchangeable with any other heroine in history" (30). Yet it is
precisely this exchangeability that gives power to the mythic method, that
allows a single character to signify beyond the boundaries of history and
nation. Cha's granting of agency to Yu is less a matter of narration than of
mythic invocation: "She calls the name of Jeanne d'Arc three times" (28).
Cha's Yu Guan Soon is a martyr, but somehow a self-conscious one, aware
of how her own story echoes that of others.

It is Yu's mythic existence—and her martyrdom—that allows her life to
be objectified, becoming a monument whose boundaries can be known.
The ephemeral events of a life become "duration," a period with a marked
beginning and end. Yu's acting out of the martyr's role grants her a kind of
immortality, removing her from temporality and placing her in the timeless
realm of myth: "Some will not know age. . . . Time stops. . . . Their image,
the memory of them is not given to deterioration" (37). This is a realm of
Messianic time, in which Cha, as historian, forms what Walter Benjamin

calls a "constellation" between one era and another (Benjamin 263). Joan of Arc and Yu Guan Soon, though separated by centuries and continents—and hence unlinked in the chronicles of history—are a pairing that "flashes up at the instant when it can be recognized" (255), existing not in empty, homogeneous time but simultaneously, in the "time of the now" (263).

If we embrace this notion of Cha as materialist historian, however, we neglect her deep unease with the timeless realm of myth and its potential for stasis. If Yu Guan Soon gains agency by invoking her mythical predecessors, she simultaneously loses agency by submitting to a predetermined (and doomed) role. History threatens to become mere repetition—a threat realized in "Melpomene/Tragedy," where the speaker identifies the Korean upheavals of 1980 as a repetition of the struggles of Yu's era and of subsequent conflicts: "Nothing has changed, we are at a standstill. . . . I am in the same crowd, the same coup, the same revolt, nothing has changed. . . . I am locked inside the crowd and carried in its movement" (80–1).

Cha thus rejects the dialectic of myth and history that animates both the mythic method and Benjamin's Messianic temporality. In these models, history provides the particulars, the sequence of events that are united and redeemed by the flashing up of the archetypal figure. But for Cha, myth and history collude in creating stasis and in robbing the individual of her singularity—even as they provide our only means of knowing not only our pasts but ourselves. Neither can provide change; each ends in repetition. What is needed is "the reply that will not repeat history in oblivion" (33), a response to historical and mythological discourses that would break the "standstill" in which they place us.

The refusal of myth/history is in part a signal that narrative is no longer a relevant mode for Cha. For Eliot, the narrative of the *Odyssey* orders the anarchy of contemporary history; for Benjamin, historical progress is the narrative that mythical structures must "blast open." But in *Dictée*, the narratives of both history and myth stand equally still, and the stories they tell have been repeated so often as to represent no movement or progress at all. Ultimately, neither can suitably animate Cha's work.

"Clio/History" thus ends in deadlock. "Calliope/Epic Poetry" marks a concerted attempt to think beyond myth/history through a second-person recounting of the experiences of Cha's mother. This suggests another possible principle of organization: biography and personal experience, as opposed to the official discourses of history and myth. L. Hyun Yi Kang, for instance, argues that "Calliope / Epic Poetry" offers an "alternative method-ology of re-membering the past" that "takes storytelling away from the im-personal recording of History to the more immediate, self-conscious vehicle of personal memory" (Kim and Alarcón 81). But personal memory is not quite as immediate as it might seem; Cha describes not her own memories but those of her mother, and her mother's experiences, as Cha remarks in an end note, are not simply channeled but derived from an encounter with another text, "based on the journals of Hyung Soon Huo" (181). Cha's use of the second person is less a gesture of immediacy than an acknowledgment of her mother's experience as radically separate.

Elaine Kim suggests that the opening pages of "Calliope" construct a na-tionalist narrative, evoking the mother's sense of her essential Korean spirit, or "MAH-UHM"—a sense against which the daughter must position her-self. But a closer reading reveals that "Korea" as homeland cannot be under-stood in merely national terms. Geographically, Korea can only be defined negatively; for the mother, born in Manchuria after her family flees the Japa-nese occupation, Korea is known only as "the land that is not your own" (45). China itself is a kind of blank space, "large. Larger than large. . . . As large and as silent." In this empty geography, at least six definitions and discourses of "home" emerge, none of which relies upon history, mythology, or even the geographical space of Korea:

as *spirit*: "[Y]our MAH-UHM, spirit has not left . . . your spirit-heart" (45–6).

as *memory*: "It is burned into your ever-present memory. . . . Because it is not in the past" (45).

as *language*: "Mother tongue is your refuge. It is being home. Being who you are. Truly" (45–6).

as *song*: Cha includes a section of the folk song "Bong Sun Hwa," which Elaine Kim notes was a sign of national defiance to Japanese rule (Kim and Alarcón 4). "You sing . . . the national song forbidden to be sung" (Cha 46).

as *writing*: "You carry at center the mark of the red above and the mark of blue below. . . . You carry the mark in your chest. . . . You write . . . from one mouth to another" (46–8).

as *mother*: "You are home now your mother your home. Mother insepa-rable from her identity, her presence" (49).

For many critics, sections like these demonstrate Cha's construction of a Korean or Korean American identity that is multiple and shifting, not reducible to any single vector of identification. What is also happening, however, is the blurring of markers that would continue to identify this "home" as Korea. "Korea" is continually deferred, replaced by a series of provisional homes—in memory, in language, in the family—so that to identify Korea as the ultimate source, or destination, of this text becomes increasingly difficult. The space to which Cha's mother "comes home" from her teaching assignment is not Korean, much less Korean American, but the place of her family's exile in Manchuria; it is defined as "home" not in national or cultural but in familial terms. Cha replaces a national discourse of "home" with a Wittgensteinian analysis of the myriad ways in which "home" is actually used, a taxonomy of the language-games in which "home" plays a part.[10]

To argue that Cha declines to identify "home" with "Korea" is not to say that her discourses of home are merely heterogeneous and chaotic. In fact, Cha attempts to provide a very particular path through these discourses, one that departs from a simple description of her mother's experiences and moves into a much more abstract realm. Although "Calliope" opens nostalgically, thematizing and yearning for a lost Korea, the dreamlike passage in the section's center—a fevered hallucination of the mother's, the text suggests—takes dislocation as both its starting point and its destination: "You are going somewhere. You are somewhere" (50). We soon realize, however, that something else is going on entirely; this "somewhere" is not a physical place but an experience of time and movement: "Such stillness. It is endless. . . . Total duration without need for verification of time. . . . You say this is how it must be death" (50–1). The language here echoes Cha's characterization of the stasis of myth in "Clio/History," suggesting that we should not understand this passage as a depiction of the mother as person moving through a physical space but as a linguistic subject's movement through a discursive and textual space. The deathlike stillness of this space recapitulates the paralyzing effects of myth and history diagnosed in "Clio," threatening the subject with erasure: "You move. You are being moved. . . . None. Nothing" (51).

"Clio" ends with the desire to move beyond this stalemate, and the following section of "Calliope" makes the first concerted attempt to do so, an attempt that will be continued throughout the book's second half. Cha's remarkable gesture is to portray this frozen space as inhabitable, as built, in an echo of the mother who makes a "home" in the blank spaces of China:

> You come to a house. Enormous in size. There are women standing before the house dressed in costumes made of a strange and beautiful cloth. . . . From the distance their movements are reduced to make almost clearer the movement.
>
> . . . On the other side, some women draped in long silk cloths are dancing. They entrance you. Numb you. You watch in awe for what seems to be a very long time. Such calm, you cannot imagine an expression that would describe it. . . . There are people very well dressed in not our native costumes and not foreign costumes. (51–2)

Cha's response to the stillness of history is to reinterpret it as dance, as controlled and contained movement—a gesture indicated in the very structure of the book, which begins with Clio, but whose penultimate figure is Terpsichore. The negation of stillness instead becomes calm. Perhaps the most striking aspect of this new space, though, is its apparent position outside the discourse of nation that ostensibly dominates *Dictée*: its inhabitants cannot be identified, as they wear "not our native costumes and not foreign costumes."

The slightly awkward phrasing here suggests that Cha is not creating what many critics have seen in *Dictée*: a "hybrid" (Lowe) or "in-between" (Kim) space that somehow combines or lies between the native and the foreign, the Korean and the American. Cha's phrasing—specifically, her placement of the *not*—does not suggest a third term ("neither our native costumes nor foreign costumes but . . ."). Rather, it suggests a space that can be defined only as the negation of the native *and* the foreign, or, as we might put it, the "not our" and the "not their." Such positions of ownership are simply not tenable in this deconstructed space. But neither is this simply a neutral zone; only by moving through the landscape of nation, myth, and history can one reach this place of their negation.

As the discourse of nation falls away, others emerge to take its place. What Cha stages in this desertlike landscape is a temptation scene, complete with biblical quotations from the temptation of Jesus; in Cha's parallel narrative, Satan's role is taken by three women who offer plates of food to the mother. The framing of the story suggests that to accept the food would be to surrender to fever and death, but there is also a suggestion that it represents a yielding to another language, as in the scenes of dictation that open the book: "You are yielding to them. . . . They force their speech upon you" (50).

The mother's refusal of the food allows her to return home, where religious discourse is replaced by family—the apparent end point of this discursive journey. Family seems to be the final "home," an escape from the binaries of historical thinking and a reclaiming of the singularity denied to Yu Guan Soon and other archetypal women: "No more sentence to exile, Mother, no black crows to mourn you. Neither takes you neither will take you Heaven nor Hell they fall too near you let them fall to each other you come back you come back to your one mother to your one father" (53). This end to exile is not a restoration of the homeland, Korea; rather, it is a product of having moved through a space where "native" and "foreign" are negated, where the very binaries that produce the condition of exile have been denied. But the homecoming is a somewhat uneasy one; the woman's first act on waking from her fever is to take food from her parents, suggesting the yielding to temptation that was previously rejected. And the family has its own binaries of gender: one mother, one father. Although it may be possible to escape certain kinds of binaries, there is no outside to discourse and its structures.

It is writing itself that finally provides the largest possible frame, giving Cha the means to navigate the many discourses that structure her work. The conclusion of the mother's story is followed by two pages with a large Chinese character written on each, followed by the appearance of the authorial voice: "I write. I write you" (56). The discourses of myth, history, nation, religion are all ultimately forms of writing; Cha's mother is a creation in writing (both through her journals and Cha's reading of them), and the space through which she moves away from nation and toward family exists only in writing. That the body itself is a written composition is suggested in "Urania/Astronomy," which opens with a Chinese medical diagram in which the body's very contours are made up of written characters.

Cha's shift of focus from nation to writing could be read as a depoliticizing of her project, if one follows Asian American critics' rejection of "postmodern" or "avant-garde" interpretations of Cha as a writer primarily concerned with stylistic issues. Most Asian American critics thus shy away from Cha's emphasis on writing, reversing the text's structure by making nation and history the telos of *Dictée*. But Cha herself offers a defense of writing that grounds it in political concerns while simultaneously insisting, to echo Stevens, that it must be abstract. Cha could have chosen many different ways to dramatize the Japanese colonization of Korea, but even though some of these methods—historical documents, personal narratives—exist in fragmentary form in *Dictée*, Cha suggests that conventional methods cannot show how the colonizer becomes embedded in language itself:

> The "enemy." One's enemy. Enemy nation. Entire nation against the other nation. . . . The enemy becomes abstract. The relationship becomes abstract. The nation the enemy the name becomes larger than its own identity. . . . Larger than its own properties. Larger than its own signification. For *this* people. For the people who is their enemy. . . .
>
> Japan has become the sign. The alphabet. The vocabulary. To *this* enemy people. (32)

The colonizer, Cha argues, presents itself to the colonized through language. For all the force of its repressive apparatus, the imperial power's most insidious presence is within the structures of language themselves. Lest this be thought a merely theoretical proposition, Cha insists that this is precisely how imperialism is experienced by the colonized, by "*this* people . . . who is their enemy"; for Koreans, Japan becomes "the sign," signification itself. This is not, as critics have suggested, only an acknowledgment of the Japanese suppression of the Korean language; it also shows how imperialism produces the very binary structures of language that divide a "nation" from its "enemy." The colonial relationship thus "becomes abstract" by moving onto the terrain of writing, language, and linguistic structure, where it becomes all the more insidious because it is no longer explicitly attached to markers of race and nation. Cha can be seen as adopting toward the colonial situation a Wittgensteinian insight: "A *picture* held us captive. And we could not get outside it, for it lay in our language and language seemed to repeat it to us inexorably" (Wittgenstein 48).

This foregrounding of language also provides the link between Japanese colonialism and post–World War II American neocolonialism. In "Melpomene/Tragedy," Cha notes that although Japan's defeat in the war put an end to Japanese occupation of Korea, the colonial binaries remain present within language, ready to be exploited by the new powers of capitalism and communism: "We fight the same war. . . . We are severed in Two by an invisible enemy under the title of liberators who have conveniently named the severance, Civil War. Cold War. Stalemate" (81). The players are not the same, but the structures of opposition and the language in which they are articulated remain fixed, blunting agency.

For Cha, then, politics must be first and foremost a question of language, and thus it is writing that must provide the basis for any attempt to resist domination. Toward the end of "Clio," the discourse of history is critiqued as "not physical enough," leading several critics to read Cha as insisting on the materiality of the body as the site of resistance to discourse.[11] But Cha's language here makes clear that this turn to corporeality is, at its core, written, and that it can lead only to writing: "[T]o the very flesh and bone, to the core, to the mark, to the point where it is necessary to intervene, even if to invent anew, expressions, for *this* experience, for this *outcome*, that does not cease to continue" (32). The "mark" of writing is what constitutes the body; what this means, though, is not that the body is undermined as a site of resistance, but that it becomes possible to intervene in material existence through language, through writing.

It is this turn to writing, and in particular the turn to the abstractions of writing, that animates the later, neglected sections of *Dictée*, which become increasingly less narrative, less grounded, less identifiable in their character and location. It may seem paradoxical that many of these later sections are staged in cinemas; but Cha's work as a video artist demonstrates her sense of a deep connection between film and writing. The cinematic apparatus is Cha's model for the ideological workings of language, and the movie screen becomes not only a surface of projection but a surface of writing, as evident in Cha's numerous video pieces in which text plays across the screen.

If colonizer and colonized were the dominant subject positions of *Dictée*'s early sections, it is the cinematic positions of viewer and viewed that become central as the text progresses. Rather than relying on history to determine such positions, Cha now seeks to work outward from the semiotic system itself. She uses the motif of a female spectator in a cinema to frame at least three sections, refiguring the "stillness" of history and myth as a cinematic experience; the film screen is the "empty window" through which the spectator gazes out into "the correct setting, immobile. Placid. Extreme stillness. . . . The submission is complete. Relinquishes even the vision to immobility" (79). At first, Cha seems to be doing little more than rehearsing a tenet of film theory. But the repetitions of this scene of viewing are also rewritings that offer different metaphors of the cinematic experience, seeking to find spaces for agency, and for writing.

Just as "Calliope" breaks up "home" by demonstrating its multiple locations, "Elitere / Lyric Poetry" breaks up the cinematic scene by offering various senses of the "screen" on which images are projected. Whereas the film screen as object presents an imperial reality, *screen* as word has multiple valences that may help mitigate film's ideological effects. The screen can be a "partition" between rooms, "Fine grain sanded velvet wood and between the frames the pale sheet of paper" (131); "partition" also suggests here the Cold War partition of the Korean peninsula. This sense of a barrier between two spaces also presents the screen not as a depthless surface of projection but as a medium through which communication might pass: "If words are to be uttered, they would be from behind the partition. . . . If words are to be sounded, impress through the partition" (132). And the paper screen can be a medium not just for sound but for writing: "the other signature the other hearing the other speech the other grasp."

Perhaps Cha's most interesting rewriting of the screen, however, is as not a two-dimensional but a three-dimensional space. Cha's stated interest, in her video work, in the "in-between" moment emerges here as an enhanced sense of the medium's role in refracting the message, a claim for what happens inside the apparently depthless screen: "Stands the partition absorbing the light illuminating it then filtering it through. Caught in its light, you would be cast. Inside" (131). Cha understands the screen's depth in temporal terms. What we call "the present" is in one respect a durationless boundary between "the past" and "the future"; but it is also the place where any action must occur. Cha imagines the screen as a space where a pure experience of the present is possible, "Breaking loose all associations" and erasing the "stain" of memory. And this can happen only through writing, by reinterpreting the screen as a surface to be inscribed rather than as a window: "If within its white shadow-shroud, all stain should vanish, all past all memory of having been cast, left, through the absolution and power of these words" (132).

Cha's conviction that memory and agency can be rewritten through new metaphors leads to several climactic scenes, recapitulations of the mother's fever dream, that try to create abstract parables of the move from historical paralysis to present agency through writing. These are often self-referential scenes that use motifs not only from *Dictée* itself but from Cha's visual and performance work, suggesting the unity of Cha's aesthetic and political project. "Terpsichore / Choral Dance," the penultimate section, presents a scene that evokes the faceless ruins of *Dictée*'s cover: "Stands now, an empty column of artery, of vein, fixed in stone. . . . Then without visible mark of transition, it takes the identity of a duration. It stays. All chronology lost, indecipherable, the passage of time, until it is forgotten. Forgotten how it stays, how it endures" (161). If we read this as an allegory of *Dictée*'s own development, we see that Cha begins with the historical record, which serves as a monument to past experience. Yet over time that record becomes an "empty column"—a ruin, a mere "duration," without any marker or memory of how it came to be. The stillness that Cha finds characteristic of historical memory is a kind of forgetting, a reduction of experience to an object whose only virtue is its mere being.

It is precisely that endurance, however, that allows the hollowed-out ruin to become the ground of present action. Cha presents the growth of this potential agency as an impersonal, almost geological process, in terms of water slowly gathering within the stone: "A new sign of moisture appears in the barren column that had congealed to stone. Floods the stone from within, collects water as to a mere, layering first the very bottom. . . . Water inhabits the stone" (161–2). Then, through a remarkable series of metaphors, Cha suggests that this process of loss, abstraction, and accumulation is what provides the literal substance of writing:

> Water on the surface of the stone captures the light in motion and appeals
> for entry. . . . Muted colors appear from the transparency of the white and
> wash the stone's periphery, staining the hue-less stone. . . . Draw from
> stains the pigment as it spills from within, with in each repetition, extract
> even darker, the stain, until it falls in a single stroke of color, crimson, red,
> as a flame caught in air for its sustenance. (162)

Water, whose accumulation Cha analogizes to the endless repetitions of history, becomes a medium, like the screen, that refracts light and gives color to the featureless stone and transparent liquid. Water thus can become pigment, which in turn becomes the substance of the composed body: "stone, water, teinture, blood" (162).

Cha offers here a model of how blood—the basis of race and nation—can be the product of writing rather than its basis. Although Cha begins from the discourse of history, historical monuments must become abstract, unmarked, before they can be reclaimed for the project of writing. The objects of history must become meaningless before they can become meaningful again; they must become arbitrary markers, like linguistic signs, before they can be used as language. In Cha's avant-garde insight, culture is not inherited but created; natural, filiative connections are replaced with affiliative connections, grounded in the artifice of writing.

Cha's final parable, which appears in the book's final section, "Polymnia/ Sacred Poetry," specifies the role of art, and in particular Cha's own work, in this process. The section presents itself, again, as a kind of capsule version of *Dictée*, opening with a photograph of ruined monuments that echoes the cover art. The section relates the story of a girl bringing remedies home for her sick mother; stopping at a well to rest, she encounters a woman who offers her water and gives her medicine to give to her mother. The girl and woman seem to be doubles in some way, as they are described as wearing similar clothing, "a white kerchief around her thick black hair braided in a single knot down to her back . . . [with] an apron over the skirt which she had gathered and tied to keep it from the water" (167). This outfit bears a striking resemblance to the white headband and robes Cha frequently wore in her performance pieces, suggesting that both women are figures not just for Cha but for the artist more generally. The chipped porcelain bowl in which the woman offers the girl water to drink also echoes an image of a bowl in Cha's video piece *Re Dis Appearing*. The scene as a whole suggests the ritual function of art in reclaiming agency from abstraction; Cha presents herself not only as the shamanistic figure dispensing medicine (in nine doses, echoing the book's nine-part structure) but as the girl bringing the medicines home to her mother. "Home" itself is a destination that can be reached only through this ritual, one that is explicitly marked as happening in writing, in the in-between: "The landscape exists inside the screen. On the other side of it and beyond" (167).

Even as she foregrounds the role of art as ritual, Cha brings the text full circle to concerns of nation and myth; the story told in "Polymnia," as Shu-mei Shih notes, echoes the Korean myth of Princess Pali, who travels to the well of the Western sky and serves for nine years to obtain healing water for her mother.[12] But this is a repetition with a difference. Cha does not cite the story of Princess Pali, as she does with Joan of Arc and Yu Guan Soon; instead, she abstracts and reenacts it, removing it from its Korean context and making it a figure for her own art. The move out of history and through abstraction is paradoxically necessary to construct a founding myth that can endure beyond the stasis of nation and race.

What does *Dictée's* move from history through abstraction to writing tell us about the competing claims of Asian American and experimental writing, at whose critical intersection it has thus far existed? Asian American critics have read the early sections of the text as a grounding in history, nation, and race that establishes a Korean (American) subject position, albeit a complex one; for such readers, this establishes *Dictée* as a mode of Asian American cultural critique directed at dominant discourses of history and nation. But such claims are eroded as the book moves forward and Cha insists on leaving history behind in favor of increasingly ungrounded and abstract scenarios. What emerges is a rejection of historical discourse in favor of a focus on language itself, and a move toward writing as a way of beginning again from a position of mythical stasis. This is what we could broadly call the "experimental" thrust of the book; and it ultimately seems incompatible with maintaining a focus on issues marked as Korean or Korean American, as Cha comes to understand the positions of colonizer and colonized as abstract positions within language. The subject Cha evokes in these sections is better understood in terms of "receiver" and "sender" than in national or racial terms. Yet this is not to say that such a move is a rejection of politics or an easy transcendence. For Cha insists that the move through this "experimental" phase is crucial to finding a new kind of agency, one that can return again to the world of the present; only in language can we find a new kind of "home." It is an insight identified less with standard paradigms of Asian American reading than with the broader project of the avant-garde.

Asian American critics' neglect of the later parts of *Dictée*, then, becomes perfectly explicable. Asian American criticism cannot afford to acknowledge fully this experimental turn, since it threatens the very founding concerns that animate Asian American criticism and politics. Yet it must grapple with the course through the experimental that Cha—a writer who has now been labeled "Asian American"—insists on charting, and with Cha's indictment of the paralysis of all historical thinking. Indeed, Asian American critics might do well to reject *Dictée*—or at least the second half of it—as an Asian American text, since accepting it would be to question the very wisdom of doing Asian American criticism in the first place.

This is not to say, however, that *Dictée* represents the triumph of the experimental over the Asian American. The reception of *Dictée* by white avant-garde writers suggests that even the discourse of experimental writing contains its own idealization of otherness, expressed in this case through an orientalism that locates Cha's origins outside American national discourse.

More significant, Cha's insistence on starting from history—even if she ulti-mately rejects historical discourse—marks her ambivalent desire to ground the politics of writing outside the text, a desire that also haunts contemporary experimental writing.

Cha's strategies thus align her more with writers such as Susan Howe, whose visual-art training and use of historical documents parallel Cha's, than with better-known polemicists like Charles Bernstein or Ron Silliman. Howe's recent text *The Midnight*, for example, echoes *Dictée* in its struggle to unearth the figure of the mother. And like Cha, Howe seeks her mother not through direct portrayal but through the mediation of shared texts and historical documents: a glimpse in a magazine article, a Michael Drayton sonnet, an inscribed copy of Yeats's poems. Howe also shares Cha's interest in the visual, reproducing and commenting on often enigmatic photographs of marginalia, folded-over pages, and persons who may or may not be cor-rectly identified: "What if what we actually see is mistakenly dubbed appear-ance?" (Howe 56). Such artifacts, in Howe's work, never simply speak for themselves; hers is an "aesthetics of erasure" (45), in which poetry emerges from textual fragments and gaps. But just as sections of documents and prose alternate with poetic passages in *The Midnight*, so history provides the necessary scaffolding for Howe's writing, as it does for Cha's. Both Howe and Cha suggest to us that gestures of historical grounding remain necessary for experimental writing to maintain its angle of political critique.

Dictée illustrates the contradictions within our current systems of literary classification and forces us to reconsider the political claims we make on the basis of such classifications. *Dictée* charts a kind of path from the Asian American to the experimental and (perhaps) back again. It offers us its own model of literary agency, insisting on writing as the only means of resis-tance; yet it also seeks a new grounding for its own project. Like modes of contemporary political criticism, it cannot escape the tension between the need for a foundation for action and the knowledge that no such founda-tion can any longer be taken for granted.

FIVE

Mr. Moto's Monologue

John Yau and Experimental Asian American Writing

The divided structure of Theresa Hak Kyung Cha's *Dictée* reveals the limits of the paradigms of Asian American and experimental reading that developed in the 1980s and early 1990s. Such paradigms largely neglected the contexts of avant-garde writing that produced such bodies of work in the 1970s. In this chapter, I argue that the poetry of John Yau points the way to a return to, and a revision of, the idea of the Asian American avant-garde. Although Yau's poetry has often been seen as a new synthesis of the Asian American and the experimental, it might best be read as a restoration of the links between politics, form, and race that characterize the avant-garde Asian American poetry of the 1970s and that were obscured in the rise of the 1980s Asian American lyric. But if Yau, whose body of work itself stretches back to the 1970s, shows us that Asian American avant-gardism is not a novelty of the late 1990s, his work has provided the first opportunity for most readers to recognize the existence of an Asian American avant-garde, and to read the presence of that avant-garde back into the very origins of Asian American writing.

The reception of Yau's work, like that of Cha's, shifted significantly during the 1990s. Yau had previously been identified with the avant-gardists of the New York school, with little or no reference to his race. By the 1990s, however, he was suddenly being read as an Asian American writer—a shift that cannot be attributed to any change in the content or style of his work—and recent years have seen a significant rise in interest in his poetry among academic critics. But Yau's work remains an uneasy fit with dominant paradigms of reading. Yau himself continues to express discomfort with his categoriza-

tion as an Asian American writer, and, indeed, his aesthetic bears little resemblance to that of more widely read Asian American poets, such as David
Mura and Li-Young Lee. While Mura and Lee offer autobiographical lyrics of
personal experience and family history, Yau's biography appears only in fragmentary, distorted, or parodic form in poems that are as likely to reference
Boris Karloff or late-night TV. A Yau poem is thus as likely to be corrosive of
a particularized ethnic identity as it is supportive of one. At the same time,
Yau's continuing engagement with narrative, lyric, and racialized personae
has made his poetry appear, to some critics, less experimental than the most
radical writings of the Language poets. So Yau remains, as he himself puts
it in "Between the Forest and Its Trees (Second Version)," "the poet who is
too postmodern for the modernists and too modern for the postmodernists"
(45)—a formulation that also suggests the ways in which "Asian American"
and "experimental" continue to seem like mutually exclusive categories. Yau's
work, in short, shows us not so much a means of bridging Asian American
and experimental modes as a map of the continuing conflicts between the
two, while affirming the continuing relevance of the avant-garde as a controlling category in understanding Yau's work.

The distinctiveness of Yau's achievement—and the difficulty of labeling
it definitively "Asian American"—can perhaps best be demonstrated by returning, once again, to Garrett Hongo's anthology *The Open Boat*. Hongo's
anthology, I have argued, represented the triumph of lyric subjectivity in
Asian American poetry, an aesthetic consonant with the "MFA mainstream"
of the 1980s and 1990s. As Hongo argues in his introduction, this aesthetic
is one in which subjective experience is balanced with a consciousness of
poetic form:

> One of us can write out of strongly held Christian religious convictions
> instilled by a refugee, theologian father who preached in a small town
> church in Western Pennsylvania, and another from a grounding in French
> semiotic theory, poststructuralist cultural critique, and American postmod-
> ernist art criticism. One voice could have the feeling and flavor of Hawai-
> ian pidgin . . . [another the] smoothness of Mallarmé's French or . . . the
> bric-a-brac of Frank O'Hara's pop art lunch poems. (xx)

The biographical, or viscerally subjective, is here opposed to the theoretical
or intellectual; the former is vernacular and provincial, whereas the latter
is polished, cosmopolitan, European. Representing the latter position, the

extreme end point, is John Yau, who quite literally closes the spectrum as the final poet in the anthology. Yau is referred to twice in Hongo's introduction, first as "the Chinese American poet who is a postmodernist art critic and had been a student of John Ashbery's" (xxxi), then again as "East Village postmodernist John Yau" (xxxiv). Who is this curious figure, who seems to represent everything opposed to the personal and subjective, who seems more readily identified by his New York intellectual allegiances (art critic, postmodern, East Villager, Ashberyite) than by his membership in an ethnic community, whose work presents not Muraesque scenes of domesticity but abstract, surreal, playful images?

To understand the challenge Yau poses to the aesthetic of *The Open Boat*, I examine two poems from the anthology that work within that aesthetic, by two of the most widely read of Asian American poets: David Mura's "Gardens We Have Left" and Li-Young Lee's "This Room and Everything in It." These poems show both the accomplishments and the limits of what, by the early 1990s, had become the mainstream of Asian American writing. Both poems grapple with and thematize memory; Mura's poem is explicitly historical and ethnically "marked" in its content but finds its project of reclaiming the past beyond its resources. Lee's work locates the limits that frustrate Mura in the limits of poetry and poetic form to articulate what needs to be said, but in the end Lee is still thrown back upon those resources as the only ones available to the writer. The issues raised by both suggest that Yau's work is, indeed, in dialogue with the central concerns of Asian American writing, even as his work departs from its tenets in crucial ways.

Mura's "Gardens We Have Left" is transparently and insistently autobiographical, with references to the poet's childhood, the "Pilgrim face" of his white wife, and their daughter, Samantha. But the public, representative "I" of 1970s ethnic writing gives way to a private "I" performing on a domestic stage; the project of history is personalized, so that the poet's family drama, along with his personal frailties, becomes the grounding for the poem. Such intensely personal details are made to bear the weight of representation, serving as microcosms of larger social issues of race. The domestic opening of the poem provides an example:

> As Sam crumbles lumps of tofu on her tray,
> I sizzle onions in oil, shoyu, rice wine,
> add noodles, ginger, sugar, *shiitake*;

shoots of bamboo and chrysanthemum leaves.
Before the beef, veined with fat, thin as gauze,
I stir what for years I could not love.

(As a child, I shunned *mochi, futomaki,*
loved hot dogs, baseball, the GI John Wayne.
Now my *hashi* hauls up steaming *sukiyaki.*)

Later I take Sam out back, dressed in her *happi,*
and humming like my grandfather *sakura,*
think of a trip to Ise, her learning Japanese.

(Hongo 212)

The catalog that opens the poem creates a familiar, sentimental domestic scene: a young daughter (clumsily) helping her father cook, the listed ingredients providing a mouthwatering realism and immediacy. But ginger, shiitake, and bamboo also serve as ethnic markers, helping to give the scene its "Asian" aura. This function of the ingredients is emphasized by Mura, who exoticizes and reifies the food: the simple beef is made strange (gauzy and fat-lined), while the catalog of ingredients becomes a stand-in for his rejected Japanese identity, "what . . . I could not love." Mura's italicization of the words is not an attempt to disrupt the Anglophone voice of the poem; rather, he emphasizes their foreignness as such, using them solely as markers of difference, even italicizing words (*sukiyaki, shiitake*) that are commonplaces on American menus. (Imagine, as an analogy, a poet of Italian descent italicizing the words *gnocchi* or *linguine.*)

The use of the ingredients as markers of identity becomes even more questionable in the third stanza, when Mura describes his childhood desire to identify as "American." The "American" identity Mura presents— hot dogs, baseball, John Wayne—is a tour-guide, Hollywood America, constructed solely through the crudest mass-culture categories. Are we to be convinced, then, by Mura's reversal: "Now my *hashi* hauls up steaming *sukiyaki*"? What the juxtaposition demonstrates is Mura's own tourist attitude toward Asian Americanness: if eating hot dogs makes one American, then eating sukiyaki must make one Japanese. Mura's strategy here brings to mind Jorge Luis Borges's objection to attempts to generate an authentic Argentinian literature through "a profusion of local color"; Borges notes that the Koran never mentions the camel, a commonplace of the Middle Eastern tourist brochure, but that Muhammad apparently felt quite able to "be an Arab without camels" (181). Borges's insight shows how easily the self-consciously "ethnic" writer can enter into complicity with the expectations of mainstream, white readers, and, by extension, with the categories of the culture industry. In Mura's poem, indeed—to borrow Horkheimer and Adorno's phrase (166)—words have become trademarks, markers that identify the "ethnic" in comfortably exotic terms (whatever white Americans' attitudes toward Asian American cultures, certainly they love Asian food) and present cultural identity as a consumable commodity.

This positioning of Asian American identity seems linked to the failures of history and memory in the body of Mura's poem. Mura's vision of history, circumscribed within the personal, becomes a vision of the past, both family and individual, as radically inaccessible:

> I know so little even of father's fatigue
>
> at his dim-lit desk at INS, as he rested on
> his typewriter, deadline approaching, the keys
> leaving little circles of letters on his brow.
>
> Neither he nor my mother talk of the past;
> my childhood myths are Saturday's cartoons.
>
> (Hongo 213–4)

As in the poem's opening, memory is completely structured by the categories of mass culture. This structuring is so profound that it reflects back onto any attempt to move beyond it into an authentic, ancestral past: the father's experience, inaccessible and willfully withheld, is reduced to a single image—vivid and striking, but itself a kind of cartoon, empty of content.[1] The threat that this could be anybody's father, anybody's history is constantly present. Mura's own anxieties about justifying his Asian American project reflect the threat of assimilation, of simple absorption into a homogenized domesticity:

> Of course, it's an old tune—people migrating
> across a river, a mountain, an ocean;
> embarking, disembarking, leaving luggage,
>
> customs, finding homes, lovers, children . . .
> Who cares about past gardens, relocations, or race?
> You and Sam take a bath; I wash dishes.
>
> (Hongo 215)

Ostensibly, it should be Mura's project to resist the flattening and forgetting of that final line. But the poem's own terms lead inexorably to such a flattening—its grounding in the purely personal and in the sphere of the nuclear family, its reductive approach to identity, and, finally, its allegiance to the homogenizing conventions of the MFA mainstream. In reaching for a transcendent conclusion, Mura presents what is almost a parody of what Charles Bernstein calls the "well-wrought epiphany of predictable measure" (2):

> When you hold a great sorrow, it lasts
>
> almost too long. And then it lasts some more.
> But the same is true also of a great joy.
> In the island of light we make with our bodies,
>
> in the lullabyes where our daughter sleeps,
> we open a picture book, and the images are
> for the first time. Once I lost something
>
> of great value. And then I sought it.
> Everything changed then. Everything changed.
>
> (Hongo 222)

In the vagueness of "something" and "everything," there is no answer to the question, "Who cares about past gardens, relocations or race?" In reaching for the universal human statement, Mura achieves only a flattening of the complex issues he has raised, the poetic equivalent of "You and Sam take a bath; I wash dishes." The attempt to find an "island of light," a pure and innocent image "seen for the first time," succeeds only in finding a place indistinguishable from that any other poem could reach. The repetitions ("lasts . . . too long . . . lasts some more"; "Everything changed . . . Everything changed") show the strains of the form, the attempt to squeeze a transcendent meaning out of a generic, commodified language. Juxtaposed to the catalogs of the opening, this conclusion presents Asian American identity as modular, capable of being inserted into predetermined slots in a poem that moves toward a seamless, American epiphany.

Against this example, Li-Young Lee's "This Room and Everything in It" can be read as moving beyond Mura's limits, relocating the dilemma of identity as a problem of poetic language and form. Lee's work does not thematize the category of the Asian American as explicitly; when it does, its elaboration of that identity is multifaceted, heavily figurative, as in his portrait of a Chinese butcher in "The Cleaving":

> . . . the sorrow of his Shang
> dynasty face,
> African face with slit eyes. He is
> my sister, this
> beautiful Bedouin, this Shulamite,
> keeper of sabbaths, diviner
> of holy texts, this dark
> dancer, this Jew, this Asian, this one
> with the Cambodian face, Vietnamese face, this Chinese
> I daily face,
> this immigrant,
> this man with my own face.
>
> (Hongo 156–7)

Lee's refusal to thematize, as Mura does, the categories of "Asian" and "American," and his insistent exploration of his own subjectivity may paradoxically make his work more effective as a comment on the position of the Asian American. As Adorno argues in "On Lyric Poetry and Society," "The less the work thematizes the relationship of 'I' and society, the more spontaneously it crystallizes of its own accord in the poem, the more complete this process of precipitation"—the indicator of the subject's relation to society—"will be" (Adorno 42). The conscious adoption of rigid racial categories can itself become ideological (visible in Mura's culinary commodification of ethnicity), blocking access to the writer's actual historical moment.

As in Mura's work, memory and history are crucial to Lee, as shown by his obsessive writing and rewriting of his relationship with his father. But Lee's more fluid sense of identity, as well as the greater self-consciousness of his writing, allows him to move beyond the limits of memory we encounter in Mura. Lee—to borrow the title of a work from his collection *The City in Which I Love You*—presents his poems as so many "furious versions" of a past, none definitive; at the same time, he is in a dynamic relationship with that past, which writes him just as he writes it: "Memory revises me" (14).

Lee's poem "This Room and Everything in It" is a meditation on memory and its limits. The poem's opening describes memory as a necessary foundation for future action:

> Lie still now
> while I prepare for my future,
> certain hard days ahead,
> when I'll need what I know so clearly this moment.
>
> I am making use
> of the one thing I learned
> of all the things my father tried to teach me:
> the art of memory.
>
> (Hongo 158)

Although memory, as in Mura, is portrayed as an ancestral inheritance, that inheritance is described not in terms of substance but in terms of form: memory as art. This notion of memory serves as a framework for the poem's project: choosing objects from "this room / and everything in it"—a room in which the speaker and a woman have been making love—the speaker attempts to create an entire symbolic system to "stand for my ideas about love / and its difficulties."

The discipline required for the art of memory is reflected in the form of the first half of the poem, which is tightly organized into quatrains, each quatrain presenting a single metaphor. The tension between this rigorous organization and the colloquial, even awkward quality of the speaker's voice reflects the strain of memory's discipline, the effort necessary to force the subjective into the objectivity of the aesthetic form that is memory. By halfway through the poem the struggle with form has been lost: the seventh quatrain, the first not to end with a period, is a turning point, as the attempt to create a complex image, to grapple with God and the self, leads to a disintegration into irregular stanzas:

> The sun on the face
> of the wall
> is God, the face
> I can't see, my soul,
>
> and so on . . .
>
> (Hongo 158–9)

Crucially, it is the attempt to conceptualize the "face"—which, in its spiritual form, becomes the essentialized self of the soul—that derails the project of memory, as if the speaker's identity is the single unstable variable. The entire structure of memory crumbles, and when the speaker attempts to recall the system he has just constructed, it is lost: "Now I've forgotten my / idea. The book / on the windowsill, riffled by wind . . ." (Hongo 159). The action of the outside world disrupts the writerly project of memory, and in the final stanza the speaker grasps desperately at the fragments:

> useless, useless . . .
> your cries are song, my body's not me . . .
> no good . . . my idea
> has evaporated . . . your hair is time, your thighs are song . . .
> it had something to do
> with death . . . it had something
> to do with love.
>
> (Hongo 159)

The failure of memory staged here becomes a moving admission of the failure of poetry and poetic form: the speaker losing a hold on memory becomes a figure for the writer losing control over his poetic materials, as metaphors come unmoored from their referents. Oddly enough, in the vagueness of the last three lines, in the repeated "something," we are left in much the same place Mura left us, unsure what, if any, epiphany has been reached—although here, there is much more self-consciousness and a much greater sense that the limits of the project are in part the limits of poetic form itself.

Lee's move toward the consideration of poetic form—toward, in Adornian terms, the objectivity of poetic material—raises another risk: the bracketing of subjectivity, of "who speaks." What allows us to read "This Room and Everything in It" as an Asian American poem? How did Garrett Hongo know to include this poem in an anthology of poems "from Asian America," since at no time in the poem is ethnicity thematized or even mentioned? Certainly, one can point to other works of Lee's that do thematize ethnicity. But ultimately, what holds all these works together if not the author-function of the ethnically marked name "Li-Young Lee"—the notion that we know a Chinese American subjectivity is behind these poems?

The work of a poet like John Yau helps to foreground these questions. In Yau's work, ethnicity is marked by the presence of obvious, even clichéd signifiers—fried rice, dim sum, Chinatown, Charlie Chan—and by the injection of biographical elements into the work. But even though Yau's use of such elements acknowledges the way in which we read his work (or any work) as already "marked" by the ethnicity of its author, his playful emptying out of them cautions us that such markers are unreliable. Although we do still wish to ask, "Who speaks?" Yau shows us that we should never be comfortable with our answer.

John Yau's relationship to the category of Asian American writing has been ambivalent enough that Marjorie Perloff, in a review of Yau's *Forbidden Entries*, could remark of Yau's early work, "[T]here was no indication, at this stage of Yau's career, that the poet is in fact Chinese-American" (39), while citing a book-jacket description of him as "the most important Chinese-American poet of our time" (40). Indeed, for much of his early career Yau was seen not as an Asian American writer but as a disciple of John Ashbery, with whom Yau studied at Brooklyn College; Ashbery chose Yau's *Corpse and Mirror* to be published in the National Poetry Series in 1983. In a 1990 interview in *Talisman*, Yau lists a number of influences on his work: the procedural experiments of Harry Mathews and Raymond Roussel, the work of Ashbery, Ron Padgett, Clark Coolidge, Michael Palmer, Barbara Guest, Jack Spicer. But it's not clear that Yau has allegiances to any of the "movements" of recent American poetry. Although Yau is of the same generation as most Language poets and cites many of the same influences, his work is not generally associated with theirs. Nor does Yau identify with what he calls in the *Talisman* interview the "gabby" and "social" poetics of the New York school: "I didn't find my day-to-day life all that interesting. I didn't want to either celebrate or lament my own life in any particular fashion" (Yau "Interview" 45).[2]

What about Yau as Asian American poet? Perloff's remark would suggest that ethnic identity was not part of Yau's self-positioning early in his career; in the past decade, however, Yau has become increasingly prominent in Asian American literary circles.[3] Yau's ethnic identity does not figure heavily in his self-presentation in his interview, which is mostly a discussion of Yau's art criticism and his poetic influences. The only Chinese or Chinese American influence Yau cites is Pound's *Cathay*, and even here Yau is suspicious of seeking an authentic "China": "For me, they were about being Chinese, about some kind of identity; they were something I could get ahold of, or at least had the illusion I could get ahold of" (43).

Yau does give a brief sketch of his family history: his mother was from a wealthy Shanghainese family, while his father was half Chinese and half English, and the family settled in working-class Lynn, Massachusetts, after fleeing China. Even in this capsule story, though, we see the same inaccessibility of the past that Mura and Lee grapple with: "My father has never talked about it, won't" (39). And there is even some doubt about the veracity of the story—"At least this is the version I have heard most often in my life"—suggesting the presence of alternative versions. When Yau is questioned about his own background, the same evasiveness and instability are apparent, sometimes to comic effect:

> E[dward]F[oster]: You grew up in Lynn?
> J[ohn]Y[au]: No, in Brookline. We only lived in Lynn for a short time.
> EF: So then you grew up in Brookline?
> JY: No, actually, we lived on Beacon Hill in Boston until the sixth grade. . . .
> EF: And then you went to Bard?
> JY: No, I went to Boston University for two years. (40)

Yau's response to this crisis of history and memory is not like that of Mura, who proposes a return to his "lost" cultural identity through the consumption of a commodified Asianness; the title of his memoir of his trip to Japan, *Turning Japanese*, suggests that such a move is possible. Yau rejects this idea: "In my case, my parents left China. They could never go back to live there, so the notion of return seems to me both an impossibility and a repressive illusion" (39). Repressive, perhaps, because it is a kind of false consciousness, deflecting the Asian American identity into a reified "Asianness." Nor does Yau turn to the kind of obsession with his past that led to Lee's extensively researched memoir of his family, *The Winged Seed*. In opposition to Lee's engagement, Yau chooses distance and understatement, setting his work consciously against the confessionalism of Robert Lowell:

> You know, who you are is simply an accident of birth. . . . A Boston Brahmin or a first-generation child of an immigrant. You can make a bigger case about that, or you can try to use it. . . . It just simply is what happened. And I don't want to deal with the accident of my birth as a right or entitlement.

But I don't want to ignore it either, and so it becomes to me an interesting dilemma: how do I deal with it? How do I write about it? (48–9)

History and memory are not the impetus to write; rather, they become materials to be incorporated, along with others, into writing. "How do I deal with it?" becomes "How do I write about it?"

Here Yau pushes beyond the awareness of poetic form that characterizes Lee's work. For Lee, although poetic form is the necessary art of memory, the experience of the self is still primary; the struggle of memory is the attempt to find lasting forms for experience, to find metaphors for "my ideas about love." By continuing to ground his work in a coherent, physical self, Lee continues to run up against the limits of what both Adorno and Language poets would recognize as a contaminated language of subjectivity. Yau, in contrast, is willing to let go of the self, in part because of his reaction against confessionalism and the personalized poetics of the New York school, in part because of his reading of proto-Language poets such as Coolidge. But letting go of the self can also be read as a tactical response both to the inaccessibility of the past and to the commodification of subjective language. If recent Asian American poetry's retreat into a private, commodified "I" shows the limits of that project, Yau's work suggests that a different site must be found for Asian American poetry:

> To write about one's life in terms of a subjective "I" is to accept an academicized, historical legacy—it is to fulfill the terms of the oppressor. I suppose I don't know who this "I" would or could speak for. Myself, what for? Maybe because I don't think what's autobiographical is necessarily interesting because it happens to one but because it might happen to more than one. Maybe I'm trying to figure out a way to get beyond the location of simply my life and see if something can happen out there instead of saying this is what happened here. So I try to find ways to find out there, in words. (49)

The "I," Yau suggests, has lost its ability to be representative. To move into the realm of action, "out there," one must move away from the subjective and into writing, into words. As Yau writes in "Between the Forest and Its Trees (Second Version)," "Where the I begins is in a sentence" (43).

Yau's critique of subjectivity has much in common with that of Charles Bernstein and other Language poets. Yet it's clear that Yau's shift of focus from the self to writing is not as radical as the Language poets' interest in "language itself." Yau's work does not seem to break the back of syntax and sense quite as relentlessly, nor does there seem to be a corresponding interest in the individual signifier as material. Narrative—rejected in almost all Language writing—figures heavily in Yau's work, though certainly not in terms of straightforward autobiography. One might say that the I, broken down into component discourses by Language poetry, is retained in Yau's work as an unstable but storytelling I, one that is constantly in revision. And the need for such an I may be explained by the pressure of the inaccessible yet necessary past, as Yau suggests in his *Talisman* interview:

> I think history is something constantly changing, and one's sense of it is changing, too, and one is constantly writing it, trying to write it, and it's fluid even though it is past. History is how one—we—ground ourselves. The past is as fluid as the present. And that kind of rewriting interests me. The writing of it is an attempt to have access to it, to understand, to discover connections, echoes. . . . [T]he connections are both real and part of the writing. (36)

If Yau's work can, indeed, be read as an extension of the project of Asian American poetry, hanging on to history is crucial if the project of ethnic writing is to remain coherent. And I would argue that Yau's work forces this kind of reading through its explicit deployment of Asian American signifiers. But it often reduces "Chinese" or "Chinese American" to a mere marker with an ambiguous relationship to the materials of the text, an identity constantly in revision. Yau's work can thus be read as a critique of the Foucauldian author-function in Asian American writing. For what marks a piece of Asian American writing if not its explicitly ethnic signifiers, beginning with the Asian name of the author—a marker that is all too easily essentialized into some notion of Asian American identity or consciousness? Perloff's doubt about Yau's Chinese Americanness can thus be seen as a crucial effect of Yau's work: the nagging sense that we do not know what it means to be "Chinese" anymore, even as we are constantly reminded of its centrality.

"Toy Trucks and Fried Rice," a work in *Radiant Silhouette* from 1980, is an extended meditation on memory, reflecting the turn toward prose and narrative that dominates much of Yau's later work. The narrator, looking back upon himself as a child, experiences "Chinese" identity as something defamiliarized:

> His parents brought him to the party. He had been told ever since he could remember that he was Chinese. He never lived in Chinatown and he didn't speak a word of Chinese. It was more complicated than that, however. His

mother was from Shanghai and spoke the dialect common to that area. The people at the party . . . spoke another dialect, Cantonese, and were, according to his mother, only farmers anyway. . . .

The differences were more than just those of language and economics, urban and rural. His mother reminded him that his grandfather was taller than anyone in this room, as were most people from Shanghai. His mother, however, was only a shade above five feet tall, and was thus indistinguishable from the rest of the women in the room. (68–9)

The narrator first experiences Chinese identity not as something interior but as something imposed from the outside, something "he had been told." Neither language nor the geography of Chinatown, both conventional locations of Chinese American culture, is available to the speaker. This double bind—of being regarded as "Chinese" while having no essentially "Chinese" experiences to draw upon—is the classic dilemma of the late-generation Asian American. Whereas a writer like Mura goes in search of an "authentic" Japan to remedy the situation, Yau, by probing the dilemma further, finds that the double bind, far from being the unique property of the American-born Asian, opens up into the situation of his immigrant mother. How can one attempt to become "Chinese" when being Chinese is itself complicated by internal divisions of language and class? And lest anyone think that the axes of culture and class exhaust the complexities of identity, the narrator's mother pushes difference to its absurd extreme by noting that Shanghainese are taller than (and hence superior to) other Chinese.

But it is here that the insistence on difference collapses under its own weight. The mother, a paragon of difference, demanding distinction to the finest degree, becomes herself "indistinguishable" from the others at the party. In one sense, the child's eye is here aligned with that of white America, which will view the self-differentiating mother as simply "Chinese" or, even more broadly, "Asian." But it is also a testament to Yau's insight that all identities are suspect—an insight echoed in the father's subsequent statement that "the Indians were the only true Americans and everyone else was a fake" (69). Although the positing of Native Americans as authentic Americans may be read as complicit with the ideology of white America,[4] the power of this position is that it allows the reading of all other Americans as "fake" and white Americanness itself as a construction. If the identity of white America is as "fake" as that of the son who is told by his parents that he is Chinese, then the political project of Asian American poetry shifts from a negotiation between two "authentic" cultures (Asian and American) to a use of Asian American identity to show that all identities, all selves, are "fake" in some way.[5]

What differentiates Yau's insight from the argument against the metaphysical "I" mounted by Language poetry is that, for Yau, the presence of the Chinese American "I" is paradoxically necessary to the insight that all identity is fake. Just as the father's argument requires the dubious positing of the "authentic" Indian, Yau uses the emptied-out category of the Chinese American as the foundation of his assault on identity. The personal experience of the Chinese American is still crucial as content; what the content shows, however, is not "what it's really like" to be Chinese American, but that no single set of terms, no single narrative, can capture this experience, or the experience of any identity.

"Toy Trucks" also helps explain why simply bracketing "history" or "content," as much Language poetry does, is not an option for Yau. The speaker's mother is usually able not to read her lost life of privilege in China as "an ironic commentary on the present" (69). But at certain moments—such as at the party—this rigid separation of past and present is not possible, and the mother is "thrown irretrievably into the past." History is inescapable, but the mother tries to cope with it through a proud individuality: "She tried to convey to her son the belief that isolation, whether social or spiritual, was the inevitable result of being better than what was around you" (69–70). While the son recognizes this as a fiction, he also realizes that it is a necessary fiction, a version of history that makes it possible to go on with life: "It was one of the ways she comforted herself." Yau's turn to narrative can be read as a search for this comfort, always coupled with an awareness that such comfort is provisional, even fake. The conclusion of the poem suggests that the pull of history, despite its hazards, is irresistible, figuring memory in erotic terms: earlier in the poem, the speaker stares at "a young woman in a turquoise satin dress" who in the end becomes a symbol of the entire experience: "All around them was bright embroidered satin, a kind of tinsel he will be attracted to for years" (71). In a striking metonymic shift, the speaker's attraction is focused not on the woman but on her clothing, on a surface image that becomes an erotic marker of memory. It is with such markers, rather than with human essences, that Yau fashions his poems.

Yau's use of narrative and his play with ethnic markers keep the racialized, storytelling I in view, while complicating it by presenting multiple versions of a given story or by filling the emptied-out ethnic self with a range of new materials. Yau's method allows us to read his work not only as a project of formal innovation but also as an extension of the project of Asian American poetry. By thematizing history, storytelling, and ethnicity, while emptying them of static content, Yau both engages with the terms of Asian American poetic practice and avoids the pitfalls of work like Mura's and Lee's.

"Childhood," a sequence of four poems dating from 1984, demonstrates Yau's use of his formal strategies to approach the writing of childhood. Yau's title places the sequence squarely within the generic conventions of the Asian American memoir—witness the centrality of childhood to the writing of a poet like Li-Young Lee. The first poem in the sequence, "Cenotaph," refers even more specifically to these conventions, taking as its subject a family photo album—a clichéd occasion for reminiscence and the topic of numerous poems by Asian American writers.[6] For Yau, however, the photograph is not presence but, like a cenotaph, an empty tomb whose referent is absent. Thus, the photographs bear an ambiguous relationship to the past: "The clues to what they remembered had been pasted into an album" (*Radiant* 151).

Curiously, the speaker's attention is caught not by the photos in the album but by the album's second half, where "someone (most likely her [his mother]) had carefully removed the snapshots. It was here I always slowed down and inspected the pages." The lost pictures are yet another figure for the inaccessibility of the past, a past whose traces outside forces have sought to eliminate: "I understood someone had tried to erase this history of excerpts" (152). But the captions remain, and become more compelling than the pictures themselves would have been, as attested by the speaker's failure to mention the pictures in the album's first half: "The words continued echoing long after I returned the album to its place on the shelf."

Why are these cryptic captions—like *Mound of Heads, Shanghai, 1946*—more compelling than images? The answer can be found in the spaces left behind: "Those black rectangles surrounded by faded black almost blue frames." These spaces, black and unfaded in contrast to the faded page, are framed and aestheticized, becoming blank canvases to be filled. In contrast to photographs, which present a static image and generate what Yau views as the repressive illusion of a return to the past, these empty spaces provide a field for the play of the speaker's imagination: "I tried imagining the pictures the black rectangles held. . . . Movies showed me everything but this." Yau's link of the visual to the totalizing experience of film will become crucial in his later work; here it suggests the way in which the visual experience of the past is appropriated and commodified by the culture industry and, specifically, by a film industry that has stereotyped or erased Asians.

The move from the visual to the written is experienced as a loss, but also as liberating. The space writing gives to the imagination is enacted in the poem, as Yau juxtaposes descriptions of the album with fragments of the speaker's personal memory. Writing, Yau suggests, answers the need to position oneself actively in relation to the past rather than remaining a passive spectator; mediated through the objectivity of language, it acknowledges both the individual's role in constructing the past and the past's role in constructing the individual. In the poem's final two sections, words themselves become the objects through which the speaker constructs history:

> At the beach I saw the words transformed by the sun. Saw them become hills of bleached skulls. Now they were smooth and round, white as the words describing them.

> Lying beside the sagging castles, watching the sand trickle through my fingers. Tiny examples of what I read. All afternoon I played beneath the sun with the skulls, molding them into little mountains.

(152–3)

The magical transformation of the caption into its referents, and the speaker's subsequent use of those referents as macabre building blocks, suggests Yau's crucial divergence from the practice of Language poetry. By describing the compulsion under which a phrase from an album puts him, Yau demonstrates that the received discourses of history that shape the individual cannot be easily discarded or challenged through fragmentation; "Cenotaph" demonstrates how those discourses get inside, how irresistibly attractive they are. And those discourses are taken quite literally: "heads" become actual heads. The poet's linguistic field of action is limited by the few words that he has received. But by refiguring words as objects of play and building, Yau emphasizes memory as a constructive and productive process, one that makes things rather than looks backward into an inaccessible past.

"Cenotaph" erases the photograph in favor of writing, a move that Yau views as a necessary first step to the process of constructing history. But the poem's mention of the movies also acknowledges its presence in a culture that is relentlessly visual. Yau's increasing use of film motifs in his recent work shows writing pressured by two different visual discourses: the (repressive) discourse of memory, represented by the photograph, and the (racist) discourse of mass culture, represented by film.

Many Asian American writers and critics have cited film as the most powerful agent in perpetuating racial stereotypes of Asians in American culture. Indeed, one of the goals of Asian American poetry's project of presenting history and identity is to combat such stereotypes and to present a different image of Asian Americans; this impulse is epitomized in a pair of recent anthologies titled *Charlie Chan Is Dead*. But in Yau's work, the Asian on film is very much alive, as in the curious figure of "Genghis Chan: Private Eye," the title of a long sequence begun in the late 1980s. Rather than reject such figures, Yau chooses to appropriate and deform them, creating bizarre hybrids who both draw upon the rhetoric of popular narrative and undermine it.

The interaction between the title of "Genghis Chan: Private Eye" and its content is a case study in Yau's deployment and emptying out of overdetermined ethnic signifiers. "Genghis Chan" is an absurd play on the film character Charlie Chan, a classic example of Asian stereotyping. But the first name "Genghis" refigures the effeminate, deferential Chan as a Mongol warrior, and the title "Private Eye" alludes to the conventions of film noir, suggesting Chan as hard-bitten gumshoe. Yau's title presents an outrageous hybrid, one constructed out of stereotypes and mass-culture clichés; although this creates an ethnically marked character who can "speak" and who occupies a certain space within popular discourse, the identity of the character is unstable.

In the first few poems of the sequence in *Radiant Silhouette*, Yau's diction operates on the border between film noir and the surreal, with phrases that sound familiar in their rhetoric but nonsensical in content: "I was floating through a cross section / with my dusty wine glass, when she entered . . ." (189). "Genghis Chan" becomes a kind of linguistic junkyard where Asian signifiers and clichés are collected, dissected, and stitched together; this process is made most explicit in the sequence's later poems, collected in *Forbidden Entries*:

Dump fun
Dim sum

Slum rubble
Gong sob

Strong song
Oolong

   (*Forbidden* 103)

Asian food, which for Mura is the essence of authentic Asian culture, is transformed through a perverse literalness into something grotesque: "Moo goo / Milk mush // Guy pan / Piss pot" (105).

What holds this play together and marks it as a specifically Asian American project is only the figure of Genghis Chan himself, the overdetermined/empty hybrid. The figure of Chan makes the question of "Who speaks?"—which Bernstein would like to make central to Language poetry—meaningful, but it also shows the danger of accepting any answer. The location of the poem is marked as "Asian," but "Asianness" itself is a mask.

Yau further thematizes the speaker's indeterminate identity in another film-based poem, "Peter Lorre Improvises Mr. Moto's Monologue." Lorre, an Austrian-born actor, starred in Fritz Lang's *M* and gave classic film noir performances in such movies as *The Maltese Falcon* and *Casablanca*. One of the most curious phases in Lorre's career was his portrayal, in a series of films in the late 1930s, of Mr. Moto, a Japanese detective based on Charlie Chan. Chan, like Moto, was always played by a white actor, a fact often seen as a racist slight to Asian American actors. Such a criticism relies on the apparently commonsensical idea that an Asian role ought to be played by an Asian actor. Yau's poem, however, asks us to think more deeply about the problem and reworks it as a situation of poetic potential. The title complicates the question of "who speaks": the speaker is an Austrian actor, but he is delivering a monologue that is "Mr. Moto's," the property of a Japanese character; the speech is not scripted but improvised, making the monologue both spontaneous and artificial; and the poem is written by a poet who is neither Austrian nor Japanese but Chinese American. In contrast to the speaker of Ron Silliman's *Ketjak*, whose perspective is fragmented but whose social location (as white male) remains intact, the identity of Yau's speaker is constantly shifting, pressuring the reading of the poem.

The speaker's self-characterization is as a pieced-together mechanical monster: "My mechanized eyes are spherical rooms bisected by new dancing knives. . . . Upgraded teeth pressed closed together. Matching black eyebrows and hair. I'm better than a laboratory frog because I don't need batteries to send my electricity. . . . Hoist a little red switch . . . and I begin to twist and bend like tall grass on a spring day" (*Forbidden* 77). Asian eyebrows and hair are part of the actor's makeup, of course, but the costume seems to penetrate so that even the eyes are mechanical. The male Asian body—the source of self in Mura and Lee—has been fragmented and mechanized. Moto/Lorre seems a puppet who will "[t]witch and quiver on hidden command," but at the same time the character has a menacing relationship toward the "you" that is ostensibly in control: "I float outside your window on rainy nights, a blanket of gray mist you can't peel from the glass. . . . I'm a rug of glistening grit settling on the shelves of atomized fat lodged beneath your epidermal layers. . . . I'm a high-end pastoral inmate, an ingratiating drip of diseased music scratching against your fidelity" (77). If "you" is read as the white movie audience, then the monster that is Lorre/Moto has been disturbingly interiorized, fundamental to perception (the film on the glass), part of the flesh. As such, the character is a source of pleasure—"pastoral" and "ingratiating"—but also of irritation. This is a monster that has not only turned against its creator but has, to some degree, contaminated its creator's very being—a move duplicated in the fusion of the white Lorre and the Japanese Moto.

In the poem's third paragraph, Lorre and Moto are even more closely linked through memory, "a black hole or tunnel sucking me back toward birth" (77). Memory first leads to Lorre's own youth in "the cobbled alleyways of Berlin," where his career began. But Lorre's foreign origins become conflated with Moto's: "Hollywood didn't mold me into what I am, a diminutive silk hurricane approaching America's crafty shores, dapper neon silhouette slipping behind a foil moon, draped bones in a metallic black suit" (77–8). The foreign other, arriving in America, becomes a dashing trickster, emptied of human essence; but the character's disembodiment paradoxically allows him to become ubiquitous, a cliché at large in the culture: "It is my voice that seeps through windows, under doormats. I rise through floorboards, leak out of phones, all warm pomade and smooth walking topped by a blazing boutonniere" (78).

Lorre/Moto is constantly faced with forces that wish to limit him to a single role and hence kill him: "Morticians wanted to get their boiled forceps on me, shove me into an economy box" (78). The character's origin as a movie commodity is inescapable and threatens to end the dapper detective's career. But the power of improvisation and role-playing transformation allows the character to stay one step ahead: "I was a snotty snot rag, a juicy hobbler, a meal ticket delivered in three languages" (79). Lorre/Moto's very lack of essential identity—his existence across the linguistic spaces of German, Japanese, English—is what keeps him mobile, immortal. At the same time, his position as commodity, his pandering study of "Americanness," allows him to get inside the American identity, to know it and become a part of it: "I learned to embroider your name perfectly. . . . I swallowed the elongated syllables of dusty, broken pills with gusto. A celluloid renegade in possession of all his neurons, a radar dish picking up telepathic wavelengths curdling in the rumpled checkerboards of America's dairy farms" (79). Lorre/Moto as "radar dish" is reminiscent of Adorno's description of the lyric subjectivity as a "precipitate," registering the pressure of society on the individual; as the outsider who has perfectly learned Americanness, Lorre/Moto is able to diagnose its fakeness, the "curdling" of the clichéd heartland.

The character's full potential as a weapon against American mass culture is realized in the final paragraph, where Lorre/Moto is transformed from insinuating voice to receiver and interpreter of the voices of America: "I hear your voices clamoring . . . demanding the silos be full and straight as the arrows entering General Custer's eyes" (79). The insatiable desire of the mass-culture audience for the commodified image of the Asian, here figured in terms of the myth of American plenty, contains the seeds of its own destruction and can be turned against mass culture by the commodity himself: "I'm one of those arrows. I fly again and again, spin through the wind. My yellow scarf hanging like spit from my chin. You can't disown me because you've never worn out my cashmere coat. I'm an engine of rebuilt fur. I'm what slips through your purified crave" (79).

The costume of Asianness that Lorre dons exposes American identity itself as a costume. The consumable, fake Asian is ingested by the "purified crave" of the mass-culture audience, the commodifying, essentializing desire; it is only by riding the clichés, the markers of Asian ethnicity, that the monster that is Lorre/Moto can penetrate into the interior of America. Once there, however, the emptied-out character, composed only of shifting costumes, can become an "engine of rebuilt fur," a dynamic entity built from exterior scraps, reanimated like the child's mound of heads. Retaining the shell of identity, Yau suggests, is necessary to slip past the gatekeepers while defending a space for identity's reconstruction.

The meeting in John Yau's work of ethnic signifiers and avant-garde techniques can best be understood not as a new development in American writing but as a continuation of the strategies that characterized the Asian American avant-garde of the 1970s. Like those earlier avant-gardists, Yau takes Asian American identity not as a given but as a product of the poem's own formal strategies—an identity that is thus provisional, shifting from poem to poem and even from line to line. Yau's work restores the historical links between experimental and ethnic writing, reminding us of the ethnicization of the avant-garde that characterized the 1970s.

A reading of Yau thus serves as a dual corrective. When seen against the mainstream of Asian American writing, Yau shows how seeing Asian American poetry as a poetry of pure content can lead to a deadening commodification, as ethnic "themes" become mass-culture clichés. Yau's own play with popular culture is a response to this threat. But Yau's poetry also warns us against reading "experimental" poetic techniques too abstractly, showing us a self that remains, like that of Ron Silliman's *Ketjak*, grounded in a particular social community. This simultaneous consciousness of the aesthetic and of the social, present not only in Yau's work but in the most powerful writings of Asian American and Language poets of the past thirty-five years, is the avant-garde's ongoing contribution to contemporary American culture.

Conclusion

In a 1988 essay, "Poetry and the Politics of the Subject," Ron Silliman describes a persistent divide in the practice of recent American poetry:

> Progressive poets who identify as members of groups that have been the subject of history—many white male heterosexuals, for example—are apt to challenge all that is supposedly "natural" about the formation of their own subjectivity. That their writing today is apt to call into question, if not actually explode, such conventions as narrative, persona and even reference can hardly be surprising. At the other end of this spectrum are poets who do not identify as members of groups that have been the subject of history, for they instead have been its objects. . . . These writers and readers—women, people of color, sexual minorities, the entire spectrum of the "marginal"— have a manifest political need to *have their stories told.* That their writing should often appear much more conventional, with the notable difference as to whom is the subject of these conventions, illuminates the relationship between form and audience. (61)

Silliman's formulation starkly separates the field of contemporary writing along lines of race, gender, and sexuality. Experiments with form and critiques of literary conventions are largely, if not exclusively, the province of straight white men. The writing of women, minorities, and gays, in contrast, adheres to poetic conventions—particularly those of personal narrative and direct speech—because its major goal is to tell stories that have been previously suppressed. But perhaps Silliman's most striking claim is that this division is necessary and even valuable, serving the different political needs and historical situations of the writers he describes.

Silliman's vision of a divided literary landscape has been sharply criticized, including by several of his fellow Language writers.[1] But there can be little doubt that the divisions Silliman describes are widely felt. The new *Cambridge History of American Literature* splits its treatment of contemporary American fiction into two sections: "Postmodern Fictions," which deals primarily with the "experimental" work of writers such as John Barth, Kurt Vonnegut, and Thomas Pynchon; and "Emergent Literatures," which surveys Asian American, Chicano, Native American, and gay and lesbian writing. Harryette Mullen—an African American woman poet whose work features a great deal of formal experimentation—notes in her 1996 essay "Poetry and Identity" that the division described by Silliman has proven tenacious, affecting the reception of her own work: "The assumption remains, however unexamined, that 'avant-garde' poetry is not 'black' and that 'black' poetry, however singular its 'voice,' is not 'formally innovative'" (30).

The history of the contemporary American avant-garde I have offered in the preceding chapters helps account for this sense of racialized and gendered divisions in American poetry, as well as for Silliman's paradoxical sense that "experimental" and "ethnic" modes of writing share a common purpose. I have argued that in the 1970s American poetic avant-gardes underwent a process of ethnicization, in which aesthetic innovations were seen as a means of articulating the distinctive social position of an artistic group. This was as true for a group such as Language writing, which consisted largely of white male writers, as it was for a group such as Asian American poets. But as such avant-gardes achieved a modicum of success within the poetry world, the aesthetic and the social were uncoupled, as avant-garde writing was reinscribed into mainstream categories. The unmarked, "white male" location of Language writing was erased in favor of the more abstract category of "experimental" technique, while Asian American writing—led by the MFA-trained writers who came to prominence in the 1980s—came to be seen as a purely social category, grounded solely in the poetry's "ethnic" content. The work of writers like John Yau, widely seen as a new synthesis of the experimental and the ethnic, is in fact a reminder of the avant-garde origins of experimental and ethnic writing, in which both modes shared a sense of the link between the aesthetic and the social.

After revisiting this recent history of the avant-garde, we can begin to see the field of contemporary poetic practice as something other than deeply divided along racial and gender lines—those "sharp ideological disagreements," as Charles Bernstein puts it in *A Poetics*, that seem to "lacerate" the literary landscape (1). Instead, we see provisional and shifting groups of writers adapting the strategies of the avant-garde to a common historical context—the political, social, and literary aftermath of the 1960s, in which writers find themselves acutely aware of how race produces and circumscribes communities. The concept of the avant-garde allows us to undertake a far more nuanced sociology of contemporary American poets, one that avoids essentializing racial differences while demonstrating the role race plays even in the work of ostensibly formalist white writers.

Just as this book critiques the notion of sharp divides in contemporary poetry, it also challenges the tendency to divorce form from content in contemporary poetic analysis. The work of white experimental writers such as the Language poets has frequently been read entirely in terms of its formal innovations, as an expression of recent developments in linguistic and literary theory. I have argued, however, that the work of a writer like Ron Silliman does indeed have discernible content—material that marks its observations as those of a white working-class man. Silliman's work registers its social location in the interplay between this determinate content and the formal techniques that attempt a more universalizing, leftist critique of language. I have also suggested that Asian American poetry, usually recognized by its ethnically distinctive content, must be understood as simultaneously an attempt to create distinctive poetic forms for Asian American expression. That the claims of Asian American poetry are made in both form and content is made clear in the work of John Yau, who self-consciously plays upon readers' expectations about what constitutes either an Asian American story or an Asian American poetic style.

It may seem curious to claim, as I have, that an understanding of the avant-garde can make a profound contribution to our understanding of race and its role in literature. While I have argued for a consideration of race in the work of white and Asian American poets alike, I hope that I have also shown that "race" is not a category that precedes the literary work but one that emerges in and through the work itself. Groupings of writers along racial and ethnic lines are always coalitions, consciously constructed either by the writers themselves or by readers seeking a common thread. The avant-garde, with its distinctive form of community grounded in both aesthetic and social affinities, offers a model for the racialized communities that can emerge in poetry, communities that can be much more open and flexible than our critical preconceptions about race might lead us to believe.

Finally, this vision of the avant-garde may offer a way past some of the impasses of contemporary poetry and criticism described by Silliman and others. The confrontation of "experimental" and "ethnic" writing, and the institutionalization of both, has forced many writers and critics to feel they must choose sides—that a commitment to Asian American poetics, for instance, precludes an engagement with nonlyric or nonnarrative styles. The invocation of new, hybrid categories, such as experimental Asian American writing, can often feel detached from history, selecting a few Asian American poets whose work is sufficiently innovative and neglecting the rest. But if we can recognize groups like Language writing and Asian American writing as parallel avant-garde formations, arising from analogous explorations of language and social location—Asian American writing was always experimental, and Language writing was always ethnicized—we can understand the place new work takes in the communities created by these avant-gardes, without compromising the historical integrity of either. If the idea of *the* avant-garde is dead, I would argue for the continuing vitality of a plurality of poetic avant-gardes—an assertion that should give us grounds for optimism about the future of American poetry.

Notes

1. In his essay "The Turn to Language and the 1960s," Language writer Barrett Watten makes a brief mention of "the emergence of Asian-American writers" in Berkeley during his time as a student but names only Frank Chin and Arthur Sze (176).

2. Language writer Ron Silliman was also a student at San Francisco State during the strike, after which he transferred to the University of California, Berkeley; I discuss his remarks on the strike in Chapter 2.

3. While Watten quotes and translates a chant ("Hare om namo shiva") Ginsberg offered in response to a reporter's question, he also characterizes it as an "incomprehensible language" that demonstrates "the limits of signification" (145–6). Noting further that Black Panther leader Bobby Seale had not read Mao's *Little Red Book* before beginning to sell it on the Berkeley campus, Watten calls the book another "empty symbol" and an "obscurantist text of cryptic formulas," though he also notes that Amiri Baraka has sharply challenged his account of the book's importance (173).

4. In a letter I discuss in Chapter 2, Silliman gives a nod to each of these groups, mentioning Thomas, the Nuyorican poet Pedro Pietri, and the Native American writer Simon J. Ortiz as candidates for publication in *L=A=N=G=U=A=G=E*.

5. "The Place of Poetry in Asian American Studies," MLA Convention, Hyatt Regency Chicago, 29 Dec. 2007.

6. I am grateful to Colleen Lye for suggesting this term.

CHAPTER 1

1. One exception is Jane E. Falk, "Journal as Genre and Published Text: Beat Avant-Garde Writing Practices," *University of Toronto Quarterly* 73.4 (Fall 2004): 991–1002.

2. In her essay "A Communal Poetry," Adrienne Rich writes that San Francisco Renaissance and Beat writing was a crucial inspiration for women's political poetry in the 1970s: "That the origins and nature of poetry are not just personal but communal was an important legacy from the poetics that Kenneth Rexroth, Lawrence Ferlinghetti, Allen Ginsberg, among others, had brought to huge audiences in the 1950s and 1960s" (175).

3. Allen Ginsberg, from *Spontaneous Mind: Selected Interviews, 1958–1996*, ed. David Carter (New York: HarperCollins, 2001). © 2000, 2001 by The Allen Ginsberg Trust. Reprinted by permission of HarperCollins Publishers and the Wylie Agency, Inc.

4. Amiri Baraka, a leader of the Black Arts movement, does cite Ginsberg as a crucial early influence: "I was drawn to certain white poets, like Allen Ginsberg . . . because they legitimized things that I wanted to do and that I felt" (209).

5. To cite a few examples: In *Content's Dream*, Charles Bernstein, speaking in a forum where Ginsberg had spoken the week before, disagrees with Ginsberg's "valorization of breath and the spontaneous" but also asserts that "Ginsberg has done something of the greatest importance . . . perhaps anything I write is possible only by virtue of the work Ginsberg and others have done" (416–7). In *A Poetics* Bernstein's critique is more pointed: he refers in "Artifice of Absorption" to "simplistic / notions of absorption through unity . . . sometimes put forward by Ginsberg / (who as his work shows / knows better, but who has made an ideological / commitment to such simplicity)" (38–9). In *The Marginalization of Poetry*, Bob Perelman describes Ginsberg, along with John Ashbery, as one of the "important precursors to language writing" (115). Perelman contrasts (largely negatively) Ginsberg's privileging of the self and the body with Barrett Watten's strategy of "anti-identification" but suggests that both poets may be similar in "invoking the dimension of the sacred" (126). Watten himself, in "The Turn to Language and the 1960s," cites Ginsberg's exploration of "the limits of signification" as a form of "becoming outside" that "made sixties radicals—even those as newly constructed as myself" (146) but suggests that Ginsberg fails to take the final step into language-oriented writing because of his continuing attachment to "images and the overall coherence of biography" (159).

6. As Paul George and Jerold Starr note, Kerouac denounced his Beat peers as "socialists" and "communists," announced his support for William F. Buckley Jr., and ridiculed black militants (Starr 217).

7. To cite just a few examples: a 1973 review in *Gay Sunshine* chastises Ginsberg for his "weak" understanding of sexual politics (Hyde 213); Marjorie Perloff, in *Poetic License*, observes that "women play no role in Ginsberg's poetry" (214); and Manuel Luis Martinez finds Beat writing "neo-colonial" in its treatment of Latin America (34).

8. "Howl" was greeted by Richard Eberhart as "a howl against everything in our mechanistic civilization that kills the spirit" (Hyde 25), by M. L. Rosenthal as a significant contribution to "American literature of dissidence" by a kind of "Mad Bomber" (Hyde 30), and by Norman Podhoretz as an "assault on America . . . that rings true" (Hyde 35). Later critics have endorsed this image of the disruptive power of "Howl." John Tytell's *Naked Angels* likens Ginsberg's first reading of "Howl" to "a detonation in a museum" and calls the poem "a crucible of cultural change" (104), and Tony Trigilio argues that it "conjoin[s] religion and politics to decenter Cold War orthodoxy" (150). Indeed, it could be said that the political relevance of "Howl" has been settled as a matter of law. In his 1957 decision clearing "Howl" of obscenity charges, Judge Clayton Horn ruled that the poem "does have some redeeming social importance" as "an indictment of those elements in modern society destructive of the best qualities of human nature; such elements are predominantly identified as materialism, conformity, and mechanization leading toward war" (Ginsberg *Howl* 174).

9. Allen Ginsberg, from "Howl," in *Collected Poems 1947–1980* (New York: Harper & Row, 1988). © 1955 by Allen Ginsberg. Reprinted by permission of HarperCollins Publishers.

10. Tony Trigilio, in "'Strange Prophecies Anew': Rethinking the Politics of Matter and Spirit in Ginsberg's *Kaddish*," *American Literature* 71.4 (1999): 733–95, argues that most recent writing on Ginsberg has been merely "fan appreciations and retrospectives" (773) and that the achievements of Ginsberg's poetry have been obscured by his "self-fashioned 'hipster' mythmaking" (774).

11. Ginsberg's annotation to this line: "Author traced the words 'Fuck The Jews,' '[N.M.] Butler has no balls,' and images of male genitalia and skull and crossbones on the dirty glass of his window to draw the attention of an Irish cleaning lady who consistently overlooked it. The action was seen by Dean Nicholas D. MacKnight as offensive and author was suspended from classes for a year" (132). Ginsberg's account suggests that the event was little more than a prank, hardly an act of serious rebellion. As Michael Schumacher writes, Ginsberg was much more concerned about having been caught in bed with Jack Kerouac: "To Allen's amazement, the university chose to focus on the window writings, as if Allen had committed a tremendous moral transgression in his prank" (55).

12. Nancy McCampbell Grace traces Kerouac's "fascination with race and ethnicity" as "an allegory of Kerouac's own condition as a marginalized male, a

masculine hybrid" (40), although she acknowledges that "his prose tends to commodify people of color and white women" (42). In his annotations, Ginsberg also notes that this character was in part inspired by the "Circus of Oklahoma" in Kafka's *Amerika* (*Howl* 135).

13. Ginsberg's annotations describe his relationship with Cassady as one of "early intense erotic liaison and extended friendship" (127). Schumacher describes Ginsberg's brief sexual relationship with Cassady, along with Ginsberg's powerful yet ambivalent feelings about the affair, in some detail (74–9).

14. As Ginsberg writes in the annotated *Howl*: "As the poem accumulated public force, the private mythology bandied about between Mr. Solomon and myself solidified as an image notorious on a quasi-national scale. This had unexpected consequences: it put Mr. Solomon's actual person in the world with my stereotype—a poetic metaphor—as a large part of his social identity. . . . I came to regret my naïve use of his name. . . . I hadn't realized all the consequences of the Word" (111). He also recounts a wrenching dream of guilt for exploiting Solomon in order to "conspire with *Time* to create this Beatnik myself" (119).

15. John Tytell writes that Kerouac's editor at Viking, Malcolm Cowley, talked Kerouac into "eliminating the *actual* names of characters which Viking felt could be libelous, but which Kerouac wanted for authenticity" (157). But Kerouac's pseudonyms—such as "Alvah Goldbrook" for Allen Ginsberg—were not particularly effective in concealing his characters' real identities.

16. Ginsberg's father's family was involved in socialist politics, and his mother, the subject of "Kaddish," was active in the Communist Party during Ginsberg's youth, bringing Ginsberg to meetings and to a Communist-run summer camp. Allen Grossman's influential essay on "Kaddish" characterizes the voice of Ginsberg's early poems as "the apotheosis of the young radical Jewish intellectual, born out of his time and place" (Hyde 104). M. L. Rosenthal sees part of the daring of "Kaddish" in its portrayal of Ginsberg's "slightly exotic and generally despised Communist background, which he refuses to apologize for" (Hyde 112).

17. Allen Ginsberg, from *Collected Poems, 1947–1980* (New York: Harper & Row, 1988). © 1984 by Allen Ginsberg. Reprinted by permission of HarperCollins Publishers.

18. In *The Marginalization of Poetry*, Bob Perelman observes of this passage: "Ginsberg has to fall back on irony, with 'language' now becoming a mantra that functions as critique not as a motor of change. . . . Ginsberg's desire to change the world by language has become trapped in the realm of language" (117–8).

CHAPTER 2

1. © 2009 Ron Silliman. All material from Ron Silliman reprinted by permission of the author.

2. Charles Bernstein, from *Content's Dream: Essays 1975–1984* (Los Angeles: Sun & Moon, 1986). All material by Charles Bernstein reprinted by permission of the author.

3. In "The Turn to Language and the 1960s," Barrett Watten observes that "[t]here have been frequent, if teasing, ascriptions of 'Language poet' as an identity politics" (139).

4. Silliman's and Grenier's work is, on the surface at least, devoid of the explicit political content, imagery, and rhetoric characteristic of the work in Gitlin's anthology. Consider, for example, the opening of Marge Piercy's "Address to the Players": "The Sphynx of the Pentagon squats on the Arlington shore. / What walks on men in the morning, / wades in corpses at noon, / flies over ashes at night?" (221). Or, more directly, Dick Lourie's "Civics I: Nothing Fancy": "the President is a piece of shit. / I said the President is a piece of shit. / He started out that way if you think back. / There hasn't really been any development" (198). Todd Gitlin, ed., *Campfires of the Resistance: Poetry from the Movement* (Indianapolis: Bobbs-Merrill, 1971).

5. In the interview, conducted by Gary Sullivan, Silliman says: "[Levertov] came to teach at Berkeley in 1969 already one of the first poets of her generation to take a serious stand on the war. But she proved a terrible listener and unbelievably rigid in some of her thinking about poetry—she would say that a semicolon had twice the value of a line break, exactly, as though this was written in stone somewhere. . . . [David] Bromige, Lyn Strongin and I visited her class as guest lecturers one day . . . and David and I immediately quarreled with Levertov. From my own perspective, it was more important that things didn't add up rather than any particular sum I derived from these events. Here was somebody who'd truly grown up within the Projectivist framework and who took politics seriously, and it had not improved anything—she'd sabotaged her writing and her political credibility simultaneously." Ron Silliman, "Interview with Gary Sullivan," *Readme* 3 (Summer 2000), 21 Nov. 2004 http://home.jps.net/~nada/silliman.htm. Watten also offers a critique of Levertov in "The Turn to Language and the 1960s."

6. Most of the other Language poets are a few years younger than Silliman and would not have begun college until 1968 or later.

7. Rossinow notes, "There is truth, as well as exaggeration and diversion" in this narrative of the new left's decline, adding that "the continuity between the new left and identity politics is notable" (343–4).

8. For an overview of the SLA's short history, see Vin McLellan and Paul Avery, *The Voices of Guns* (New York: G. P. Putnam's Sons, 1977).

9. After registering as a conscientious objector to service in Vietnam in the late 1960s, Silliman worked at the Committee for Prisoner Humanity and Justice until 1977.

10. Silliman writes: "What happens when a language moves toward and passes into a capitalist stage of development is an anaesthetic transformation of the perceived tangibility of the word, with corresponding increases in its expository, descriptive and narrative capacities, preconditions for the invention of 'realism,' the illusion of reality in capitalist thought. These developments are tied directly to the function of reference in language, which under capitalism is transformed, narrowed into referentiality" (10). Language writing, like all other avant-garde movements, can be seen, according to Silliman, as "an attempt to get beyond the repressing elements of capitalist reality, toward a whole language art" (15).

11. Vickery, *Leaving Lines of Gender*. Gender has been a vexed question throughout the history of Language poetry; although a number of women, including Lyn Hejinian, Susan Howe, and Rae Armantrout, were often grouped under the Language writing umbrella, the domination of the group by men was pronounced enough that Charles Bernstein asked Armantrout to write an essay on the question, "Why Don't Women Do Language-Oriented Writing?"—later reprinted in Silliman's anthology *In the American Tree*.

12. Indeed, a talk by Glück opens *Writing/Talks* (Carbondale: Southern Illinois University Press, 1985), the seminal anthology of lectures edited by Perelman that includes many central figures of Language writing.

13. Although Silliman cites Glück's talk as unpublished, a copy of the talk can be found in Silliman's papers (Box 8, Folder 20).

14. Unpublished materials from Ron Silliman papers reprinted by permission of Mandeville Special Collections Library, University of California, San Diego.

15. Unpublished materials from Charles Bernstein papers reprinted by permission of Mandeville Special Collections Library, University of California, San Diego.

16. Unpublished letter of Bruce Andrews reprinted by permission of the author.

17. Andrews seems later to have rethought his position; in a note in the margin, he writes: "Ron—speaking w/Charles after your talk w/him, I realized I've missed yr pt. *Sorry.* Such writing may well be of crucial interest—as localized repression of certain possibilities."

18. Silliman is presumably referring to Nuyorican poet Pedro Pietri.

19. In *A Poetics*, Bernstein writes: "[I]n the last twenty years a number of self-subsistent poetry communities have emerged that have different readers and different writers . . . even, increasingly, separate hierarchies and new canons" (4). Although the term "poetry communities" is not strictly defined, it seems designed to encompass both groups organized around racial or gender identity and groups such as Language writing.

20. I am indebted to Stephen Fredman for suggesting this connection.

21. In fact, in the *Quarry West* interview Silliman even describes himself as a "Buddha-atheist," although he suggests that in California he encountered Bud-

dhism "not as an exotic other, but rather as a very practical and varied mode of being in the world" (16).

22. For example: "We cannot in conscience blame these varied sources of modality on the notion of analycity" (80).

23. Many of these critiques have focused on Silliman's essentialized notions of the differences between white male writing and that of women and minorities. Perelman notes in *Marginalization* that Leslie Scalapino accused Silliman of "defining innovation as the repository of white men who are supposedly free of connection" (172–3). In *Discrepant Engagement*, Nathaniel Mackey writes: "Failures or refusals to acknowledge complexity among writers from socially marginalized groups, no matter how 'well-intentioned,' condescend to the work and to the writers and thus . . . are part of the problem" (18).

CHAPTER 3

1. Vernon Shetley uses the term "MFA mainstream" to describe the dominant mode of the 1990s in his book *After the Death of Poetry*; this mainstream mode is a descendant of what Charles Altieri calls the "scenic mode" of the 1970s in *Self and Sensibility in Contemporary American Poetry*.

2. William Wei notes: "During the late 1960s, Asian American activists on other campuses and communities also responded to the significant issues and concerns of the period, quite independently of what occurred at San Francisco State" (9).

3. "We are the Uncle Toms of the nonwhite peoples of America . . . a race of yellow white supremacists, yellow white racists. We're hated by the blacks because the whites love us for being everything the blacks are not. Blacks are a problem: badass. Chinese Americans are not a problem: kissass" (74). Frank Chin, "Confessions of a Chinatown Cowboy," *Bulletproof Buddhists and Other Essays* (Honolulu: University of Hawaii Press, 1998), 63–110.

4. In a 1976 interview with Teri Lee in *Asian American Review*, Janice Mirikitani, one of *Aion*'s editors, says, "I think we were the first Asian American magazine" (36), a claim repeated by William Wei. Although work on *Aion* may well have begun before work on other Asian American magazines, by the time *Aion* was published in 1970, the seminal magazine *Gidra* was already in its second year of publication. Wei also repeats an assertion in the interview that the magazine was "born during the San Francisco State Third World Strike in 1968" (36).

5. Wei has a brief discussion of the Red Guards (207–10), whereas Warren Mar describes his own involvement with the group (Louie and Omatsu 33–47).

6. The June/July 1970 issue of *Gidra* is also dedicated to Oka, with an elegy by Mirikitani on the back cover.

7. The epithet "Fat Jap" refers to an incident during the 1968 campaign, when Spiro Agnew, Richard Nixon's running mate, referred to reporter Gene Oishi as a "fat Jap."

8. According to a 2003 history of City Lights Bookstore published in the *San Francisco Chronicle*, Oka worked as a clerk at City Lights in the late 1960s. Heidi Benson, Jane Ganahl, Jesse Hamlin, and James Sullivan, "And the Beat Goes On: City Lights and the Counterculture: 1961–1974," *San Francisco Chronicle* 9 June 2003: D1. http://www.sfgate.com/cgi-bin/article.cgi?f=/c/a/2003/06/09/DD158147.DTL.

9. In one famous example from "Wichita Vortex Sutra," Ginsberg asks: "How big is the prick of the President? / . . . / How big are all the Public Figures? / What kind of flesh hangs, hidden behind their Images?" (*Poems* 395–6).

10. © Lawson Fusao Inada. Poems reprinted by permission of the author.

11. In their introduction, the *Aiiieeeee!* editors write that Okimoto's "self-contempt is implicit" in his negative "assessment of Japanese American literary potential" (Chin et al. 11). Interestingly enough, the passage quoted from Okimoto in *Aiiieeeee!* asks whether "Japanese-Americans will be forced to borrow the voices of James Michener, Jerome Charyn, and other sympathetic novelists to distill their own experience," an echo of Chin and Inada's own anxiety about borrowings from African American culture.

12. Poems and prose of Janice Mirikitani reprinted by permission of the author.

13. Wei discusses the development of both the Basement Workshop (185–90) and *Bridge* (112–23). In *Asian Americans*, Chris Ijima reflects on his involvement with the Basement Workshop (Louie and Omatsu 3–14).

14. Alan Chong Lau, "my ship does not need a helmsman," from *Songs for Jadina* (Greenfield Center, N.Y.: Greenfield Review, 1980). © 1980 by Alan Chong Lau. Reprinted by permission of the author.

CHAPTER 4

1. Hongo's anthology has subsequently been subjected to a great deal of criticism. For Juliana Chang, it displays the danger of "appropriation of Asian American poetry into hegemonic narratives of immigration and assimilation" (87). Catalina Cariaga suggests that "a reader of *The Open Boat* anthology may come away . . . thinking that Asian American literature springs from one homogenous American 'Asianicity' reduced to variations on the 'immigrant trope'" (1), and Victor Bascara takes Hongo to task for separating poetry from the social. Finally, Walter K. Lew's anthology *Premonitions*, published two years after *The Open Boat*, includes work that is much more experimental in tone and that includes a number of poets prominent in 1970s writing. In his afterword to the anthology,

Lew notes that "the work in this anthology is not limited to conventional models of verse. . . . Previous anthologies have been either too small or conservative to convey the astonishing diversity and eloquence of new poetries spread out among numerous networks and poetics" (575).

2. The first anthology dedicated solely to Asian American poetry was Joseph Bruchac's *Breaking Silence*, published in 1983.

3. "These days, some of us even serve on foundation and NEA panels, sit on national awards juries, teach in and direct creative writing programs, and edit literary magazines. . . . We are included in the textbook and annual anthologies published by Norton, Heath, McGraw-Hill, Little Brown, Morrow, Godine, St. Martin's, Pushcart, and Scribner's" (Hongo xxxiii).

4. Anne Cheng's recent book follows Kim in largely dismissing readings of *Dictée* by "postmodern and avant-garde critics," who, she argues, reduced Cha's achievement to the "enigmatic quality" of "female experimentation"; *Writing Self, Writing Nation*, in contrast, was characterized by its "pioneering analysis into Cha's political negotiations" (140–1).

5. Generational conflict is a dominant theme not only in much Asian American writing but in most Asian American criticism. See, for example, the thematic framework of "necessity" and "extravagance" set up in Sau-ling Wong's *Reading Asian American Literature.*

6. For example, Susan Koshy's 1996 article "The Fiction of Asian American Literature" is a widely read polemic against cultural nationalism, which Koshy sees as theoretically bankrupt, and in favor of a transnational paradigm for Asian American studies. But Koshy's practical suggestion for this shift seems to be that we turn our attention to texts that talk explicitly about transnationalism or post-coloniality; our actual critical practices seem unaffected.

7. Theresa Hak Kyung Cha, from *Dictée* (Berkeley: University of California Press, 2001). © 2001 by The University of California Press. Reprinted by permission of The University of California Press.

8. As several critics have noted, Cha further undermines classical authority by altering the name of the Muse of lyric poetry, Euterpe, to "Elitere." Shelley Sunn Wong argues that Cha's foregrounding of genre marks "a recognition of the ways in which subjects are interpellated . . . by different generic formations," and reads the text as a critique of generic structures (Kim and Alarcón 118).

9. Yu was a student leader in the March 1, 1919, Korean uprising against the Japanese. She died in 1920 at the age of seventeen.

10. Indeed, Wittgenstein's mode of inquiry is a way of finding words' own "home" in language: "When philosophers use a word . . . and try to grasp the *essence* of one thing, one must always ask oneself: is the word ever actually used in this way in the language-game which is its original home?" (48).

11. Lisa Lowe identifies "the physical body" as the "site from which different, often fragmented, speech is uttered in resistance to the imposed competency in the colonizer's language" (Kim and Alarcón 47). Shu-mei Shih similarly reads the female body in *Dictée* as the "register of the materiality of history" that "escapes linguistic representation" (150).

12. As Shih notes, "This myth is most often evoked in Korean shamanistic rituals for the dead. Princess Pali, the little girl in Cha's tale, is considered by Koreans as the original shaman from whom the tradition has descended. During a *kut* (shamanistic performance) for the deceased, the female shaman calls the spirit of Pali by chanting the ballad of the princess and asking her to guide the deceased through the underworld" (157).

CHAPTER 5

1. Stan Yogi suggests a different reading of such failures of memory in Sansei poets, seeing them instead as products of a previous generation's silence on the experience of internment and the subsequent Sansei need to "creat[e] memories for their parents" (247). Frank Chin, in "Come All Ye Asian American Writers of the Real and the Fake," more caustically alludes to the "unique emotional problems" suffered by the Sansei "because not one of their mother and father's Nisei generation had the guts to stand their ground and fight for their constitutional rights . . . being so good at being pathological victims and wimps" (Chan 76–7). It seems to me, however, that Mura fails to account for the limits of the materials with which he must create memory; Li-Young Lee, as I will argue later, is much more conscious of the difficulties of this process.

2. All material by John Yau used by permission of the author.

3. In his introduction, Hongo notes Yau's presence at an Asian American writers' conference at Berkeley in 1991. In 1994, a version of Yau's essay "Between the Forest and Its Trees" appeared in an issue of *Amerasia Journal* on Asian American poetry—an issue that opened with a version of Hongo's introduction to *The Open Boat*. In the 1997 issue of the *Boston Review*, in which Perloff reviews *Forbidden Entries*, Yau joins four other Asian American scholars in writing a response to an earlier essay of Perloff's.

4. Priscilla Wald argues that the father's statement is itself an Americanizing strategy that "transforms the heroic Indian fighters into representatives of the culture they opposed" (144).

5. Yau's use of the "fake" here brings to mind the well-known debate between Frank Chin and Maxine Hong Kingston over Kingston's *The Woman Warrior*. Chin has argued that Kingston, by rewriting the myth of Fa Mu Lan, has presented a "fake" image of China for the consumption of a white audience. Kings-

ton's subsequent novel, *Tripmaster Monkey: His Fake Book*, appropriates Chin's accusation as a figure for writing itself. Kingston sees the "fake" as an empowering license for fiction; Yau, I would argue, is proceeding from a similar premise.

6. At least 10 of the 104 poems in *The Open Boat* take the contemplation of photographs or photo albums as their explicit occasions.

CONCLUSION

1. In *The Marginalization of Poetry*, Bob Perelman quotes a number of Silliman's critics, including Leslie Scalapino, who charges that Silliman's "authoritarian" account was "defining innovation as the repository of white men who are supposedly free of connection" (qtd. in Perelman 172–3). In her 1992 essay "Feminist Poetics and the Meaning of Clarity," Rae Armantrout asks "whether the nature of women's oppression can be expressed in the poem which . . . 'looks conventional'" (7–8). Nathaniel Mackey argues that "[f]ailures or refusals to acknowledge complexity among writers from socially marginalized groups, no matter how 'well-intentioned,' condescend to the work and to the writers and thus . . . are part of the problem" (18).

Bibliography

Adorno, Theodor W. *Notes to Literature*. Trans. Shierry Weber Nicholsen. Ed. Rolf Tiedemann. Vol. 1. 2 vols. New York: Columbia University Press, 1991.

Altieri, Charles. *Self and Sensibility in Contemporary American Poetry*. New York: Cambridge University Press, 1984.

Andrews, Bruce. Letter to Ron Silliman. 26 February 1977. Ron Silliman Papers, Mss. 0075, Mandeville Special Collections Library, University of California, San Diego.

Armantrout, Rae. "Feminist Poetics and the Meaning of Clarity." *Sagetrieb* 11.3 (1992): 7–16.

Baraka, Imamu Amiri. *Conversations with Amiri Baraka*. Ed. Charlie Reilly. Jackson: University Press of Mississippi, 1994.

Bascara, Victor. "Hitting Critical Mass (or, Do Your Parents Still Say 'Oriental,' Too?)." *Critical Mass: A Journal of Asian American Cultural Criticism* 1.1 (1993): 3–38.

Benjamin, Walter. *Illuminations*. Trans. Harry Zohn. Ed. Hannah Arendt. New York: Schocken, 1986.

Bercovitch, Sacvan, and Cyrus R. K. Patell, eds. *The Cambridge History of American Literature*, Vol. 7: *Prose Writing 1940–1990*. 8 vols. New York: Cambridge University Press, 1999.

Bernstein, Charles. *Content's Dream: Essays 1975–1984*. Los Angeles: Sun & Moon, 1986.

———. Letter to Ron Silliman. 14 February 1977. Charles Bernstein Papers, Mss. 0519, Mandeville Special Collections Library, University of California, San Diego.

———. Letter to Ron Silliman. 7 March 1977. Charles Bernstein Papers, Mss. 0519, Mandeville Special Collections Library, University of California, San Diego.

———. Letter to Ron Silliman. 13 June 1986. Ron Silliman Papers, Mss. 0075, Mandeville Special Collections Library, University of California, San Diego.

———. *A Poetics.* Cambridge, Mass.: Harvard University Press, 1992.

———. "Poetics of the Americas." *Reading Race in American Poetry: "An Area of Act."* Ed. Aldon Lynn Nielsen. Urbana: University of Illinois Press, 2000. 107–32.

Borges, Jorge Luis. *Labyrinths: Selected Stories and Other Writings.* Ed. Donald A. Yates and James E. Irby. New York: New Directions, 1964.

Brautigan, Richard. *The Pill Versus the Springhill Mine Disaster.* San Francisco: Four Seasons, 1968.

Bruchac, Joseph, ed. *Breaking Silence: An Anthology of Contemporary Asian American Poets.* Greenfield Center, N.Y.: Greenfield Review, 1983.

Bürger, Peter. *Theory of the Avant-Garde.* Trans. Michael Shaw. Minneapolis: University of Minnesota Press, 1984.

Cariaga, Catalina. "Reading the Fissures." *Poetry Flash* 240 (1993): 1, 6–9.

Cha, Theresa Hak Kyung. *Dictée.* Berkeley: University of California Press, 2001.

Chan, Jeffery Paul, Frank Chin, Lawson Fusao Inada, and Shawn Wong, eds. *The Big Aiiieeeee!: An Anthology of Chinese American and Japanese American Literature.* New York: Meridian, 1991.

Chang, Juliana. "Reading Asian American Poetry." *MELUS: The Journal of the Society for the Study of the Multi-Ethnic Literature of the United States* 21.1 (1996): 81–98.

Cheng, Anne Anlin. *The Melancholy of Race.* New York: Oxford University Press, 2001.

Chin, Frank, Jeffery Paul Chan, Lawson Fusao Inada, and Shawn Hsu Wong, eds. *Aiiieeeee!: An Anthology of Asian American Writers.* New York: Mentor, 1991.

Chin, Frank, and Frank Ching. "Who's Afraid of Frank Chin, or Is It Ching?" *Bridge* 2.2 (1972): 29–34.

Ching, Frank. "American in Disguise." *Bridge* 1.1 (1971): 4–5.

"Editorial." *Aion* 1.1 (1970): 5.

Eliot, T. S. "*Ulysses*, Order, and Myth." *Selected Prose of T. S. Eliot.* New York: Harcourt, 1975. 175–8.

Gee, Emma, ed. *Counterpoint: Perspectives on Asian America.* Los Angeles: UCLA Asian American Studies Center, 1976.

Ginsberg, Allen. Auto Poesy Recorded at Various Locations. Recorded January 1971. Audiotape. Department of Special Collections, Stanford University Libraries, Stanford, Calif. Box 226, Tape 70A1/025D.

————. *Collected Poems, 1947–1980.* New York: Harper & Row, 1988.

————. *Howl: Original Draft Facsimile, Transcript & Variant Versions, Fully Annotated by Author, with Contemporaneous Correspondence, Account of First Public Reading, Legal Skirmishes, Precursor Texts & Bibliography.* New York: Harper & Row, 1986.

————. *Spontaneous Mind: Selected Interviews, 1958–1996.* Ed. David Carter. New York: HarperCollins, 2001.

Gitlin, Todd. *The Sixties: Years of Hope, Days of Rage.* New York: Bantam, 1987.

Grace, Nancy McCampbell. "A White Man in Love: A Study of Race, Gender, Class, and Ethnicity in Jack Kerouac's *Maggie Cassidy, The Subterraneans,* and *Tristessa." College Literature* 27.1 (2000): 39–62.

Hejinian, Lyn. Letter to Ron Silliman. 12 June 1986. Ron Silliman Papers, Mss. 0075, Mandeville Special Collections Library, University of California, San Diego.

Hing, Alex. "Interview with Neil Gotanda." *Aion* 1.1 (1970): 32–43.

————. "The Need for a United Asian-American Front." *Aion* 1.1 (1970): 9–11.

Ho, Fred. "Tribute to the Black Arts Movement: Personal and Political Impact and Analysis." *CR: The New Centennial Review* 6.2 (2006): 141–89.

Hoffman, Steven K. "Lowell, Berryman, Roethke, and Ginsberg: The Communal Function of Confessional Poetry." *Literary Review: An International Journal of Contemporary Writing* 22 (1979): 329–41.

Hongo, Garrett Kaoru, ed. *The Open Boat: Poems from Asian America.* New York: Doubleday, 1993.

Horkheimer, Max, and Theodor W. Adorno. *Dialectic of Enlightenment.* Trans. John Cumming. New York: Herder & Herder, 1972.

Howe, Susan. *The Midnight.* New York: New Directions, 2003.

Hyde, Lewis, ed. *On the Poetry of Allen Ginsberg.* Ann Arbor: University of Michigan Press, 1984.

Inada, Lawson Fusao. "Asian American Poetry 1976." *Bridge* 4.4 (1976): 61.

————. *Before the War: Poems As They Happened.* New York: Morrow, 1971.

————. "Father of My Father." *Aion* 1.1 (1970): 44–5.

Jameson, Fredric. *Postmodernism, or, the Cultural Logic of Late Capitalism.* Durham, N.C.: Duke University Press, 1991.

Kim, Elaine H., and Norma Alarcón, eds. *Writing Self, Writing Nation: A Collection of Essays on* Dictée *by Theresa Hak Kyung Cha.* Berkeley: Third Woman, 1994.

Koshy, Susan. "The Fiction of Asian American Literature." *Yale Journal of Criticism* 9.2 (1996): 315–46.

Lau, Alan Chong. E-mail to the author. 22 January 2008.

————. *Songs for Jadina.* Greenfield Center, N.Y.: Greenfield Review, 1980.

Lee, Li-Young. *The City in Which I Love You.* Brockport, N.Y.: BOA, 1990.

Lew, Walter K., ed. *Premonitions: The Kaya Anthology of New Asian North American Poetry.* New York: Kaya, 1995.

Lewallen, Constance M. *The Dream of the Audience: Theresa Hak Kyung Cha (1951–1982).* Berkeley: University of California Press, 2001.

Lim, Shirley, and Amy Ling, eds. *Reading the Literatures of Asian America.* Philadelphia: Temple University Press, 1992.

Louie, Steve, and Glenn K. Omatsu, eds. *Asian Americans: The Movement and the Moment.* Los Angeles: UCLA Asian American Studies Center, 2001.

Mackey, Nathaniel. *Discrepant Engagement: Dissonance, Cross-Culturality, and Experimental Writing.* Tuscaloosa: University of Alabama Press, 2000.

Mann, Paul. *The Theory-Death of the Avant-Garde.* Bloomington: Indiana University Press, 1991.

Marshall, Thomas C. "'Nevermore' Than: Form, Content, and Gesture in *Ketjak*." *Quarry West* 34 (1998): 52–67.

Martin, Stephen-Paul. *Open Form and the Feminine Imagination: The Politics of Reading in Twentieth-Century Innovative Writing.* Washington, D.C.: Maisonneuve Press, 1988.

Martinez, Manuel Luis. "'With Imperious Eye': Kerouac, Burroughs, and Ginsberg on the Road in South America." *Aztlán* 23.1 (1998): 33–53.

Messerli, Douglas, ed. *"Language" Poetries: An Anthology.* New York: New Directions, 1987.

Mirikitani, Janice. "Broken Alleys." *Aion* 1.1 (1970): 15.

———. "Interview with Teri Lee." *Asian American Review* (1976): 34–47.

———. "Poem to the Alien/Native." *Aion* 1.1 (1970): 28–9.

———. "Tansaku." *Aion* 1.2 (1970): 56–7.

———. "The Time Is Now." *Aion* 1.2 (1970): 99.

Mullen, Harryette. "Poetry and Identity." *Telling It Slant: Avant-Garde Poetics of the 1990s.* Ed. Mark Wallace and Steven Marks. Tuscaloosa: University of Alabama Press, 2002. 27–31.

Mura, David. *Turning Japanese: Memoirs of a Sansei.* New York: Atlantic Monthly, 1993.

Nee, Dale Yu. "Asian American Writers Conference." *Bridge* 3.6 (1975): 42–8.

Nielsen, Aldon Lynn. *Black Chant: Languages of African-American Postmodernism.* New York: Cambridge University Press, 1997.

Oka, Francis. "America." *Aion* 1.2 (1970): 7.

———. "Blue Crayon Dripped in Wax." *Aion* 1.2 (1970): 5.

———. "The Cell." *Aion* 1.1 (1970): 12.

———. "Reagan Poem." *Aion* 1.2 (1970): 8.

———. "Shades Drawn Tight." *Aion* 1.2 (1970): 4.

Okimoto, Daniel I. *American in Disguise.* New York: Walker, 1971.

Park, Josephine Nock-Hee. *Apparitions of Asia: Modernist Form and Asian American Poetics.* New York: Oxford University Press, 2007.

Perelman, Bob. *The Marginalization of Poetry: Language Writing and Literary History.* Princeton, N.J.: Princeton University Press, 1996.

———, ed. *Writing/Talks.* Carbondale: Southern Illinois University Press, 1985.

Perloff, Marjorie. "Language Poetry and the Lyric Subject: Ron Silliman's Albany, Susan Howe's Buffalo." *Critical Inquiry* 25.3 (1999): 405–34.

———. *Poetic License: Essays on Modernist and Postmodernist Lyric.* Evanston, Ill.: Northwestern University Press, 1990.

———. Review of *Forbidden Entries,* by John Yau. *Boston Review* 22.3–4 (1997): 39–41.

Poggioli, Renato. *The Theory of the Avant-Garde.* Trans. Gerald Fitzgerald. Cambridge, Mass.: Harvard University Press, 1968.

Pound, Ezra. *Gaudier-Brzeska: A Memoir.* New York: New Directions, 1960.

Reich, Steve. *Writings on Music, 1965–2000.* Oxford: Oxford University Press, 2002.

Rich, Adrienne. *What Is Found There: Notebooks on Poetry and Politics.* New York: Norton, 1993.

Rossinow, Doug. *The Politics of Authenticity: Liberalism, Christianity, and the New Left in America.* New York: Columbia University Press, 1998.

Shetley, Vernon. *After the Death of Poetry: Poet and Audience in Contemporary America.* Durham, N.C.: Duke University Press, 1993.

Shih, Shu-mei. "Nationalism and Korean American Women's Writing: Theresa Hak Kyung Cha's *Dictée.*" *Speaking the Other Self: American Women Writers.* Ed. Jeanne Campbell Reesman. Athens: University of Georgia Press, 1997. 144–62.

Siegle, Robert. *Suburban Ambush: Downtown Writing and the Fiction of Insurgency.* Baltimore, Md.: Johns Hopkins University Press, 1989.

Silliman, Ron. *The Age of Huts.* New York: Roof, 1986.

———. "The Dwelling Place: 9 Poets." *Alcheringa,* n.s., 1.2 (1975): 104–20.

———, ed. *In the American Tree.* Orono, Maine: National Poetry Foundation, 1986.

———. "Interview with Thomas C. Marshall and Thomas A. Vogler." *Quarry West* 34 (1998): 10–46.

———. *Ketjak.* San Francisco: This, 1978.

———. Letter to Charles Bernstein. 10 August 1975. Charles Bernstein Papers, Mss. 0519, Mandeville Special Collections Library, University of California, San Diego.

———. Letter to Charles Bernstein. 17 February 1977. Charles Bernstein Papers, Mss. 0519, Mandeville Special Collections Library, University of California, San Diego.

———. Letter to Charles Bernstein. 28 March 1977. Charles Bernstein Papers, Mss. 0519, Mandeville Special Collections Library, University of California, San Diego.

———. Letter to Charles Bernstein. 9 June 1986. Charles Bernstein Papers, Mss. 0519, Mandeville Special Collections Library, University of California, San Diego.

———. Letter to Jessica Hagedorn. 19 August 1986. Ron Silliman Papers, Mss. 0075, Mandeville Special Collections Library, University of California, San Diego.

———. Letter to Peter Glassgold. 9 June 1986. Charles Bernstein Papers, Mss. 0519, Mandeville Special Collections Library, University of California, San Diego.

———. *The New Sentence*. New York: Roof, 1987.

———. "Poetry and the Politics of the Subject." *Socialist Review* 18.3 (1988): 61–83.

———. *Silliman's Blog*. 20 September 2003. http://ronsilliman.blogspot.com/2003/09/death-of-wayan-limbak-at-age-of-106.html.

———. "Under *Albany*." Contemporary Authors Autobiography Series. Ed. Joyce Nakamura. Vol. 29. Detroit: Gale Research, 1998. 309–52.

Song, Cathy. *Picture Bride*. New Haven, Conn.: Yale University Press, 1983.

Spahr, Juliana. *Everybody's Autonomy: Connective Reading and Collective Identity*. Tuscaloosa: University of Alabama Press, 2001.

———. "Postmodernism, Readers, and Theresa Hak Kyung Cha's *Dictée*." *College Literature* 23.3 (1996): 23–43.

Starr, Jerold M., ed. *Cultural Politics: Radical Movements in Modern History*. New York: Praeger, 1985.

Stefans, Brian Kim. "Remote Parsee: An Alternative Grammar to Asian North American Poetry." *Telling It Slant: Avant-Garde Poetics of the 1990s*. Ed. Mark Wallace and Steven Marks. Tuscaloosa: University of Alabama Press, 2002. 43–75.

Stephens, Michael Gregory. *The Dramaturgy of Style: Voice in Short Fiction*. Carbondale: Southern Illinois University Press, 1986.

Sumi, Pat. "Tule Lake." *Aion* 1.2 (1970): 100.

Tachiki, Amy, Eddie Wong, and Franklin Odo, eds. *Roots: An Asian American Reader*. Los Angeles: UCLA Asian American Studies Center, 1971.

Trigilio, Tony. *"Strange Prophecies Anew": Reading Apocalypse in Blake, H.D., and Ginsberg*. Madison, N.J.: Fairleigh Dickinson University Press, 2000.

Tytell, John. *Naked Angels: The Lives and Literature of the Beat Generation.* New York: McGraw-Hill, 1976.

Vickery, Ann. *Leaving Lines of Gender: A Feminist Genealogy of Language Writing.* Hanover, N.H.: University Press of New England, 2000.

Wakyama Group. "Why Are There So Few Sansei Writers?" *Bridge* 2.1 (1972): 17–20.

Wald, Priscilla. "'Chaos Goes Uncourted': John Yau's Dis(-)Orienting Poetics." *Cohesion and Dissent in America.* Ed. Joseph Alkana. Albany: State University of New York Press, 1994. 133–58.

Watten, Barrett. "The Turn to Language and the 1960s." *Critical Inquiry* 29 (2002): 139–83.

Wei, William. *The Asian American Movement.* Philadelphia: Temple University Press, 1993.

"What Interests Chinatown Is $, Not China!" *Bridge* 1.3 (1972): 20–9.

Wittgenstein, Ludwig. *Philosophical Investigations.* Trans. G. E. M. Anscombe. New York: Macmillan, 1968.

Wong, Sau-ling Cynthia. *Reading Asian American Literature: From Necessity to Extravagance.* Princeton, N.J.: Princeton University Press, 1993.

Wong, William. "An Indictment of White America." Review of *The Chickencoop Chinaman* by Frank Chin. *Bridge* 1.6 (1972): 26.

Yau, John. "Between the Forest and Its Trees (Second Version)." *A Poetics of Criticism.* Ed. Juliana Spahr. Buffalo, N.Y.: Leave, 1994. 43–8.

———. *Forbidden Entries.* Santa Rosa, Calif.: Black Sparrow, 1996.

———. "Interview with Edward Foster." *Talisman* 5 (1990): 31–50.

———. *Radiant Silhouette: New and Selected Work, 1974–1988.* Santa Rosa, Calif.: Black Sparrow, 1989.

Yogi, Stan. "Yearning for the Past: The Dynamics of Memory in Sansei Internment Poetry." *Memory and Cultural Politics: New Approaches to American Ethnic Literatures.* Ed. Amritjit Singh et al. Boston: Northeastern University Press, 1996. 245–65.

Yung, Eleanor S. "I Thought You Were Dead." *Bridge* 1.1 (1971): 19.

Index

Acker, Kathy, 52, 108, 110
Adam, Helen, 52
Adorno, Theodor, 142, 149, 158; "On Lyric
   Poetry and Society," 144
African American culture, 11–13, 75–77,
   84–85
African American literature, 11–13
Afro Asian Music Ensemble, 12
Agnew, Spiro, 81, 172n7
Aiiieeeee! (Chin et al.), 7, 85, 94, 113, 114,
   172n11
Aion (journal), 3, 7, 10, 74, 77–84, 86, 89–93,
   171n4
Alcheringa (journal), 51
Alienation, 41
Allen, Donald: The New American Poetry, 13
Altieri, Charles, 103, 171n1
Amerasia Journal, 174n3
Anaphora, 24, 82
Andrews, Bruce, 10, 51–52, 54, 57, 60, 121,
   170n17
Archive for New Poetry, University of
   California, San Diego, 51
Armantrout, Rae, 170n11, 175n1
Ashbery, John, 140, 147, 166n5
Asian American culture: Aion and, 77–80;
   American culture and, 76, 78–79, 81–82,
   155–58; Asian culture and, 93–94; Bridge
   and, 92–95; cultural nationalism, 75, 77,
   95, 107, 173n6; film and, 155; formation of,

5–6, 74–78; and identity, 5, 83–88, 92, 94,
   104, 108–11, 113–19, 142–44, 148, 150–53,
   155–58; literature and, 7; orientalism and,
   10–11, 106, 109, 111–12, 120, 136; poetic
   form and, 87–88, 92; and politics, 79–80;
   stereotypes of, 75, 76, 78, 95, 154, 155. See
   also Asian American poetry; Asian culture
Asian American Literature Study Group,
   MLA, 104
Asian American poetry, 73–99; and aesthetics,
   6–7, 75, 87–88, 94–95, 102–5, 107; and
   African American culture, 12, 75–77,
   84–85; Aion and, 77–93; and Asian culture,
   11, 87–88, 92; as avant-garde, 2, 7–8, 15,
   73–74, 92, 93, 99–101, 103, 138, 158–59,
   163; Beat influence on, 81–82; Bridge and,
   92–97; Bruchac's anthology of, 172n2;
   Cha and, 102–37; and generational
   conflict, 173n5; Hongo's The Open Boat
   and, 96, 98–99, 104–5, 139–40, 172n1;
   and identity, 155; Inada and, 84–86;
   individualism in, 96–99, 104 (see also
   personal history as theme of); Language
   poetry compared to, 2, 10, 102; Lau and,
   96–98; Lee and, 140, 143–46; and lyric
   poetry, 8–9, 73, 93, 102–5, 118–19, 138–39;
   and the mainstream, 8–9, 11, 13, 73–74, 96,
   101–5, 171n1; and memory, 153, 175n6;
   Mirikitani and, 86–93; Mura and, 140–43;
   Oka and, 80–83; origins of, 75–78;

Myth, 125–28

Nee, Dale Yu, 93, 96
New Directions, 57–58
New left, 3, 39–43, 47–48, 50, 66, 169 *n*7
New sentence, 39–40, 44–50, 70–71
New Yorker (magazine), 8, 103
New York school, 13, 138, 147
Nielsen, Aldon Lynn, 12, 13, 15
Nixon, Richard, 80–81

Oishi, Gene, 172 *n*7
Oka, Francis Naohiko, 7, 17, 74, 80–83, 98,
    171 *n*6, 172 *n*8; "America," 81; "Reagan
    Poem," 82–83
Okimoto, Daniel: *American in Disguise*, 85,
    172 *n*11
Olson, Charles, 1, 13
Oppenheimer, Joel, 109
Orientalism, 106, 111–12, 120, 136. *See also*
    Postmodern orientalism
Ortiz, Simon J., 57, 165 *n*4

Padgett, Ron, 147
Paik, Nam June, 112
Pali, Princess, 135, 174 *n*12
Palmer, Michael, 9, 52, 102, 147
Parataxis, 71
Paris Review (magazine), 8
Park, Josephine Nock-Hee: *Apparitions of
    Asia*, 10, 11
Parker, Charlie, 1, 13
Particularity: in Ginsberg's work, 20–21, 31,
    36; Language poetry and, 47, 53, 57, 70;
    in Silliman's work, 38–39, 50, 71–72
Perelman, Bob, 46, 58, 166 *n*5, 168 *n*18;
    "China," 63; *The Marginalization of
    Poetry*, 44, 61, 171 *n*23, 175 *n*1; *Writing/
    Talks*, 47
Perloff, Marjorie, 147, 150, 166 *n*7, 174 *n*3;
    "Language Poetry and the Lyric Subject,"
    44, 60–61
Perry, Matthew C., 80
Picasso, Pablo, 1
Piercy, Marge: "Address to the Players,"
    169 *n*4
Pietri, Pedro, 56, 165 *n*4, 170 *n*18
Piñero, Miguel, 111
Plath, Sylvia, 25
Podhoretz, Norman, 167 *n*8
Poetry (magazine), 103

Poggioli, Renato: *The Theory of the Avant-
    Garde*, 4–6
Political left, 2–3. *See also* New left
Politics: Asian American culture and,
    79–80; Asian American poetry and, 10,
    74, 78, 88–89, 93–98; avant-garde and,
    2–3, 20; Beat movement and, 21, 166 *n*6;
    Cha and, 130–32, 136–37; coalitions
    in, 39; Ginsberg and, 19–22, 25, 31–36,
    167 *n*8, 168 *n*16; Language poetry and,
    14–15, 50, 60; literary form and, 20,
    44–49; race and, 3; Silliman and, 3, 15,
    38–43, 46–49
Popular culture: avant-garde vs., 4–5. *See also*
    Culture industry
Port Huron manifesto, 41
Postmodern orientalism, 10–11, 106, 109
Pound, Ezra, 1, 10, 20, 22, 23, 58, 59, 106,
    124; *Cantos*, 68; *Cathay*, 147
Public/private space, 66–68
Public transportation, 63–64
Pynchon, Thomas, 161

Quarry West (magazine), 42, 47, 63

Race: Asian American poetry and, 2;
    avant-garde and, 1–6, 39, 160–63; Beat
    culture and, 27; Cha's work and, 120;
    Language poetry and, 2, 13–15, 52–53,
    55–57; and politics, 3; Siegle's criticism
    and, 110–12; stereotypes and, 87, 141–42,
    155; Yau's work and, 147, 150–53, 155–58.
    See also African American culture; Asian
    American culture
Raworth, Tom, 56
Reagan, Ronald, 82–83
Realism, 46
Reception: of Asian American poetry, 8–9,
    11–13, 15, 100–102, 172 *n*3; audience and,
    47–49; of Cha's *Dictée*, 102–3, 105–20,
    130, 136; of Ginsberg's "Howl," 167 *n*8; of
    Language poetry, 8–9, 48–49, 100–102; of
    Yau's work, 138. *See also* Audience
Red Guard Party, 78, 79
Reich, Steve, 10–11; *Drumming*, 10, 62
Rexroth, Kenneth, 166 *n*2
Rich, Adrienne, 38, 166 *n*2
Richie, Donald, 108
Riley, Terry, 62
Rinder, Lawrence, 120
Rivas, Bimbo, 111